D1454827

Education of Chinese Children
in Britain and the USA

Multilingual Matters

Please contact us for the latest book information:
Multilingual Matters Ltd,
Frankfurt Lodge, Clevedon Hall,
Victoria Road, Clevedon,
Avon BS21 7SJ, England

MULTILINGUAL MATTERS 82

Series Editor: Derrick Sharp

Education of Chinese Children in Britain and the USA

Lornita Yuen-Fan Wong

MULTILINGUAL MATTERS LTD

Clevedon • Philadelphia • Adelaide

To my Mother and late Father

LC
3085
.G7
W66
1992

Library of Congress Cataloging in Publication Data

Wong, Lornita Yuen-Fan, 1955-
Education of Chinese Children in Britain: A Comparative Study with the United States of America/Lornita Yuen-Fan Wong.
p. cm. (Multilingual Matters: 82)
Includes bibliographical references.
1. Chinese students–Education–Great Britain–Evaluation. 2. Chinese students–Education–United States–Evaluation. 3. Education, Bilingual–Great Britain–Evaluation. 4. Education, Bilingual–United States–Evaluation. I. Title. II. Series: Multilingual Matters (Series): 82.
LC3085.G7W66   1992
371.97'951041   dc20

British Library Cataloguing in Publication Data

A CIP catalogue record for this book is available from the British Library.

ISBN 1-85359-141-6 (hbk)
ISBN 1-85359-140-8 (pbk)

Multilingual Matters Ltd

UK: Frankfurt Lodge, Clevedon Hall, Victoria Road, Clevedon, Avon BS21 7SJ.
USA: 1900 Frost Road, Suite 101, Bristol, PA 19007, USA.
Australia: P.O. Box 6025, 83 Gilles Street, Adelaide, SA 5000, Australia.

Printed and bound in Great Britain by the Longdunn Press, Bristol.

Contents

List of Tables

Maps

Figure

Abbreviations

CAL	Center for Applied Linguistics
CERI	Center for Educational Research and Innovation
CHAMP	The Chinese Achievement and Mastery Program
CIAC	Chinese Information and Advice Center
CILT	Center for Information on Language Teaching and Research
CRC	Community Relations Commission
CRE	Commission for Racial Equality
DES	Department of Education and Science
E.C.	European Commission
EDAC	Evaluation, Dissemination and Assessment Center
EEC	European Economic Community
ESEA	Elementary and Secondary Education Act
ESL	English as a Second Language
GLC	Greater London Council
HAC	Home Affairs Committee
HCG	Haringey Chinese Group
HEW	Department of Health, Education and Welfare
HMSO	Her Majesty's Stationery Office
ILEA	Inner London Education Authority
I.S.	Intermediate School
KEYS	Knowledge of English Yields Success
LAB	Language Assessment Battery
LAS	Language Assessment Scale
LEA	Local Education Authority
LEP	Limited English Proficient
LES	Limited English Speaking
NCC	National Children Center
NDEA	National Defense Education Act
NEP	Non English Proficient
NES	Non English Speaking
OCR	Office of Civil Rights
OEA	Office of Educational Assessment
OPCS	Office of Population, Census and Surveys
P.S.	Public School
QCRC	Quaker Community Relations Committee
SFUSD	San Francisco Unified School District

Acknowledgements

This book is a revised version of my PhD thesis. A lot of people had given me assistance and support when I was carrying out the research in Britain.

I am very grateful to Dr Martin McLean who was my thesis supervisor for his patience, guidance and concern during the three years of intellectual preparation for the PhD degree at the Institute of Education University of London. I should also thank Professor Brian Holmes and Professor Guy Neave at the Institute for their advice, encouragement and comments on some parts of the thesis.

My special gratitude goes to Miss Wendy Man, one of the founders of the Haringey Chinese Group and Mr John Broadbent, the co-ordinator of the E.C. Pilot Project on the 'Community Languages in the Secondary Curriculum' who had given me a lot of support to help me to get through problems at various stages of my research in London.

My greatest debt is to all my informants of the Chinese communities in London, Los Angeles, New York City and San Francisco, headteachers and teachers of the state and Chinese supplementary schools, Chinese parents and students, and officials and workers of various institutions in the four metropolitan cities for their hospitality, time, patience, co-operation and assistance when I was making all sorts of tedious inquiries in the field.

Finally, I would like to thank the Institute of Education and the Central Research Fund Committee of the University of London for their grants to enable me to carry out field work in both Britain and the United States.

Without the assistance of Mr Stephen Ma, a former colleague of mine in the City Polytechnic of Hong Kong, and Mr Geoffrey Tam, a friend of my brother's, I would not be able to revise the PhD thesis by using a computer. Special thanks should also go to them.

To my mother and late father, I owe them gratitude for their generosity in supporting my costly studies in London and their tolerance of my temporary 'escape' from my family obligations. This book is particularly dedicated to them.

Part I:
Issues and Methodology

1 Introduction

Mother Tongue Education in the British Isles

Mother tongue education has existed in the British Isles for centuries. Before attention was given to the immigrant languages, the debate of mother tongue education focused on the Celtic languages (i.e. Welsh, Irish and Gaelic) spoken by the indigenous minorities in some specific regions of Wales, Ireland and Scotland. In order to eliminate the problems children experience in learning through a second language, and to maintain and transmit the indigenous culture to the younger generation, the Welsh-, Irish- and Gaelic-speaking people formed leagues or unions to lobby for the incorporation of their mother tongue in the national education system. By the early twentieth century, some initiatives had been taken by the national government to provide bilingual education in some non-English speaking areas where children could be taught in their mother tongue at nurseries or primary schools. At a later stage, the three Celtic languages had been incorporated in the school curriculum as a second language at primary or secondary level (Baker, C., 1988; Edwards, 1991; Hickey, 1991; Mackinnon, 1991; Sharp, 1973).

While effort was made to overcome the problems of the supply of teachers and the production of teaching materials of the Celtic languages, mother tongue education in the British Isles had shifted its focus to the teaching of immigrant languages at school in the 1970s. In order to demonstrate Britain's support of the 1977 EEC (European Economic Community) Directive, initiatives had been taken to develop pilot projects for the teaching of ethnic minority languages in the national school system in Britain. For instance, the Pilot Mother Tongue Project 1976–1980 in Bedford, being directly financed by the EEC Education Research Grant, had incorporated the teaching of Punjabi and Italian in the curriculum of some maintained schools (Commission for Racial Equality [CRE], 1980; Department of Education and Science [DES], 1982; EEC Sponsored Pilot Project, 1979; Orzechowska, 1984). While the EEC Pilot Project was in progress, a two-year bilingual programme funded by the DES and the Bradford Local Education Authority was implemented in 1978. Punjabi-speaking infants in schools in Bradford were taught in both English and Punjabi (CRE, 1980 & 1981; DES, 1982; Orzechowska,

3

1984). After the completion of the Bradford bilingual programme, with the finance and support of the EEC and the Inner London Education Authority (ILEA), a four-year mother tongue project was initiated by the Schools Council in 1981[1] to develop teaching resources in Bengali and Greek for primary school children (DES, 1982; Mother Tongue Project, 1984). At secondary level, the University of London Institute of Education had launched a E.C. (European Commission) funded pilot curriculum development project 1984–1987, known as the 'Community Languages in the Secondary Curriculum', to develop materials and explore strategies to teach Punjabi, Urdu and Italian in secondary schools (EC Pilot Project, 1987).

Significance and objectives of research

Despite the fact that more attention has been given to the teaching of immigrant languages in state schools and that the number of Chinese school children is increasing in Britain, Chinese language education has not been studied by any of the school-based pilot mother tongue projects.

In fact, Chinese in Britain has been a subject of interest to some social scientists and authors such as Broady (1955), E. Chan (1983), K.M. Cheng (1981), Cheung (1975), Ho (1977), K.C. Lai (1975), L. Lai (1975), Lynn (1982), O'Neil (1972), K.C. Ng (1968) and Yau (1983). Besides investigating various social aspects of the Chinese in Britain, some of these writers also deal with educational issues of Chinese children in Britain. Unfortunately education only forms a minor topic of their major discussion.

The pilot action project by Garvey and Jackson (1975), the Nuffield Foundation Chinese children's project (The Nuffield Foundation, 1981) and small scale studies by Fitchett (1976), I. Jones (1979) and Langton (1979) are some significant works on the education of Chinese children in Britain. However, the theme of these projects has put too much emphasis on the English language problems of Chinese children. Educational issues of mother tongue maintenance by Chinese children in Britain have been ignored.

By the early 1980s, owing to the adoption of the 1977 EEC Directive, the theme of the debate on the education of Chinese children in Britain had been shifted to mother tongue maintenance. Chann (1982), D. Jones (1980), Lue (in Quaker Community Relations Committee [QCRC], 1981), A. Ng (1982), Tsow (1980, 1983 & 1984) and D. Wong (in National

Children Centre [NCC], 1984) have drawn the public's attention to the self-help educational initiatives taken by the Chinese in Britain. However, most of them fail to explain with research evidence why there is such a need within the Chinese community in Britain.

Because of the absence of systematic research evidence, both the Chinese community and the public sector has speculated from ignorance on the educational needs of Chinese children in Britain. Chann's (1982) survey of the Chinese classes in Britain indicates that in order to meet the increasing demand for Chinese language learning, 37 out of the 53 private Chinese classes currently in existence in Britain were set up within just four years between the late 1970s and the early 1980s. In response to Articles 2 and 3 of the 1977 EEC Directive which requires member States of the EEC to provide (i) the teaching of the official language, or one of the official languages of the host country and (ii) the teaching of the mother tongue and culture of the country of origin of the school-age migrant/immigrant children (CRE, 1980; DES, 1982), the ILEA had set up 19 school-based Chinese classes by July 1985 (ILEA, 1986) in addition to the English as a Second Language (ESL) provision.

The main change that has taken place in the contemporary Chinese community is the increase in the number of British-born Chinese. Chinese parents are quite concerned about the maintenance of the Chinese language and certain Chinese traditional cultural values by their children, particularly those who are brought up and educated in Britain. On the other hand, they want their children to succeed in the mainstream English-medium education. The majority of Chinese children at school are from families where Chinese is the language of communication between parents and children. Some of these children had been educated in Chinese in a different educational system before they emigrated to Britain. To what extent has the present educational provision met the needs of Chinese children from various backgrounds as well as the aspirations of Chinese parents in Britain? How effective is the language education provision in the maintained sector as compared to that in the Chinese community?

The Chinese community in Britain is relatively new. The lack of investigation of the educational problems of Chinese pupils in Britain and the absence of published official documents on the effectiveness of the educational practice and policies makes it difficult to justify the present education provision for Chinese children in Britain.

In order to anticipate the possible outcomes of the language education policies for Chinese pupils in Britain, reference is made to countries where similar policies have been implemented in a comparable social context. Chinese communities in English-speaking societies such as Britain and the USA seem to offer a possibility of useful research and comparative analysis.

The objectives of this research are:

(i) To investigate the strength of demand for mother tongue/culture teaching by the Chinese community in Britain and the effectiveness of current educational provision, especially that of the Chinese community or supplementary schools, in meeting these demands.

(ii) To find out whether the educational problems of Chinese children in Britain are similar to those in the United States by comparing the immigration and demographic patterns, socio-economic conditions and the cultural-linguistic background of the Chinese communities in London, New York City and San Francisco where Chinese populations are of a considerable size.

(iii) To anticipate the extent to which some bilingual policies in New York City and San Francisco could be successfully transferred and incorporated into the London system to solve the problems of Chinese pupils in Britain.

Methodology

Chinese communities in Britain and the USA are reserved, conservative and complex. Many of the Chinese people are reluctant to reveal their problems as they are afraid of 'losing face'. Some business proprietors within the Chinese community worry that their personal privileges will be interfered with by the government if the information given to researchers is not treated in strictest confidence. The majority of Chinese parents work unsocial hours, including weekends, in the food-catering business. After sending their children to Chinese school at the weekend, many of the Chinese parents will rush to work in restaurants and 'take-away' shops until very late at night. Some Chinese educated professionals and politicians do not want to co-operate with researchers as knowledge of Chinese communities and weekend Chinese supplementary schools has become a key to leadership and power in the community. It is therefore not surprising that previous research by K.C. Ng (1968), Cheung (1975), K.C. Lai (1975), O'Neil (1972), Tan (1982), Taylor (1987) and Tsow (1984) indicate that gaining access to Chinese people is a major problem in conducting research on Chinese communities in Britain.

In order to solve the problems of entry and set up rapport with subjects of the research, the following techniques have been adopted during the process of data collection.

Expansion of site

As suggested by Schatzman and Strauss (1973), a researcher has to 'endeavor to negotiate his own way through every door' (p. 22) and 'create situations which invites visibility and disclosure for others' (p. 23). Instead of using supplementary schools as a base for the research, visits had been made to Chinese community centres to talk to youth and community workers about the research project. Active participation had also been taken in teacher training seminars, dinner parties and cultural activities organised by the Chinese community.

After disclosing the research to various people of the Chinese community over a couple of months, an effort was made to establish better relationships in the community. As predicted by Schatzman and Strauss (1973) and Vidich (1969), a relatively long period of residence in the field will usually lead the researcher into unanticipated places and subsequently change his actions as well as identity. Between March 1986 and April 1987, the field work was not only carried out at supplementary schools but also in different locales such as Chinese community centres, state schools, families, goverment agencies and restaurants (Appendix 4) where I had played such various roles as a community worker, an interpreter, an after-school Chinese language teacher and an English language teacher of an adult English class at a Chinese Community centre. All these research-related activities could not be planned in advance.

Participant observation and interviews

While research activities were in progress, a variety of methods had been adopted to collect and record data. Primarily interviews were used to obtain information from different subjects. If the situation permitted, semi-structured interviews with open-ended questions to allow respondents to express more of their opinion were conducted. On occasions such as dinner parties or within the family environment where the interview setting and movement of subjects could not be pre-determined, unstructured interviews were used.

Since pilot studies of the research indicated that the use of a 'walk-man' to record interviewing data had created tension and proved a distraction to interviewees, data collected in uncontrollable situations were recorded by memory. Mental notes were immediately transcribed into paper notes at the end of each interviewing activity. If the subject felt comfortable at the interview, effort would be made to jot down information while verbal interaction was taking place.

Questionnaires

Although participant observation and interviews had permitted the research to dig deeply into various situations to obtain information with greater clarity, these methods were time-consuming.

During the process of data collection, there was an opportunity for the research to study a British-born Chinese child at a greater depth in terms of his performance at school as well as his relationship with his family. Since I was a complete stranger to the family, some rapport could only be established after three or four visits to the family. Gradually access could be made to the child's Chinese and British nursery schools where observation of the child's performance and interviews with teachers were allowed.

All the observational activities of the child and interviews with the child's family members and his school teachers took place outside London. In order to perform one of these tasks, at least half a day or sometimes even a whole day would be consumed. Not only had such a case study proved that participant observation and interviews were time-consuming, but also that subjectivity as a result of too small a sample could pose a problem. In order to achieve objectivity, there was a need to obtain opinions from as many subjects as possible. Questionnaires therefore had been designed to supplement data obtained by participant observation and interviews. The main advantage of using questionnaires is that

> it permits wide coverage at a minimum expense both in money and effort. It not only affords wider geographic coverage but it also reaches persons who are difficult to contact. This greater coverage makes for greater validity in the results through promoting the selection of a larger and more representative sample (Mouly, 1970:242).

Two questionnaires had been designed — one for school children (Appendix 1) and the other for headteachers/organisers of Chinese supplementary schools (Appendix 2). Twenty-four children from two Chinese schools had been selected to test the comprehensibility and the time required for answering the questionnaire. The headteacher's questionnaire had not been tested. The main reason being that some of the headteachers had been interviewed before the questionnaire was sent to them. The purpose of the questionnaire was to check the results of the interviews and obtain some statistical data which headteachers were unable to produce at the interview. In fact many of these headteachers were quite busy. They would be annoyed if they were asked to fill in a similar questionnaire again. Out of the 13 questionnaires sent to the headteachers, only seven were returned.

After rapport had been developed through a wide range of activities, attempts were made to distribute the children's questionnaire to 13 weekend Chinese schools in London. All except one school had accepted the request. In order to guarantee a maximum return of the questionnaire, and to reduce the possibility of unanswered questions, the whole process of distribution, administration and collection of the questionnaires was done by myself. The advantage was that I would have

> an opportunity to establish rapport, to explain the purpose of the study, and to explain the meaning of items that may not be clear . . . [The most important is that it] provides a high proportion of usable responses (Best, 1977:157).

Finally 449 completed questionnaires had been collected from children of ten years or over studying in primary class three and upwards at nine supplementary schools. Out of the 449 returned questionnaires, only 14 could not be analysed as quite a large section of the questionnaire had not been completed by children who were handicapped in English.

No effort was made to distribute the questionnaire to children in maintained schools because of the lack of connection with the public sector. On the other hand, the application for permission to conduct research at schools of the ILEA takes a lot of bureaucratic procedures which would hinder the progress of the research. Instead, attempts had been made to request for observation of Chinese classes in some state schools. Because of the absence of response from these schools, no further formal application for classroom observation in the maintained sector was made.

The decision not to distribute questionnaires to the public sector was supported by Evans (1968) who does not recommend choosing subjects who are beyond the accessibility of the investigator and those with whom the researcher are not familiar. Since the majority of the pupils helping to fill in the questionnaire were attending British state school, their needs and problems to a certain extent could be quite representative.

Chinese parents were given no questionnaire as the pilot study indicated that quite a lot of Chinese parents were illiterate in both English and Chinese. Such evidence in fact corresponds to findings of a small scale survey of the social service needs of the Chinese community in Haringey[2] (Haringey Chinese Group [HCG], 1986b). Although the questionnaire of the Haringey Chinese Community Centre was in Chinese, the majority of the respondents required some assistance in answering the questionnaire. Since similar assistance could not be secured for another survey, data related to the education of Chinese children was obtained from the results of the questionnaire of the Haringey Chinese Community Centre.

Owing to the complexity of the Chinese community and the lack of guidelines from other sources in relation to the manner of conducting research on the Chinese community, a combination of methods had been adopted to operationalise the research. By having findings supplemented and checked by various methods — literature, observation, interviews and questionnaires, the study aims at producing an objective and true picture of the education of Chinese children in Britain.

By having a grant from the Central Research Fund Committee of the University of London, I had been able to carry out field work in Los Angeles, New York City and San Francisco for three months[3], from 27 April to the end of July, 1987. Basically the techniques used were similar to those in London except that questionnaires could not be designed because of insufficient information obtained from the American literature available in Britain. In other words, data collection in the two American cities relied mainly on observation and interviews. Similar to those carried out in London, observations and interviews had to be carried out in different environments in order to reach as many subjects as possible. One major difference was that some data in relation to the education of Chinese children could be obtained from state schools.

Notes to Chapter 1

1. The Mother Tongue Project was under the auspices of the Schools Council until March 1984 and was extended and funded by the School Curriculum Committee until August 1985 (Mother Tongue Project, 1984).
2. The Haringey Chinese Community was formerly known as the Haringey Chinese Group when it was founded in 1983. At the Annual General Meeting in December 1986, Haringey Chinese Community Centre became the official name of the Group.
3. About 10 days were spent in Los Angeles partly because school visit arrangements had been made before the author's departure from London,

England. Another purpose of the trip was to visit the Evaluation, Dissemination and Assessment Center at the State University of California where the majority of the bilingual education curricular materials can be found. The data obtained in Los Angeles will supplement what is lacking in New York City and San Francisco.

2 Contemporary Chinese Communities in London, San Francisco and New York City

During the last two decades, owing to the rapid immigration of Chinese people to Britain and the USA, Chinese communities in London, San Francisco and New York City had undergone changes in terms of their size, geographical distribution, and language of communication which undoubtedly would have an impact on policies in education.

Size of the Chinese Population

After the Second World War, the Chinese population in Britain and the USA had increased considerably. The causes leading to such a growth are of two main categories: (1) the 'push' factors and (2) the 'pull' factors.

The 'push' factors

In post-war China, the two major events which pushed Chinese people out of the country were the communist take-over in 1949 and the Cultural Revolution between 1966 and 1976. The confiscation of properties from the rich and land from land-owners, the radical attack on Confucianism and the degradation of intellectuals during the Cultural Revolution had resulted in frustration and turmoil in China. Under such circumstances, many of the discontented Chinese sought refuge outside the country.

Before Hong Kong was ceded to Britain in 1842 under the Treaty of Nanking, Hong Kong was part of China sharing similar culture and economy. Since the New Territories[1] (see Map 1) was located at the border of China and land was available for farming, Chinese refugees arriving in Hong Kong in the late 1940s preferred to settle in the New Territories (Brim, 1970; D. Jones, 1979; Lynn, 1982; The New Territories Development Department, 1978). The settlement of refugees from China in the New Territories not only resulted in a 317% increase in the New Territories population over the period between 1931 (population: 98,157) and 1961 (population: 409,945) (Brim, 1970) but also created keen competition for arable land. While the New Territories was facing the problem of a shortage of farm land, some of the land had been resumed by the government for development purposes resulting in still further shortage (Chiu and So, 1983). Some people in the New Territories tried to look for jobs in the city. Getting employment in town was not easy for these people as many of them did not have any basic education or specific skills. By the late 1960s, as a result of the economic recession, political instability and riots in 1966 and 1967, a lot of business had been wound up and factories had been closed down (Jones, D., 1979; Ma, 1967). Many people in the city were unemployed. People who found it

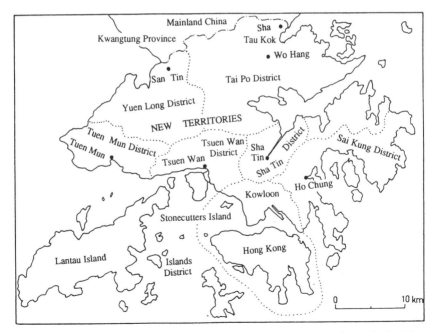

MAP 1 *HONG KONG: Hong Kong Island, Kowloon Peninsula and the New Territories*
Source: Taylor, M. (1987:27).

hard to earn a living in the New Territories therefore had to look for opportunities abroad (Aijmer, 1967; Jones, D., 1979; Krausz, 1971; Ng, K.C., 1968; Shang, 1984). Their intention of going overseas has been summarised by Crissman (1967) in such a way that

> [Chinese] did not set out adventurously to begin a new life abroad, but were pushed out of their homes by economic necessity, the unwilling victims of pressure on the land and lack of local opportunities for earning a living (p. 187).

The 'pull' factors

The external 'pull' factors which had facilitated the emigration of Chinese people were the post-war immigration policies of Britain and the United States. After the Second World War, both Britain and the United States had opened their doors to immigrants from China and Hong Kong because of diplomatic and political reasons.

In order to maintain a political relationship with China after the war, the Chinese Exclusion Acts implemented in 1882 were repealed by President Franklin D. Roosevelt in 1943 (Leary, 1971; Stone and DeNevi, 1971). Such legislation as the War Brides Act of 1945, the Immigration and Nationality (Walter-McCarran) Act of 1952, the Refugee Relief Act of 1953, which gave special consideration to the immigration of refugees, individuals with needed skills and those who came to the USA for the purpose of family reunification, were passed by Congress. As a result, the Census of 1960 which maintained a record of 237,292 Chinese showed an incredible increase of 101.7% in the Chinese population in the United States, as compared to the 117,629 in 1950 (Fessler, 1983; Wong, B., 1979).

While Britain was attempting to meet the shortage of labour after the war, there was hardly any immigration control over the people from its colonies and Commonwealth countries (Gordon and Klug, 1985). As Hong Kong had become a British colony in 1842, Hong Kong citizens could have the right of entry and abode in Britain under the 1948 British Nationality Act. Britain therefore became one of the alternatives for Chinese in Hong Kong who wanted to look for opportunities abroad (Ng, K.C., 1968). Similar to the USA, the British Census of 1961 also showed a substantial increase of 71% in the total Chinese population (from Hong Kong and China) in Britain, as compared with the record in 1951 (General Register Office, 1956 & 1966). Although the Chinese population in both countries continued to grow in the 1960s, the rate of expansion in Britain was higher as a consequence of the enactment of the new laws to control immigration into Britain.

In order to curb immigration of the coloured people, whom it was felt might increase the social costs of the country, Britain passed the Commonwealth Immigration Act of 1962 (Gordon and Klug, 1985). Since the Act would abolish the right of entry into the UK of the British colony citizens, a considerable number of Chinese people had rushed into the country before the new Act came into effect in July 1962. The *Observer* of 11 February 1962 reported that the number of Chinese immigrants in Britain in the first seven months of 1962 was 880 — more than double that of the previous statistics of 400 for the same period in 1961.

In addition to the last-minute immigrants, workers from Hong Kong taking advantage of the employment voucher system[2], which was introduced by the 1962 Commonwealth Immigrants Act, had enlarged the size of the Chinese population in the first half of the decade. The New Territories Annual Reports of 1961/62 and 1963/64 recorded that there were more than 20,000 Hong Kong workers in Britain by 1962 (Aserappa, 1962) and the number increased to about 35,000 by 1964 (Aserappa, 1964). In the same period, President Kennedy's Executive Order of 1962 had only admitted about 15,000 Chinese into the United Stated (Chen, J., 1980; Leary, 1971; Wang, L.C., 1971). Comparatively speaking, more Chinese immigrants had entered Britain in the early 1960s.

In the late 1960s the increase in the Chinese population in Britain and the USA was highlighted by the passage of two major immigration laws. In the United States the Immigration and Nationality Act of 1965 had set an annual quota of 20,000 per country in the Eastern Hemisphere[3] (Brand, 1987; Chen, J.,1980; Jung, 1972; Leary, 1971; Lum, 1971; Tsang, 1982). In Britain the Commonwealth Immigrants Act of 1968 required the wife to be sent for if the husband in Britain wanted to apply for entry of children who were under 16 (Great Britain. Parliament. House of Commons. Home Affairs Committee [GB. P. H. of C. HAC], 1985; Greater London Council Department of Planning and Transportation Intelligence Unit, 1974). While Hong Kong and China were having political unrest in the late 1960s, the opportunities promised by the prosperity of the catering business in Britain and the fairly stable and optimistic economy of the USA had attracted more Chinese into the two countries. Both the UK and USA indicated a rise in the Chinese population (General Register Office, 1966; GB. OPCS, 1974) of about

107% and 80% (Chan and Tsang, 1983; Fessler, 1983) respectively in the 1970 Census, as compared to 1960's.

Over the period of the 1970s, in spite of the strict immigration control, the figures of 1980 revealed a significant growth of 76% (GB. OPCS, 1974 & 1983a) and 85% (Fessler, 1983; Suzuki, 1983) of the Chinese population in Britain and the United States respectively.

Geographical Distribution

Owing to the tremendous increase in the Chinese population in the 1960s and 1970s, the geographical distribution of Chinese people in Britain and the USA had been affected.

Despite the fact that San Francisco has accommodated the majority of the Chinese in the United States since the nineteenth century, a comparison of the 1960 and 1970 Census statistics indicates that New York City has been leading the Chinese population since 1970 (Chang, P.M., 1983; Chen, J., 1980; Fessler, 1983; Sung, 1976). The 1970 American Census reported that there were 16.1% (69,324) of the total Chinese population in the United States in New York City but only 15.6% (58,696) in San Francisco (Chen, J., 1980). In the 1980 Census, the difference between the Chinese population in the two American cities was even larger. There were 124,372 Chinese in New York City but only 82,244 in San Francisco (U.S. Department of Commerce. Bureau of the Census, 1983a & b, Vol. 1, Parts 6 and 34).

At present about half of the total Chinese population in the UK are living in London (DES, 1985; GB. P. H. of C. HAC, 1985; GB. OPCS, 1987; Shang, 1984). The two earliest Chinese communities established before the war in East London near Pennyfields and Limehouse Causeway, and Liverpool around Pitt Street, Cleverland Square and Frederick Street lost their importance after the war due to bombing and redevelopment (Berridge, 1978; Jones, D., 1979; Lynn, 1982; Ng, K.C., 1968). Following the development of the restaurant business, Chinatown in London had been moved to the Soho area in West End, occupying Gerrard Street, Lisle Street, Wardour Street and Great Newport Street (ILEA, 1975) (see Map 2). To replace Liverpool, Manchester has now established the second largest Chinese community in Britain (DES, 1985; GB. P. H. of C. HAC, 1985).

Unlike the pre-war Chinese communities in Britain, or Chinatowns in San Francisco and New York City, not many Chinese in London reside

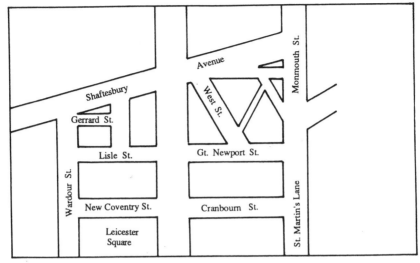

MAP 2 *London 'Chinatown' — The Soho Area*
Source: ILEA (1975:6).

in Chinatown because of high rents in the West End. On the other hand, the Chinese catering trade had reached saturation by the late 1960s. Chinese people had to look for new places to establish their businesses (Jones, D., 1979). As the geographical mobility of the Chinese in Britain is governed by the demand for catering service, their settlement is quite dispersed in the country (Garvey and Jackson, 1975; GB. P. H. of C. HAC, 1985; Shang, 1984). Besides the old concentrations in the London Boroughs of Westminster, Kensington and Camden, as indicated by the Commission for Racial Equality (1978) in their survey of ethnic minorities in Britain, the establishment of Chinese community centres in Haringey, Hackney and Islington in the last two years shows that a sizeable Chinese community is spreading out to North London (see Map 3).

In contrast with London, quite a lot of Chinese immigrants live and work in Chinatowns in San Francisco. Sung (1979) and B. Wong (1982) indicate that about half to three quarters of the Chinese in New York City live in areas close to the core Chinatown. Owing to the increase in Chinese immigrants in the last two decades, the two American Chinatowns are expanding. In addition to the San Francisco Chinatown proper which comprises 24 blocks bounded by Columbus, Montgomery, California and Powell, the Chinese community is creeping into the Richmond and Sunset districts (see Map 4) where public transport to Chinatown is convenient

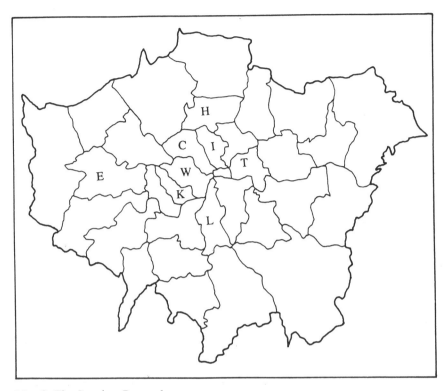

MAP 3 *The London Boroughs*
Source: General Register Office (1966)
Greater London Tables/Great Britain Tables, between p. 32 and p. 33. C: Camden,
E: Ealing, I: Islington, K: Kensington & Chelsea, H: Haringey, L: Lambeth, T:
Tower Hamlets, W: Westminster.

(Chen, J., 1980; Sung, 1976). Richmond is now regarded by the local
Chinese as the second Chinatown in San Francisco.

Although the Chinese community in New York City was only
created during the Anti-Chinese Movement (1882–1943), recent studies
of the American Chinese societies by J. Chen (1980), C. L. Kuo (1977),
Sung (1976 & 1979), B. Wong (1982), L. Wong (1976) point out that
Chinatown in New York City has expanded considerably. From its original
boundaries of Mott, Pell and Doyer, Chinatown has extended north to
14th Street, south to the piers, east to Allen Street, and west to Broadway.
Outside the Chinatown proper, scattered Chinese communities are found
near the Columbia University in north Manhattan, Jackson Heights and
Elmhust in Queens as well as Flatbush in Brooklyn (Wong, B., 1982)

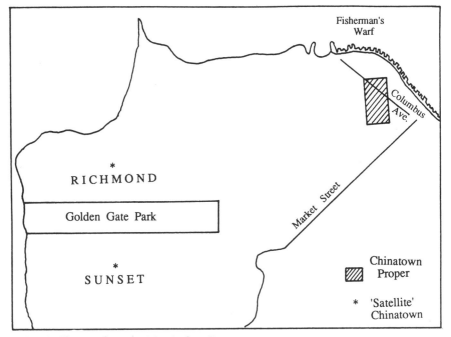

MAP 4 *Chinese Communities in San Francisco.*

(see Map 5). According to L. Wong (1976), the Chinese community in Queens is known to New Yorkers as 'little Chinatown of Queens'.

Regardless of the fact that Chinese are moving out of the core area of Chinatowns in London, San Francisco and New York City, their settlement indicates that they like to concentrate in cities. The 1970 American Census shows that Chinese in the United States have reached a total urbanisation rate of 97% (Fessler, 1983; Sung, 1976; Tsai, 1986). In Britain such data on the urbanisation of Chinese people is not available. Through interviews and observation, it was found that Chinese people prefer living in areas where Chinatown can be easily accessible by the Underground.

Linguistic Diversity

Chinese communities in Britain and the USA have become less homogeneous since the war in terms of languages/dialects brought in by new immigrants (Ng, K.C., 1968; Wong, B., 1979). Such a phenomenon is quite different from the pre-war situation.

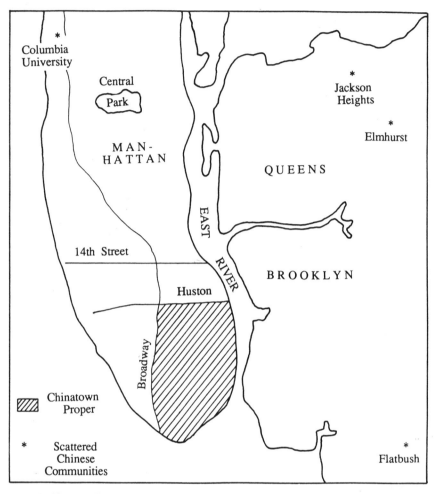

MAP 5 *Chinese Communities in New York City.*

Before the war, about 99% of the Chinese–Americans came from the southern part of Kwantung Province (Chen, J., 1980; Heyer, 1953; Kung, 1962; Kuo, C.L., 1977; Lee, 1956 & 1960; Wong, B., 1979 & 1982; Woo, 1985; Wu, 1958). The majority of the Chinese were from Sze Yup and Sam Yup Districts (see Map 6) where people speak a similar dialect called Toysanese (Wong, B., 1982; Chen, J., 1980). Therefore Toysanese had once been the lingua franca among Chinese in the United States.

Although a substantial number of Chinese in Britain originated from

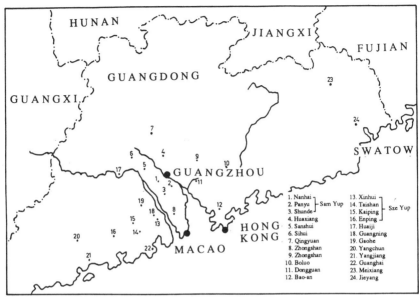

MAP 6 *Counties in Guangdong Province from which the majority of Chinese emigrants came to America*
Source: Chen, J. (1980:17).

Kwantung Province (Ng, K.C., 1968), Toysanese is not as popular as *pun tei wa* (local language/Cantonese) or Hakka (a Chinese dialect) among Chinese in Britain. The main reason is that many early Chinese immigrants in Britain came from villages such as San Tin (Watson, 1977a) and Sha Tau Kok (see Map 1) where Hakka was commonly spoken by villagers. Besides Hakka, people from the New Territories also know Cantonese which is the lingua franca in Hong Kong. Within the Chinese community in Britain, Cantonese remains to be the lingua franca. Hakka is confined to intra-group communication only.

Similar to Hakka, Toysanese is losing its importance in Chinese communities in New York City and San Francisco. Cantonese-speaking Chinese have already outnumbered the Toysanese-speaking people. The language of communication in American Chinatowns has been dominated by Cantonese. In addition to the Cantonese dialect, Hakka, Toysanese, Putonghua, Fukienese and Vietnamese have been brought into Chinatowns in London, New York City and San Francisco by new immigrants.

Many Chinese parents in Britain or the USA speak at least one of the Chinese dialects. Although Chinese children are exposed to the

Chinese language at home and have contact with the Chinese community in the UK or USA on certain occasions, the mother tongue proficiency of the younger Chinese generation is usually weaker than English. In their daily life, English is the language of communication with the majority people. At school their mother tongue is not supported. At home Chinese parents are more concerned that their children should give priority to assignments from English-medium schools. The learning of Chinese has become less important. There has been research evidence in Britain and the USA showing the phenomenon of language dominance among Chinese. The one% sample of the 1970 US Census indicated that 14% of the Chinese–Americans claimed English as their mother tongue. These figures had included 12% in California and 4% in New York City (Sung, 1976). Of the 435 Chinese children within the age range of 10 to 23 in London, about 6 to 8% of the group used English with their siblings and friends[4]. Findings of the studies indicate that in addition to various Chinese dialects, English is commonly spoken by the younger generation within the Chinese communities in Britain and the USA.

Occupational Patterns

New Chinese immigrants had not only diversified the linguistic situation, but also brought with them skills and capital which had changed the occupational patterns of the Chinese communities in Britain and USA. Such traditional jobs as seamen and laundrymen among Chinese in Britain (Jones, D., 1979; Lynn, 1982; May, 1978; Ng, K.C., 1968) and railroad builders and miners among Chinese–Americans (Chun, 1980; Tom, 1941; Wang, L.C., 1971; Wong, L., 1976; Wright, K., 1979) have almost disappeared. In addition to the popular catering business and Chinese grocery stores, a variety of service industries such as tourism, gift shops, barber shops, printing, banking, etc. have been opened in Chinatowns in London, San Francisco and New York City.

The cost of living in the three metropolitan cities is relatively high. Many Chinese women have to help to support the family by sewing. In London most Chinese women sew at home whereas their American counterparts work in garment factories in Chinatowns. Besides the stereotyped menial jobs and service industries, some prestigious professions such as lawyers, doctors and accountants have been taken up by a certain proportion of Chinese–Americans who are either new immigrants or Chinese who have gone through schooling in the United States. According to the 1970 US Census, about 25% of the Chinese in the USA were engaged in professional jobs. The percentage was higher than that of other ethnic groups (Chang, P.M., 1983).

In London, findings of a small scale survey of the needs of the Chinese in Haringey conducted by the Haringey Chinese Group in July 1986 indicated that the majority of Chinese parents (27 out of 52) had only achieved primary level education (HCG, 1986b). A similar survey carried out by Yau (1983) in Lambeth discovered that many Chinese people who were 25 years of age or over did not have a working knowledge of English. The educational attainment of the Chinese in London is far behind Chinese–Americans. The 1970 US Census showed that of the age group 25 and over, 57.8% had completed high school (Chang, P.M., 1983). Statistics compiled by the Commission on Civil Rights pointed out that in 1976, 60% of the Chinese male and 44% of the Chinese female aged 25 to 29 had achieved some form of higher education (Chan and Tsang, 1983). A lot of Chinese in Britain came from the New Territories where education provision was inadequate prior to the universalisation of primary education in Hong Kong in 1971. It would not be too suprising that only 2 to 3% of the Chinese in Britain were regarded as professionals. More than 90% were engaged in the restaurant business (GB. P. H. of C. HAC, 1985).

Community Associations

When the Chinese were boycotted by the discriminatory legislation in the United States during the Anti-Chinese Movement (1882–1943) (Fan, 1981; Ow et al., 1975; Wong, L., 1976; Yu, 1976) and suffered from racist harassment in Britain in the early twentieth century (May, 1978; Jones, D., 1979), they hardly got any assistance and protection from the local or the Chinese government.

Chinese have a very strong sense of clanship and lineage[5] (Baker, 1966; Crissman, 1967; Watson, 1977a). In their country of origin, some Chinese had acquired some knowledge of self government through the practice of a village representative system (Brim, 1970). In order to protect themselves from racism in Britain and the USA, overseas Chinese have set up among themselves clan or district associations such as the Sam Yup Association and Sze Yup Association in San Francisco (Ow et al., 1975; Wong, L., 1976), the Lees', Chans', Engs', Wongs' 'Jung Chun Wui' (Common Descent Relatives Association) and 'Jung Wa Gung So' (the Chinese Six Companies)[6] in New York City (Wong, B., 1982), the Oi T'ung Kung Sheung Wui (Oi T'ung Association) in East London (Ng,

K.C.,1968; Shang, 1984), the Chinese Mutual Aid Workers Club in London and the Chi Kung Tong (Chinese Masonic Lodge) in Liverpool (Collins, 1957; Shang, 1984). The major function of the clan societies is to look after overseas Chinese welfare, combat discrimination, provide shelter for overseas Chinese and liaise between the host society and the local Chinese community in matters concerning Chinese (Collins, 1957; Ng, K.C., 1968; Ow *et al.*, 1975; Shang, 1984).

Although the clan associations are more of a charitable nature, some of them, especially those known as 'tongs' in the USA, have political affiliation either with the Communist China or the Taiwan government (Collins, 1957; Kuo, C.L., 1977; Shang, 1984; Wong, B., 1982). Since the majority of Chinese supplementary schools are established by benevolent associations, their political background will have some influence on the curriculum of Chinese supplementary schools in Britain and the USA. The educational contribution of these associations will be discussed in more detail in part two of the book.

Owing to the influx of immigrants, such social problems as housing, unemployment, juvenile delinquency and schooling became quite serious in Chinatowns in both countries. Some educated people familiar with the local government structure become more conscious of the welfare and the future development of their community. They get together to form voluntary working groups to provide services for their people. At the same time, they apply for resources from the local government to support those services. Gradually modern service associations, as called by C.L. Kuo (1977), such as the Community Educational Services in San Francisco, the Chinatown Planning Council, the Chinatown Development Council, the Immigrant Social Service, Inc. in New York City, the Chinese Information and Advice Centre (CIAC), the Chinese Community Centre and the Haringey Chinese Community Centre in London flourished between the 1970s and 1980s[7].

Unlike traditional associations, modern service associations and their projects are financially supported by the government (Kuo, C.L., 1977). They therefore can take a more active role in providing services of various types to meet the needs of the community and act as watch-dogs and political pressure groups of the community. In Britain and the United States, some of these new associations also play a role in providing educational service for Chinese children.

It can now be concluded that as a result of the increase in Chinese immigrants, the social structure of the Chinese communities in Britain and the USA has already changed. Although they are only minorities in the two countries, they have become more visible in terms of their number. Despite the fact that many of the Chinese in both countries do not speak English, their rights and needs are represented by Chinese community associations/organisations founded by the more educated and enthusiastic Chinese.

Notes to Chapter 2

1. Under the Convention of Peking, the New Territories were leased to Britain for 99 years from July 1, 1898. The total area of the New Territories is 370 square miles and comprises four main administrative districts: Tai Po, Yuen Long, Tsuen Wan and Sai Kung and islands (Hong Kong Government, 1965) (See Map 2). Before urbanisation, the New Territories was considered to be the rural part of Hong Kong where people grew rice and vegetables.
2. There were three types of vouchers, A, B and C, in the voucher system. Category A vouchers were for those who had specific jobs to come to Britain; category B vouchers were for those with skills useful to Britain; and category C vouchers were for unskilled labourers (Gordon and Klug, 1985). According to O'Neil (1972), many of the Chinese in Britain came with the 'A' vouchers.
3. Only 105 quota for Chinese was set by the Chinese Exclusion Laws 1882 (Chen, J., 1980; Wong, L., 1976).
4. The information was obtained from the questionnaire filled in by Chinese children studying at Chinese supplementary schools.
5. 'Clan' refers to the grouping of people sharing the same name but the lines of descent are often fictional. 'Lineage' aggregates people on the basis of known descent from a specific ancestor. It is usually localised in a given village (Watson, 1977a).
6. There are two Chinese Six Companies (also known as the Chinese Consolidated Benevolent Association). One is in San Francisco which was established in 1869 (Hoy, 1942). The other one was founded in 1884 but is located in New York City (Kuo, 1977; Wong, B., 1979 & 1982). The Six Companies in San Francisco namely Ning Yung, Kong Chow, Hop Wu, Yan Wu, Young Wo and Sam Yup District Associations were merged in 1858 (Almquist, 1979; Chang, P.M., 1983) and was incorporated under the laws of California in 1901 (Kuo, C.L., 1977). The Chinese Six Companies in New York City was incorporated under the Societies Act of New York State in 1890. At that time, it was known as the Chinese Charitable and Benevolent Association. Before the incorporation, it was registered with the Peking Imperial Government in 1884 under the title of 'Jung Wa Gung So' (Wong, B., 1982). Therefore the Chinese Six Companies in New York City is commonly known to the local Chinese as 'Jung Wa Kung So'.
7. The information was obtained by making reference to the annual reports of the Chinese Information and Advice Centre (CIAC) and the Haringey Chinese Group (HCG). The two centres were opened in 1983 and 1986 respectively (CIAC, 1984; HCG, 1986a). Lue (1981) in his speech given at the Open Day at the North London Polytechnic on 4 November 1981 stated that the Chinese Community Centre at Gerrard Street was opened in July 1980.

Part II:
Education Provision for
Chinese Children in the UK

3 Analysis of Chinese Children's Educational Problems in Britain

Owing to the changing political situation in Hong Kong, and Chinese parents' belief that English-medium education will lead to social and economic advancement, Chinese parents in Britain are quite willing to send their children to schools in the maintained sector. Although Chinese children can enjoy the same educational facilities, Chinese parents in Britain are not satisfied that Chinese language education does not officially form part of the curriculum in British schools as that in Hong Kong. From Chinese parents' point of view, the ignorance of the Chinese language is an educational problem of their children.

Despite the fact that Chinese children in Britian are educated in English, some of them have not acquired the basic English language skills to enable them to benefit from the British education. Underachievement and failure at school among Chinese children have not been tackled.

In order to analyse the educational problems of Chinese children in Britain, Holmes' (1981) classificatory taxonomy and John Dewey's theory of asynchronous change have been applied in this research. There are four basic patterns in Holmes' classificatory taxonomy namely: (1) normative patterns, (2) institutional patterns, (3) natural environment or the physical world and (4) the pattern of mental states. If a change takes place in any of the first three patterns but there is a relative lack of change in other patterns, especially in mental states, problems will arise (Holmes, 1965). In the case of Chinese communities in Britain, the 'change' and 'no-change' elements have been detected in the natural environment patterns and the patterns of mental states which are elaborated as follows.

Changes in the Natural Environment

Increase of Chinese children in Britain

The increase of Chinese children in individual schools is a normative effect of the demographic change in the natural environment. It has been explained in Chapter 2 that owing to the political and economic instability in Hong Kong in the late 1960s and the promise of opportunities by the prosperity of Chinese restaurants in Britain, there has been a drastic increase in the Chinese in Britain since the late 1960s. By the 1980s there were about 100,000 Chinese in Britain; forming the third largest ethnic group after the Afro-Caribbeans and Asians (GB. P. H. of C. HAC, 1985; GB. OPCS, 1983a).

In the past, it was quite common practice among Chinese parents in Britain to leave their children, who were either born in Hong Kong or in the UK, to be brought up by their grandmothers or mothers in Hong Kong so that parents could be free to work in Britain (Jones, D., 1980; Fitchett, 1976; Garvey and Jackson, 1975). Four children interviewed and a few respondents to the questionnaire confirmed such a practice. After family reunion between the late 1960s and the early 1970s, because of the strict immigration control due to the 1971 Immigration Act[1] which came into effect in January 1973 (Dummett, 1982; Gordon and Klug, 1985), the sending of Chinese children back and forth between Britain and Hong Kong became less popular.

By the early 1980s, the confirmation of the return of Hong Kong's sovereignty to China by the Sino-British Agreement (Hong Kong Government, 1984) further discouraged Chinese in Britain from returning to Hong Kong. Because of the fear of communism, which had been experienced by some Chinese before they fled to Hong Kong or Britain, and the lack of confidence in the government of the People's Republic of China in maintaining two social systems within one political framework, Chinese who had settled in Britain with their families were more determined to abandon their 'sojourner' mentality and settle in Britain permanently. Nine out of the 13 Chinese parents in interviews conducted in 1986 indicated that because of the political instability of Hong Kong and the problems of readjustment for them as well as for their children, they had no intention of going back and settling in Hong Kong.

As a result of immigration, family reunion and the change from sojourner to permanent settlers, the number of Chinese children in Britain has grown considerably since the 1970s. According to the immigration statistics of the Home Office, among all Chinese immigrants from Hong Kong who were given the right of abode on their arrival in Britain in the 1970s, the majority were children (CRE, 1978; Great Britain. Home Office, 1974 & 1975; NCC, 1979 & 1984). Table 1 illustrates the pattern of continuous immigration of children from Hong Kong in the 1970s.

Since the 1968 Commonwealth Immigrants Act requires both parents to be in Britain if the father wants to apply for entry of his children who are under sixteen (Greater London Council Department of Planning and Transportation Intelligence Unit, 1974), the immigration statistics in Table 1 show that many women had entered the country to join their husbands in the early 1970s. The number of female Chinese immigrants was very close to that of Chinese children. In 1973 and 1974 the proportion between the number of children and women accepted for settlement in Britain upon their arrival was 1.3 : 1.

After the reunion of husbands and wives, more Chinese children have been born in Britain. According to the Home Affairs Committee's (1985) Second Report on the Chinese Community in Britain and the Labour Force Survey of 1984 (GB. OPCS, 1986), about a quarter (24,000) of the Chinese in Britain are British-born.

Increase of Chinese children in British schools

The number of Chinese children in British schools becomes more significant as a result of immigrantion and natural growth. Among 178 immigrant children of Chinese origin, 72.5% arrived in the UK at school age, i.e. between 5 and 15[2]. The Labour Force Survey of 1984 (GB.

TABLE 1 *Acceptance of people from Hong Kong for settlement in UK on arrival in the 1970s*

Year of arrival	Number of different age-groups given the right of abode in UK			
	Men (%)	Women (%)	Children (%)	Total
1973	161 (10)	617 (40)	783 (50)	1,561
1974	434 (22)	686 (34)	880 (44)	1,990
1976	51 (4)	315 (23)	1,000 (73)	1,366
1977	34 (4)	186 (20)	729 (77)	949

Sources: CRE (1978, Table 25(a), pp. 24–25).
        Clough and Quarmby (1978:64).

OPCS, 1986) indicated that about 80% (24,000) of the Chinese children in British schools (about 30,000) were born in the UK. These statistics suggest that a specific proportion of the school population in Britain derives from Chinese children.

Since most of the Chinese in Britain have re-united with their families, including grandparents, not many of the Chinese children in Britain will be sent back to the native country to be brought up and educated in a Chinese cultural environment. In other words, the school-age Chinese children who are either immigrant or British-born will have to go to schools in Britain. Consequently individual schools in Britain, particularly those under the administration of the ILEA, have demonstrated a substantial increase of children of Chinese origin.

In Linda Lai's (1975) visits to five schools while she was investigating the social needs of Chinese families in London, she pointed out that in one primary school in the ILEA, more than half of the pupils were of Chinese origin. The presence of such a considerable number of Chinese children within one school is quite a recent phenomenon. A part-time youth worker at a Chinese community centre claimed that when she had primary education at a school in Chinatown in London, about 80% of the pupils in her school were Chinese[3].

Despite the fact that Chinese are scattered all over the country where they could possibly set up their catering business, their small concentrations in such Boroughs as Westminster, Kensington, Camden (see Map 3) (CRE, 1978) and recent settlement in North London has led to an increase of Chinese children in ILEA schools. The four Language Censuses on pupils whose first language is not English, conducted by the ILEA in 1978, 1981, 1983 and 1985 (ILEA, 1979; ILEA Research & Statistics, 1982; Kysel, 1983 & 1985) showed that there had been an average increase of 26% of Chinese children in ILEA schools in each Census. By comparing the number of children whose home language is Chinese[4], it has been noticed that most of these children are concentrated in schools in Divisions 2 (Westminster and Camden) and 3 (Islington) (See Map 7). Tables 2 and 3 demonstrate the pattern of increase and distribution of Chinese children in ILEA schools.

Table 3 indicates that Chinese children in the 10 ILEA Divisions (see Map 7)[5] continued to increase in each Language Census. In the 1978, 1981 and 1983 Language Census, Divisions 2 (Westminster and Camden) and 3 (Islington) had the largest number of Chinese children. Although Division 2 was heading Chinese pupils in 1985, there was a slight drop in the number of Chinese children. Divisions 9 (Lambeth)

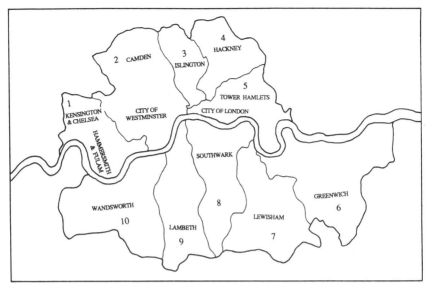

MAP 7 *The 10 Divisions of the Inner London Education Authority*
Source: ILEA (1983b:1).

TABLE 2 *Pattern of increase of Chinese pupils in ILEA schools*

Year of Census	Number of Chinese children	Change percentage
1978	1,712	—
1981	2,237	+30.7
1983	2,825	+23.1
1985	3,546	+25.5

Sources: ILEA Research & Statistics (1982, Table 4:16).
        Kysel (1983, Table 5:9).
        Kysel (1985, Table 5:9).

and 8 (Southwark) (see Map 7) demonstrated a significant growth of 44 and 50% of Chinese pupils respectively in 1985. Division 3 (Islington), which had been accommodating a considerable number of Chinese children since 1978, was outnumbered by Divisions 8 and 9 which had become the second and the third largest divisons with pupils of Chinese origin. Such a phenomenon signalled that some Chinese were moving out of their traditional concentrations to places adjacent to the City of London. As a result, the rate of growth of Chinese pupils in Divisions

TABLE 3 *Distribution of Chinese pupils in ILEA's 10 administrative divisions*

Year of Census	ILEA Divisions									
	1	2	3	4	5	6	7	8	9	10
1978	155	483	240	128	136	50	84	133	187	116
1981	188	576	316	147	176	73	126	197	262	175
1983	190	641	374	192	233	179	199	280	321	212
1985	197	607	413	251	329	302	242	422	462	317

Sources: ILEA Research & Statistics (1979), Table 1 (page number not indicated).
ILEA Research & Statistics (1982, Appendix 2 p. 25).
Kysel (1983), Appendix 2, (page number not indicated).
Kysel (1985), Appendix 2, (page number not indicated).

with newly developed Chinese communities was higher than that in Divisions which traditionally had the largest number of Chinese pupils.

Besides evidence from the four ILEA Language Censuses, interviews with teachers and students had also confirmed the increase of Chinese pupils in British schools. Some teachers at two ILEA secondary schools admitted that the number of Chinese pupils in their school had been increasing in recent years. In 1986/87 there were about 20 and 30 Chinese pupils in each of these schools. Two sisters studying at a secondary school in Haringey claimed that they used to be the only Chinese at school. When the new academic year 1986/87 began, some more Chinese pupils had been admitted to the school. There were at least one or two Chinese pupils at each grade level that year.

No-change in Mental States

The aspirations of Chinese parents in Britain

Holmes and other social theorists such as William Sumner, William Ogburn and Gunnar Myrdal indicate that it is very difficult for people to change their deeply held sentiments immediately in response to social innovations (Holmes, 1981). Such a notion also applies to Chinese parents in Britain.

Although more Chinese children go to schools in Britain where prestigious jobs may not be secured by academic achievement, Chinese parents' aspirations for their children's success in education have never changed. On the other hand, Chinese parents often presume that western concepts of democracy and individualism in the British society will not be compatible with the traditional Chinese cultural values. Therefore many Chinese parents expect that their children will only take advantage of the British education system to earn more academic credentials to prepare them for work. Their children should have a strong link with the Chinese culture which will help them to maintain certain traditional cultural values.

In order to understand Chinese parents' ideologies, an 'ideal typical model' (Holmes, 1981) based on the philosophies of Confucius has been constructed. In such a model, the ideal 'mental states' of Chinese parents can be revealed.

Success in education

Similar to the western philosophies of Plato, Aristotle, Marx and Dewey, Confucius' concepts of man, society and knowledge could be understood through some of his great works. In the Great Learning (in Woo, 1985), Confucius says,

> The aims of the great learning consist of illuminating the bright virtue, renewing the people, and resting only in perfection . . . Thus in ancient times those who wanted to illumine the bright virtue in the whole world first sought to govern the country well. Those who want to govern the country well first sought to manage their own families. Those who wanted to manage their own families first sought to control their own hearts. Those who wanted to control their own hearts first sought to purify their motives. Those who wanted to purify their motives first sought to extend their knowledge . . . (p. 17).

Such a quotation from the Great Learning reveals some of Confucius' perception of knowledge. Knowledge viewed by Confucius is of paramount importance. It not only develops a person intellectually and morally but also provides an educated person with an insight into the management of one's family, the administration of a country as well as the illumination of the 'bright virtues' of the world.

Confucius' notion of knowledge in fact has an impact on the development of 'kwun tsi' (perfect men) and the administration of society. The emphasis on the achievement in classics (e.g. odes, records of history and music) in the civil service examinations in old China indicated that scholars or perfect men were preferred for government officials (Fan, 1981; Kiang, 1948; Woo, 1985). Among the hierarchy of professions in the traditional society, '*si*' (scholars/officials) were on top of the social ladder, followed by '*nong*' (agriculturalists), '*gong*' (artisans) and '*soeng*' (merchants) (Baker, 1981; Creel, 1954; Fan, 1981; Nee and Nee, 1973). Therefore in old China, literacy training was seen by the common people as the high road to public service, and subsequently to wealth and prestige (Kiang, 1948). Nowadays many Chinese parents still believe that success in education will lead to what Ogbu & Matute-Bianchi (1986) calls 'status mobility'.

The majority of the Chinese in Britain come from the rural parts of Hong Kong where 'status mobility' can be achieved by education. In Hong Kong executive positions in the civil service are normally filled by university graduates. It implies that university education is the key to social and economic advancement.

In order to enter a university in Hong Kong, one has to demonstrate an outstanding performance in all the examinations at various stages of schooling. Before the implementation of free compulsory primary education in 1971 (Education Department, Hong Kong, 1972), a student had to do extremely well in the Secondary School Entrance Examination (SSEE)[6] in order to be admitted into a government or subsidised school. Simpson's (1966) report on the Future Development in Education pointed out that only about 15% of the primary school graduates could enter a government or an aided secondary school. At the end of the fifth year of secondary education, all students are normally required to sit for the Hong Kong Certificate of Education Examination (HKCEE) the results of which will determine the prospective candidates to be admitted into the sixth form where students are prepared for the university entrance examinations. Since there are only very limited places at the two universities in Hong Kong, students being admitted into any of the universities are regarded as the cream of the society. When they graduate, many of them can earn quite a respectable salary by joining the civil service or private firms in executive or administrative positions.

Such a road to social and economic advancement demonstrates that the modern society of Hong Kong is very much under the influence of Confucius' concept of man, knowledge and society. Chinese parents in Hong Kong therefore place a very high value on education. While Baker (1968) was conducting his field-work in the New Territories in Hong Kong, he noticed that successful scholars such as university graduates were highly respected on the return to their own village. A feast would be organised by their own clan to celebrate their trip back home. Such a practice indicated that people in the rural area also had high expectations of their children — to succeed in education and bring honour to the family or the clan.

Many of the Chinese in Britain, especially those who come from the New Territories, are not well-educated (Baker, 1968; Wong and Fong-Lee, 1980; Yau, 1983). Because of their illiteracy and their agrarian background, they were not much respected in Hong Kong despite the fact that agriculturalists were ranked the second in the social hierarchy in old China. After having experienced hardships and frustration in looking for jobs in the city of Hong Kong and in Britain, less educated Chinese immigrants begin to realise the importance of education for personal advancement. Their attitude towards education has been changed. They insist that their sons, daughters, brothers and sisters should go to school and they are not required to help in the fields. They believe that an educated boy will have better prospects in the city or abroad (Ng, R., 1964). After family re-union, both immigrant and British-born Chinese children go to British schools. Regardless of the fact that many highly educated people in Britain are unemployed, Chinese parents' aspirations for their children's success in education have not changed. According to a survey on the Chinese community in Lambeth, more than half (55%) of the parents indicated that they expect their children to reach university education (Yau, 1983).

Although many Chinese parents send their children to Chinese supplementary schools, they '. . . do not want to see their children learn the mother tongue at the expense of learning English or to be a priority over English' (Tsow, 1984:20). When Chinese children reach senior secondary level (third and fourth year in particular) in British schools, those who are not interested in learning the Chinese language will take the opportunity to make excuses to drop out of Chinese classes. At this stage, most Chinese parents will let their children decide whether to continue to go to Chinese classes as they are more concerned that their children should one day escape from the vicious circle of ghetto by the successful completion of their mainstream education (Clough and Quarmby, 1978).

Maintenance of the hierarchy of relationships

According to Confucius' theory of society, society ought to be governed by the most capable men (scholars). In order to achieve harmony in society, Confucius had created a set of principles known as '*ng lun*' (five relationships) which outlines the expectations and obligations of the parties engaging in a certain relationship. In the Chinese society, five relationships can be identified, viz: (i) the governor and the governed, (ii) father and son, (iii) husband and wife, (iv) the elder brother and the younger brother and (v) friends (Creel, 1954; Lang, 1946). Among the five relationships, three are more concerned with relationships within a family. The emphasis on the family relationships has an implication that the state should be rooted in the family. The family ought to be regarded as a primary unit of the society. Confucianism believes that the administration of a state should start from the family. If a person is properly brought up and taught to respect authorities within his family, he should be able to respect authorities outside the family and become an obedient citizen of the empire (Lang, 1946). As a result of the influence of Confucianism, family ethics in old China emphasised filial piety and unreserved obedience of children to parents and of the younger to the elder (Baker, 1981; Creel, 1954; Fan, 1981; Lang, 1946). Nowadays although not many Chinese believe that harmony in society can be achieved in the Confucian manner, they would like to see that some discipline in the family can be maintained by transmitting Confucius' concept of family relationships to their children.

In Britain the orientation of society as well as education is more influenced by the Aristotelian concept of man, society and knowledge. The British believe that all people in society are 'free men' who are capable of reasoning and rationality. The administration of society should allow the democratic participation of free men. Knowledge should put an emphasis on logical explanations as free men are logical animals (Holmes, 1981). Because of the influence of the Aristotelian philosophies, the governing power in Britain is subject to challenge from people. The Confucius' idea of the unreserved submission to authority is not accepted in the British society.

Chinese people in Britain have realised these philosophical and cultural differences between Britain and their home country. They understand that if their children are brought up and go to schools in Britain, the concept of democracy, rationality and individuality will be inculcated in their children. Chinese parents' authority in the family can be threatened if they do not have a good educational background to enable them to think logically when they argue with their children. On the other hand, many Chinese parents in Britain are ignorant of English. According to an unofficial estimate, about 65 to 75% of the first generation Chinese are unable to speak English (GB. P. H. of C. HAC, 1985). The language of communication among Chinese children in Britain is quite different from the early Chinese immigrants. As the younger generation are exposed to the English language more often at school, only very few of them can hold a conversation solely in Chinese. In a sample of 244 school pupils, there was only an average of 20% who spoke to their siblings in Chinese. About 65 to 70% would use two languages, English and a Chinese dialect (mainly Cantonese)[7]. Chinese parents without much knowledge of English find it very difficult to participate in their children's conversation or communicate with their children. When they have 'close encounter' with their children, they feel a gap between them and their children as their children do not seem to have anything to talk to them about. When children are left alone to play, the house can be noisy. Unfortunately the parents do not know what the talk among the children is about because the conversation is usually predominantly English[8]. Such a failure to communicate with children will inevitably develop a sense of psychological insecurity among the non-English speaking parents (Khan, 1977).

Before the Chinese arrived in Britain, many of them lived in villages in the New Territories where people are close to one another and bear the same family name (Baker, 1966; Chann, 1976b). In some villages, people speak the same dialect. The '*Mans*' in Britain are one of the typical examples. Many of them are from San Tin (see Map 2) (Watson, 1977a) where '*wai tau wa*' (a Chinese dialect) is commonly spoken. Besides the '*Mans*', the '*Cheungs*' have also formed a considerable group in Britain (Jones, D., 1979). They may have come from the Sai Kung Area (see Map 2) as Williams (1964) says that many people in Ho Chung in Sai Kung bear the '*Cheung*' family name. Because of the clan relationship and the dense settlement, people in the same village know one another well. When there are problems within the village, villagers will gather at the ancestral hall to discuss their problems.

Although Chinese in Britain can find a lot of their clansmen in this country as a result of chain migration, they seldom see or live close to one another. Instead of having their own people around, Chinese are surrounded by people who have no knowledge of the Chinese language except Chinese 'take-aways' and restaurants. The living environment in Britain is totally different from what Chinese people were so used to in Hong Kong. Chinese villagers in Britain can no longer share their emotions with their neighbours who can speak the same Chinese dialect as before. On the other hand, the unforgettable racist experience in Britain has discouraged some Chinese from socialising with the majority people. As a result, their own family has become a target of verbal communication and an outlet for the release of frustration of the non-English speaking Chinese parents. At home parents would expect to share one another's emotions by the use of Chinese. At the same time, some would demand respect and filial piety from their children so that they could re-develop a sense of self-esteem and dignity which they fail to establish in the majority society.

Chinese parents realise that there is a difference between the Chinese (Confucius') concept of society and that of the British. It would be difficult for children who are educated in Britain to respect and obey their parents in a traditional Chinese manner. Chinese settlement in Britain is quite dispersed. Chinese children would not be able to acquire traditional Chinese cultural values by having limited contact with the Chinese in Britain. Many Chinese parents have to work 'unsocial hours' in restaurants and do not see their children very often. How can Chinese children know the expectations of their parents? In order to ensure that Chinese children should maintain some of the Chinese traditional cultural values which are not taught in British schools, many Chinese parents send their children to Chinese supplementary schools where Chinese children are expected to identify themselves with one another and acquire some knowledge of Chinese culture through the learning of the Chinese language.

Lack of change in language policies in British state schools

Despite the fact that there has been an increasing number of Chinese children in British schools since the 1970s, initiatives taken by the ILEA to incorporate Chinese language education into the curriculum in a few state schools only began in the early 1980s. There are a few reasons to account for such a 'lag'.

Reluctance to change the English-only tradition

Prior to the influx of immigrants from the Caribbean Islands and the Indian Sub-continent to meet the shortage of labour in Britain after the Second World War, the population in Britain was fairly homogeneous. Language policies at school had never been challenged. English was the sole medium of instruction in the classroom. The learning of a second language was only confined to the five popular European languages — French, German, Italian, Russian and Spanish (ILEA, 1986). Although there have been debates on the improvement of the educational status of Welsh and Gaelic which are spoken by a sizeable population in Wales and Scotland respectively, English prevails in the British national education system.

Despite the fact that Welsh and Scottish are nationals of Britain, they have failed to gain support from the central government to change the language policies in education in Britain. There is little optimism that minority immigrants from New Commonwealth countries, who were citizens of Britain's former colonies, could receive recognition of their language in British schools. The main reason could be that Britain would like to maintain its 'superiority' over citizens of her former colonies through the implementation of the English-only education for all children in British schools. Even though there have been signs of under-achievement among immigrant children in school in the last two decades, the British government insists that the provision of more English education is the only panacea. The belief that the learning of more English will help non-English speaking children to cope with their educational problems is revealed in Circular 7/65 (DES, 1966) as follows.

From the beginning the major educational task is the teaching of English. Where a school contains a number of children with little or no knowledge of English, it is desirable to arrange one or more special reception classes in which they may learn English as quickly and as effectively as possible (p. 2).

As the aims of the education of immigrant children had been stated clearly in Circular 7/65, innovations to meet the needs of immigrant children in the 1960s and the early 1970s tended to focus on the teaching of English. In 1963 Pamphlet No. 43 on the 'English for Immigrants' (Ministry of Education[9], 1963), it was recommended that 'a carefully planned intensive course making full use of modern methods of language teaching' (in DES, 1971a:16) should be developed. In response to the recommendations of the Pamphlet, a three-year project funded by the Schools Council for the Curriculum and Examinations was set up in September 1966 at the University of Leeds to develop course materials for teachers to teach English to non-English speaking children (DES, 1971a; Derrick, 1967; Edwards, 1984).

Following the Leeds Project, three surveys on the language needs of immigrant children namely the Potential and Progress in a Second Culture (DES, 1971b), the Education of Immigrants: Education Survey 13 (DES, 1971a) and the Continuing Needs of Immigrants (DES, 1972) were conducted by the DES in the early 1970s (Edwards, 1984). Based on findings of the three surveys, the Bullock Report (DES, 1975) pointed out that there was a need to extend the initial English language training for non-English speaking children and suggested that such a task should be done by specialist language teachers. The rationale of the proposal was that although after a year [the immigrant child] may seem able to follow the normal school curriculum, especially where oral work is concerned, the limitations to his English may be disguised; they become immediately apparent when he reads and writes. He reads slowly and often without a full understanding of vocabulary and syntax, let alone the nuances of expression. His writing betrays his lack of grasp of the subject and a very unsteady control of syntax and style . . . [The Education Committee] regard it as a grave disservice to such children to deprive them of sustained language teaching after they have been learning English for only a comparatively short time. In [the Committee's] view they need far more intensive help with language in English lessons. This should be the task of a specialist language teacher, whose aim should be to help them achieve fluency in all the language skills (p. 290).

Although changes had taken place to solve the language problems of immigrant children, all projects, surveys and policy statements in relation to innovations had reflected Britain's persistence in the English-only tradition and her rejection of minority languages irrespective of the growing numbers of immigrant children in British schools.

Absence of statistics on language-minority pupils

Although statistics of immigrant children are crucial in the formulation and implementation of policies, the Green Paper of 1977 (DES, 1977) points out that there has been an absence of information on ethnic minorities in the British education system as the collection of such data on ethnic minority groups could be viewed as discriminatory. On the recommendation of the HMSO White Paper of 1965 (HMSO, 1965), attempts had been made by the DES between 1966 and 1972 to identify the number of immigrant children in British schools. Owing to the anomalies resulting from the definition of 'immigrants', Margaret Thatcher, being the Secretary of State for the Department of Education and Science, stated that '[the Department makes] no use of [the statistics] whatsoever except to publish them' (The Runnymede Trust and Radical Statistics Race Group, 1980:93). Subsequently the collection of educational data concerning children's ethnic origin had to cease in 1972 (Edwards, 1984). As a result of such a termination of data collection, the Bullock Report (DES, 1975) and the Select Committee on Race Relations and Immigration (HMSO, 1977) have difficulties in quantifying and identfying the needs of immigrants.

The Chinese community seems to be an alterntive for the collection of information on Chinese children in Britain. However, they also have problems in compiling such kinds of statistics.

Despite the fact that various Chinese associations have been set up in Britain since the early twentieth century, their major function is the provision of ceremonial activities and mutual aid for their clansmen and members (Collins, 1957). The government-funded Chinese community centres established in the early 1980s are quite concerned about the development and well-being of Chinese children in this country, but they have to give priority to the general welfare of all Chinese in Britain. As revealed by the annual reports of the Chinese Information and Advice Centre (1985a) and the Haringey Chinese Group (1985), most of their resources have been channelled into the handling of cases concerned with housing, interpretation and immigration as records have shown that cases of an educational nature are very few. Among the 202 cases handled by the Haringey Chinese Community Group in 1983–85, about 11% (22 cases) were concerned with education (HGC, 1985). Educational cases dealt with by the Chinese Information and Advisory Centre in 1984/85 were hardly visible. Only 1% (2 cases) of the total 144 cases were of an educational nature (CIAC, 1985a). On the other hand, there is a lack of expertise, personnel and finance within the Chinese community centres. It would be far beyond the ability of these agencies to conduct surveys on the Chinese community in Britain.

The Hong Kong Government Office (London) and the China Embassy are the official respresentatives of the Hong Kong and China government in Britain. Their main duty is to handle matters in relation to their government and nationals in Britain. The majority of the Chinese in Britain have already become British nationals. It would be inappropriate for the overseas government bodies to take over the responsibility of the British government to have an official count of the minority Chinese in Britain[10].

Registration records at Chinese supplementary schools were considered to be the best source for information on Chinese children. However, not many of the schools have designed any enrolment or registration forms to record details of their pupils. Even though an enrolment record is available, the information obtained may not be useful and reliable. In a Chinese school in London, it was found that many of the forms were not filled in completely or properly. In the space where the place of birth was expected, some pupils put in the name of the hospital where they were born. Some children had left out the occupation of their parents and address. As Chinese teachers only work on a voluntary basis and the time for teaching is limited, schools do not want to give extra work to their teachers by expecting them to check the registration forms of their pupils in detail.

Both the Chinese community and the British government have their own problems in compiling detailed statistics on the Chinese in Britain. Therefore no specific education policies catering for the needs of Chinese children in Britain could be formulated before the 1980s. It was only until 1978 when the ILEA conducted a survey on the non-English speaking children in the ILEA schools that some official statistics on Chinese children were available.

Lack of support of the EEC Directive's mother tongue issue

In the Council Statement attached to the EEC Directive, the EEC Member States are required

> to offer nationals and children of nationals of other member-states of the countries and of non-member countries who are not covered by this Directive, better facilities for their education and training (CRE, 1980:1).

In response to the Statement, Mr Carlisle, the Secretary of State for Education and Science agreed that Britain would 'intend to apply the Directive without regard to the country of origin of the children concerned' (*ibid.*). Subsequently, some legislation in Britain had made it the statutory responsibility of the local education authorities to provide education for all children without discrimination against any particular racial group. Under Section 7 of the 1944 Education Act, the local education authorities in Britain are required to make primary, secondary and further education available 'to meet the needs of the population of their own area' (Liell and Saunders, 1986: B10). Chapter 74 of the Race Relations Act 1976 (Great Britain, 1979) states that it is unlawful to refuse or deliberately omit

> to provide [any person] with goods, facilities or services [including facilities for education] of the like quality, in the like manner and on the like terms as are normal in the first-mentioned person's case in relation to other members of the public or (where the person so seeking belongs to a section of the public) to other members of that section (p. 14).

Despite the fact that there are laws in Britain to ensure that ethnic minority people are not excluded from the national education provision, there has not been any nation-wide mother tongue education programme to demonstrate Britain's full support of Article 3 of the EEC Directive which requires the provision of mother tongue education for non-English speaking school children. The main reason is that Britain has a different interpretation of the objectives of the Directive.

Based on the Action Programme of February 1976, the CRE (1980) believes that the main objective of the Directive is 'to assist the movement of workers from member states and their families within the community' (p. 1). The objective could have been based on the assumption that children of the migrant workers would return home one day. The provision of mother tongue/culture education of the country of origin of these children in member States will facilitate the reintegration of migrant children when they return to their native country (Brook, 1980; DES, 1985; Wright, J., 1982).

The rationale of the Directive does not seem to be the case in Britain. Many of the Asian immigrants in Britain

have become permanent settlers in Britain and may not return home. Their children intend to remain and compete for life with the majority-language speakers in Britain (Wright, J., 1982:12).

The Swann Report (DES, 1985) notes that it will be illogical to extend the provision of mother tongue/culture education to language-minority children as

the great majority of [these children] are unlikely to 'return home' and neither perceive themselves nor wish to be perceived as in any sense 'transitory' citizens of this country (p. 402).

Evidence has shown that many of the ethnic minority children will be settling in Britain permanently. They must accept the fact that English is the key to equality of opportunity, academic success and to full participation in the British life (CRE, 1982; DES, 1975 & 1985; Perren, 1976). In order to help language-minority children to compete equally in the majority society, both the Bullock Report (DES, 1975) and the Swann Report (DES, 1985) recommend that emphasis should be put on the learning of English in the education of non/limited English-speaking children.

The policy statement in the Bullock Report (DES, 1975) and the Swann Report (DES, 1985) implies that Britain would adopt the assimilation policy in education. As the EEC Directive is legally-binding and member States are required by Article 4 of the Directive to inform the Commission of measures taken to comply with the Directive (Brook, 1980; CRE, 1980), Britain has tactfully made an effort to indicate its intent of support to the Directive in some of the education documents. Before the Directive was finally adopted in July 1977, the Bullock Report (DES, 1975) in 1975, a year after the proposal of the Programme of Action, gave an impression that ethnic minority children's mother tongue would be recognised by schools. The Report says:

> In a linguistically conscious nation in the modern world we should see [bilingualism] as an asset, as something to be nurtured, and one of the agencies which should nurture it is the school. Certainly the school should adopt a positive attitude to its pupils' bilingualism and wherever possible would help to maintain and deepen their knowledge of their mother tongue (pp. 293–294).

Although it was suggested in the Bullock Report that children's bilingual skills should be nutured in school, the Report had not stated precisely what policies and strategies schools would adopt to maintain the bilingual skills of the ethnic minority children. It seemed that the British government's support of mother tongue/culture education at school was only 'a statement of intent' (Brook, 1980).

When the Directive was adopted in 1977, a similar statement of intent to support mother tongue teaching was reiterated in the 1977 Green Paper, Education in Schools: A Consultative Document (DES, 1977). The Green Paper suggested that '. . . the curriculum should reflect a sympathetic understanding of the different cultures and races that now make up [the society of] Britain' (p. 4). Unfortunately it had failed to elaborate how the curriculum should be designed in order to achieve such an aim in education.

Circular 5/81 (DES, 1982) tried to inform the LEAs how the DES interpreted the Directive and what the LEAs were expected to do in order to comply with the Directive. It was mentioned in the Circular that

> for the local education authorities in this country, this [Directive] implies that they should explore ways in which mother-tongue teaching might be provided, whether during or outside school hours, but not that they are required to give such tuition to all individuals as of right (p. 51).

There have been some ambiguities in the Circular. First of all, the use of the word 'promotion' in Article 3 of the Directive is open to interpretation and therefore provides a loophole for LEA's to avoid their obligation to provide mother tongue/culture education. Secondly, the Circular gives an impression that there is an absence of practical leadership to show the LEAs how they should explore ways to teach mother tongues at school. Owing to the DES' lack of support to the Directive, the ambiguity of the national policy statements and the decentralised nature of the British education system, there are variations in the LEAs' mother tongue education policies in school.

With funding from Section 11 of the Local Government Act 1966[11] (HMSO, 1966), individual LEAs formulate their own policies to provide mother tongue teaching. LEAs in Manchester, Coventry and Inner London have employed full-time teachers/specialists/advisors to supervise mother tongue teaching at school. Instead of setting up their own mother tongue classes, some LEAs give financial assistance and permission to minority communities for the use of school premises at the weekend to run mother tongue classes (CRE, 1980; DES, 1984). Some local authorities such as those in Bedford, Bradford and Inner London had obtained additional financial support from the EEC, the DES and the European Commission. They were able to carry out school-based projects to explore ways of incorporating mother tongue teaching into the mainstream curriculum (CRE, 1980 & 1981; DES, 1982; EC Pilot Project, 1987; Mother Tongue Project, 1984; Orzechowska, 1984).

All these mother tongue projects in Britain reveal the fact that the official support of the EEC Directive varies in Britain depending on individual LEAs' and teachers' attitudes towards ethnic minority languages and funding available. Many of the resources have been directed to the promotion of the South Asian languages in state schools. The Chinese language has hardly received any support in this respect.

While more Chinese parents have chosen to send their children to British schools, they are quite anxious that their children should be taught the Chinese language to help them to maintain their cultural identity and some traditional Chinese cultural values. Owing to the English-only tradition in the British education system and the traditional practice of teaching 'prestigious' European languages as a second language at school, the support of incorporating the Chinese language into the curriculum by the British government is rather reluctant and piecemeal. As a result, Chinese parents' aspirations cannot be satisfied by the British education system. Such dissatisfaction, according to Dewey's theory of asynchronous change, will give rise to problems in the education of Chinese children in Britain.

Notes to Chapter 3

1. The 1971 Immigration Act stated that wives and children of Commonwealth citizens who settled in the UK on or after 1 January 1973 no longer had an automatic statutory right to settlement. The employment voucher system introduced by the Commonwealth Immigrants Act 1962 came to an end and was replaced by the work permit system (Dummett, 1982; Gordon and Klug, 1985).
2. Source of information: Questions 3 and 4 in Questionnaire A.
3. The information was obtained in an interview with a youth worker in her early twenties at a Chinese community centre in London.
4. The ILEA only uses a general term 'Chinese' to include such dialects as Cantonese, Hakka, Mandarin, etc. spoken by Chinese pupils in Britain. Although the dialect has not been identified in the language surveys, it can be assumed that the majority of Chinese pupils speak Cantonese as their home language because the figures compiled by the DES indicate that 70% of the Chinese pupils in British schools speak Cantonese as their mother tongue (GB. P. H. of C. HAC, 1985).
5. The 10 Divisions are: (1) Hammersmith and Fulham, Kensington and Chelsea, (2) Westminster and Camden, (3) Islington, (4) Hackney, (5) Tower Hamlets, (6) Greenwich, (7) Lewisham, (8) Southwark, (9) Lambeth and (10) Wandsworth (ILEA, 1983a) (see Map 7).
6. It was promised by the 1974 White Paper to abolish the SSEE when sufficient subsidised junior secondary places were available (Hong Kong Government, 1974). The last SSEE was held in May 1977. A new system known as the Secondary School Places Allocation (SSPA) Scheme was implemented in 1978 to control the flow of students from primary to secondary schools.
7. Source of information: Question 5 in Questionnaire A.
8. The information was obtained by interviews with Chinese parents.
9. The first Ministry of Education was appointed on 10 August 1944 and was dissolved on 1 April 1964. After the dissolution of the Ministry of Education, all functions of the Minister of Education were transferred to the newly-appointed Secretary of State for Education and Science by the Secretary of State for Education and Science Order 1964, SI 1964/490 (Liell and Saunders, 1986).
10. The information was supplied by officials of the Hong Kong Government Office (London) and the China Embassy (London).
11. According to Section 11 of the Local Government Act 1966, LEAs with a substantial number of Commonwealth immigrants whose language or customs differ from those of the indigenous community can apply for a maximum grant of 75% to cover the cost of the employment of additional staff to meet the special needs of the immigrant population.

4 Problems of Chinese Pupils in the British Context: Some Case Studies

Most Chinese children in Britain are brought up in traditional Chinese families where they are not supposed to challenge authorities. Because of the absence of Chinese mother tongue and culture education in most British schools, especially before the adoption of the EEC Directive, many Chinese children fail to recognise the change in the cultural setting and the expectations of teachers when they first join the British education system. In order to show their respect for the school authority, many of the Chinese children are relatively quiet. They seldom discuss their difficulties or queries with teachers. Chinese are often stereotyped as hard-working people. Teachers who do not have much knowledge of the cultural and family background of Chinese children usually presume that Chinese children do not have many problems at school.

Some research and conferences on the Chinese community and Chinese children in Britain (CRC, 1975; Garvey and Jackson, 1975; NCC, 1979 & 1984; National Educational Research and Development Trust, 1977 & 1978; QCRC, 1981; Taylor, M., 1987) have pointed out that Chinese children in Britain do have some psycho-educational problems which arise from the dilemmas faced in meeting the expectations of their parents and teachers at school. The various problems of Chinese children in Britain are analysed below and supported with some case studies.

Maintenance of Cultural Identity

The major problems encountered by Chinese children in maintaining their cultural identity are (1) the complexity of the linguistic identity, (2) the ambiguity of the concept of Chinese culture, and (3) Chinese children's perception of identity and integration.

Complexity of the linguistic identity

Chinese people are proud of the complex, aesthetic nature of the Chinese script. Besides embodying approximately 80,000 ideograms (Jeffery, 1949), the Chinese script requires a specific technique to combine the strokes and radicals together to form a Chinese word (Wang, 1973) which by itself can convey its meaning in the form of a picture. Other languages do not seem to possess such distinctive features as the Chinese language, therefore Chinese people usually regard·the Chinese script as an intrinsic part of the Chinese culture. In order to identify oneself as Chinese, many Chinese people would insist that the person ought to know the Chinese language. As the Chinese language competence of many Chinese children in Britain has been dominated by the English language, Chinese parents in Britain are more anxious that their children should maintain their cultural identity through the learning of the Chinese language.

Owing to the complexity of the Chinese language and the lack of exposure to the language in Britain, there are difficulties for Chinese children to identify themselves linguistically with Chinese.

Phonetically the Chinese language consists of at least eight *fanyan*[1] which are mutually unintelligible. Within the Chinese community in Britain, Cantonese and Hakka are commonly spoken. Other dialects such as Putonghua (Mandarin), Toishan and Hokkien are found among Chinese who are from Taiwan, mainland China or Singapore (GB. H. of P., HAC, II, 1985). Putonghua, which is supported by a phonetic system known as *pinyin*, has been declared as the national language of Communist China. Except in Taiwan, and recently in Singapore, Putonghua is not widely spoken in Chinese societies outside mainland China.

In addition to the dialectic variations, the two forms of *hanzi* (written Chinese) have led to some discrepancies in Chinese people's linguistic identity. In the People's Republic of China, *hanzi* refers to the official national simplified Chinese characters which were developed during the language reform movement between the 1950s and 1960s (Alitto, 1969; DeFrancis, 1984; Lehmann, 1975). In Taiwan, Hong Kong and other Chinese communities overseas, the complicated form of written Chinese is maintained. Despite the fact that the *hanzi* used in Communist China is easier to learn, most Chinese parents expect their children to learn the complicated form as the simplified *hanzi* has lost some of the aesthetic characteristics of the traditional script.

Although language is seen as a unifying force of a nation (Hans,

1949; Kloss, 1971), the national spoken and written Chinese used in mainland China is not much supported by overseas Chinese. Chinese immigrants in different Chinese communities abroad prefer to retain their own dialect and written form. If Chinese children are expected to identify themselves linguistically with Chinese, should they maintain the variety which is commonly spoken and written in their own community; or the one used by their parents; or the national form adopted in mainland China?

Ambiguity of the concept of Chinese culture

Besides the linguistic complexity, the political influence on the Chinese culture in different societies has created problems in defining Chinese culture to the younger generation of Chinese overseas.

After the Communist Party took over China in 1949, old China was divided into two political entities — the People's Republic of China (Communist China) and the Republic of China (Taiwan). The two Chinas have different political ideologies. Many of the educated people and land owners in old China were scared off by communist ideas and left the country. Some of them went to Taiwan and some to countries overseas such as those in south-east Asia, America and Europe.

During the Cultural Revolution in mainland China in 1966–1976, Confucianism, which had been a basis of the Chinese culture and philosophy, was under attack. Educated people at universities were not respected. Many of them had to go through tough labour training and were forced to join the production line of the country. The only authority that young people would respect was the leader of the country — the Communist Party. If parents did not support the Party, they would be reported and challenged by their own children. Traditional Chinese culture was on the point of disintegration.

Hong Kong was ceded to Great Britain in 1842 under the Treaty of Nanking. After being administered by Britain, Hong Kong has become a free market for trade and an international centre for commerce and finance. In a capitalist city like Hong Kong, Chinese parents realise that success in the English-medium education will lead to social and economic advancement. Many of the parents prefer having their children educated in Anglo-Chinese schools[2] although they can anticipate that some of the traditional Chinese cultural values such as absolute obedience to parents will be abandoned by their children. Through the mass media and exposure to people from the western world, a new set of values have been developed in Hong Kong. The perception of family and human relationships is completely different from that in a traditional Chinese society.

Chinese culture has already changed under different political regimes and in different geographical localities. What aspects of Chinese culture do Chinese parents want their children in Britain to maintain — remnants of Chinese culture in Hong Kong, the new Chinese culture evolved in Chairman Mao's regime in Communist China or the traditional Chinese culture in the old history of China?

Chinese children's perception of identity and integration

As there is ambiguity in the concept of cultural identity and culture, Chinese children in Britain maintain their own cultural identity in their own manner which is in conflict with the expectations of the school and parents. The following examples are to illustrate such kinds of conflict.

At school, some Chinese children would like to separate themselves from the majority pupils. In an after-school Chinese class in a secondary school in London, two Chinese immigrant girls always liked to sit together. They seldom had verbal exchange with the other three British classmates except when required by the teacher of the Chinese language to participate in classroom discussions. It seemed that there might be some racial antagonism between the two groups of pupils[3].

In another secondary school, it was found that two British-born Chinese girls who had no problems with spoken English seldom mixed with other children. The two girls often stayed with one another as a group. Teachers were not able to understand the reasons for the two Chinese girls' reluctance to integrate with other children but simply worried about the social and psychological development of the two pupils[4].

Outside the school, it was noticed that a group of eight immigrant and British-born Chinese secondary school boys and girls went to a Chinese community centre quite regularly after school. Their main purpose was to socialise — chatting, playing games, watching Chinese videos, etc. Chinese pupils' preference for games at Chinese community centres instead of participating in the extra-curricular activities at school is not appreciated by some state school teachers.

Without understanding the needs of Chinese children, teachers are quite negative about the 'withdrawn' attitude of some Chinese children. In fact, children in the three cases were quite conscious of their cultural identity. Because of the pervasive influence of English at school and at home through the mass media, they found it difficult to maintain their cultural identity by speaking the Chinese language as their parents expect. They had no intention of separating themselves from children of other races. They simply felt that they could study with the majority students and talk to them at school but would prefer to be close to friends of their own race and culture in their own social life outside school[5].

The union of Chinese children is a signal of their inclination to maintain their cultural identity. Unfortunately their inability to use the Chinese language for communication with their parents or Chinese people in their community often leads to complaints from parents that their children are like 'bananas' (with Chinese yellow skin but white people's mind) and have forgotten their roots. Their lack of interest in socialising with other children at school is often misinterpreted by state school teachers as a typical emotional problem of Chinese pupils.

Maintenance of Traditional Chinese Values

After having experienced racism, frustration and hardships in Britain, Chinese parents are anxious for their children to make social and economic advancement through success in education. On the other hand, they hope that some kind of refuge and dignity can be provided at home so that they can maintain a psychological balance. Therefore Chinese children in Britain are always expected by parents to maintain two traditional Chinese values based on Confucianism: (1) respect for parents and (2) achievement in education.

Respect for parents

In a welfare state such as Britain, education is free to children up to the age of sixteen. When people are unemployed, they can live on the dole. When they get old, they can survive on a pension or other old-age benefits. Unlike their counterparts in Hong Kong, Chinese children in Britain theoretically do not have to rely on their parents for support of their education or their living if they cannot get a job when they finish their studies. They therefore tend to feel less obliged to show respect for their parents or look after them when they get old.

Teaching in British schools is child-centred. Children are encouraged to explore their environment actively to seek knowledge. Therefore children are given a certain degree of freedom to move around in the classroom. Classrooms in Britain seem to be less disciplined than those in Hong Kong. Teachers are less authoritarian as they understand that they have to respect the rights of children in a democratic society. Students are encouraged to debate with teachers to reach their own conclusions.

At home some of the western cultural values acquired by Chinese children at school are exhibited. Many Chinese children do not think that there is a need to be absolutely obedient to parents, especially if their parents are wrong. They also expect to have the right to voice their opinion in the family. If such a right is not respected, children will regard their parents as dictators.

The conflict between Chinese parents and their children does not simply arise from the differences in the value system between Britain and that maintained by Chinese parents. The traditional practice of sending children back to Hong Kong to be brought up by their grandmother is a major factor (The Community Relations Commission, 1975; The Quaker Community Relations Committee, 1981; National Children's Centre, 1979). The following are two examples to explain why some Chinese children in Britain are reluctant to show absolute respect for their parents as a result of separation from their parents when they were young.

Example 1

Lai Ping was seventeen years old in 1987. She was born in Britain but was sent back to Hong Kong to receive a Chinese education. She came back to Britain with her mother to join her father when she was nine years old in 1979. While she was growing up in Hong Kong, she sometimes came to Britain to see her father. Since the stay with her father was short and she was quite young at that time, she only had a very vague idea of what her father looked like. She had been living with her parents since she arrived in Britain. She felt that there was always a big gap between her and her father. It was difficult for her to communicate with her father. Since she found staying home boring, she went to three Chinese classes a week — one at her own school on Thursday and two private classes on Saturday and Sunday. Her main purpose was to avoid having confrontations with her parents.

Example 2

Tsing Tsing was a very close friend of Lai Ping. She was sixteen in 1987. She was born in Hong Kong. When she was three years old, her mother went to Britain and left her with her grandmother to be brought up in Hong Kong. Tsing Tsing came to Britain with her grandmother to join her parents when she was twelve. She remembers that when she was re-united with her family in Britain, her parents, especially her father whom she only saw once in Hong Kong when she was seven, were like complete strangers to her. Before Tsing Tsing left for Britain, she had some expectations of her parents. After living with her parents for a while in Britain, she did not feel as if she had parents of her own. Apart from being able to see her parents more often than before, she could not sense any affection from her parents though the family lived together. She did not like living with her parents as she was expected to help out in her father's 'take-away' shop. Later she became quite hostile towards her parents because they stopped her from seeing her grandmother at the old people's home. The girl found her parents unreasonable as her grandmother was the one whom she had lived with for twelve years since she was a baby. Her grandmother was left at the old people's home to live on her own in Britain. Tsing Tsing felt that she was obliged to look after her grandmother. However, the conflict between her parents and grandmother had prevented her from fulfilling her obligations expected in a conservative Chinese family.

After having been exposed to the western world for a few years, Tsing Tsing began to question her tolerance of her parents. She noticed that the labour which she contributed to her father's 'take-away' shop and family was not appreciated. She did not feel as if she had parents of her own. Although Tsing Tsing was a teenager, she also needed somebody to show some concern and affection for her. Unfortunately she could not stay with her grandmother in the old people's home. When she could no longer stand the pressure exerted by her parents and the traditional Chinese culture, she finally decided to live with her sister's family where she would have her brother-in-law to give her advice and guidance in life[6].

The unhappy relationship between Lai Ping, Tsing Tsing and their parents indicates that during the period of adjustment to a new environment and culture, some immigrant Chinese children require support and tolerance by parents. If parents are impatient and too demanding, it will be difficult for parents to re-establish their relationship with their separated children. After knowing more about the rights of children at school, it is more unlikely for Chinese children in Britain to show respect for their parents if their parents fail to impress these children that they have fulfilled their duties as parents.

Achievement in education

As Chinese parents learnt from Hong Kong that success in the English-medium education will lead to economic and social advancement, they place a high value on the achievement in the mainstream education in Britain. Owing to the non-English speaking family background, the lack of appropriate support for limited/non-English speaking children at school and the declining economy in Britain, there has been evidence of underachievement and the lack of motivation to succeed in school among Chinese children in Britain.

According to the statistics compiled by the DES, about 70% of Chinese pupils in British schools speak Cantonese and 25% speak Hakka as their home language. Among the Chinese in Britain, the Home Affairs Committee (1985) estimates that about 65 to 75% of the first generation Chinese are unable to speak English. In other words, before Chinese children enter British school, the majority of them are brought up in Chinese families where they first learn to speak Chinese for at least four or five years. When they begin schooling in Britain, many of the Chinese children have problems with the English language.

Of 416 Chinese pupils in a sample, 64% reported that they understood less than half of the classroom instructions[7]. More than half (55%) of these children simply followed what other children did in the classroom. Some 23% retreated into a 'silent misery' (Langton, 1979) and waited quietly and passively for teachers to come to help[8].

The English proficiency of Chinese children in the school system has been assessed by other studies too. Rosen and Burgess (1980) found that only 46% of the Cantonese-speaking Chinese pupils in London were rated as fluent speakers of English. The ILEA's three Language Censuses (ILEA Research & Statistics, 1982; Kysel, 1983 & 1985) (see Table 4) showed that there was only an average of 34% fluent speakers of English among Chinese pupils at ILEA schools. The percentage of fluent speakers of English among Chinese pupils at ILEA schools dropped slightly in each succeeding Language Census. The survey exclusively on Chinese children in Britain shows that only 38% of the 431 Chinese pupils would consider their English good [9].

The findings above indicate that Chinese pupils are relatively weak

TABLE 4 *Fluent speakers of English of Chinese-speaking pupils in ILEA*

Year of Census	Percentage of fluent English speakers	Total number of Chinese pupils
1981	36.4	2,237
1983	35.5	2,825
1985	31.2	3,546

Sources: ILEA Research & Statistics (1982), Appendix 4, p. 27.
Kysel (1983), Appendix 4 (page number not indicated).
Kysel (1985), Appendix 5 (page number not indicated).

in the English language. There ought to be some language support at school to help Chinese children to cope with the English-medium education. However, the support is not available for all Chinese school children. Among 432 Chinese pupils, only 26% had been placed in a special English or an ESL (English as a Second Language) class. 73% had not been given any assistance in their English language[10].

As Chinese children are not well prepared for the English-medium education in Britain, many of them have difficulties in learning at school. They

> have to struggle with the spoken form of the language while their peers are learning new concepts and how to read and write. By the time they have mastered spoken English, they have fallen behind in reading, writing and conceptual development (GB. P. H. of C. HAC, 1985, Vol. III:159).

The English language seems to be the major obstacle of some Chinese children in making progress at school. The three case studies below elaborate how some Chinese pupils in this country fail in the system.

Case 1

Kwok Wah was an eight-year-old British born Chinese boy. According to some assessments made by the school in December 1985 and comments of an educational psychologist, Kwok Wah's performance at school was not too satisfactory. His verbal communication skills at the age of six years and nine months were below average. His number work was poor too. He could only match amounts with numbers from one to three and had been able to count up to ten on occasion. He was seen by his teachers as a passive and withdrawn child who had moderate learning difficulties and ought to be sent to a special school.

In order to understand the real problem of Kwok Wah, observation in the classroom and family, as well as interviews with Kwok Wah's teachers at his infant and Chinese schools had been carried out. When Kwok Wah was observed in class at his infant school, he was found sitting quietly at the back and not concentrating. Later Kwok Wah's withdrawn behaviour was checked with teachers at his Chinese school. Teachers there saw nothing strange about Kwok Wah's behaviour as there were a couple of other students in the same class who were as quiet as Kwok Wah. His class teacher even emphasised that he saw these children as 'introverts' but they were normal.

Kwok Wah behaved quite differently at his Chinese school and at home. At the Chinese school, it was found that Kwok Wah had been complained about by a Chinese parent several times for making fun of her child who was physically handicapped. While Kwok Wah was queuing up to go out of the classroom at recess time, the girl in the front was very angry with Kwok Wah because her hair was disturbed by him. At Kwok Wah's eighth birthday party at home, he ate, sang and played with other children among whom there were four Indian/Pakistani neighbours and one British girl who was a friend of his sister's. When appropriate stimulation such as picture books and animal postcards was given to Kwok Wah, he showed a great interest in reading and drawing. Kwok Wah's talent for drawing was only discovered by teachers at his nursery school at a later stage.

Kwok Wah, his older brother and sister studied in the same school where they were the only Chinese. According to the three children, they were often bullied and laughed at by other children at school. They understood that they were not accepted. In order to avoid trouble, they were taught by parents to withdraw from the majority.

Kwok Wah's different behaviour at his nursery school, Chinese school and at home indicates that in addition to the English language problem, the sense of insecurity at school and the lack of understanding and tolerance of teachers will affect the academic performance of some Chinese children. Tests used to assess local English-speaking children in Britain may not be able to detect the real problem of children from a Chinese background. Transferring less able Chinese children at an early stage of schooling to special schools could not be a solution to their problem[11].

Case 2

Lai Ying was a sixteen-year-old Chinese immigrant girl. She was twelve years old when she arrived in Britain in 1983. Before she left Hong Kong, she had not yet completed Primary 5. After being placed in a language centre to learn English for three months, she was allocated to the second year at a secondary school. It implied that Lai Ying had been deprived of her right to basic knowledge which is supposed to be learnt in the two years of schooling which she had missed.

The two years' gap in Lai Ying's education is crucial as one of these years marks the end of primary education and the other opens up the second stage of schooling. In these two years, learning is supposed to be relatively more serious and difficult as new concepts are introduced to pupils in a more formal manner. Even though English-speaking children learn through their mother tongue, some of them also encounter problems at this stage of schooling. Lai Ying had only been taught the basic skills of English for three months after her arrival in Britain. She had not been given any opportunities to learn what she had missed in the two years of schooling. Although she remained in the system until the final year of secondary education, she had never developed any interest in her studies. Very often she skipped classes. In the spring of 1987 while she was moving home, she dropped out from school without the knowledge of her family. She did not sit for the Certificate of Secondary Education (CSE) examination which she had entered before she left school[12].

Case 3

Siu Ha is another immigrant Chinese pupil who claimed that she was born in England but was sent back to Hong Kong where she was brought up. She came to Britain in 1979 when she was nine and a half years. Although she joined the British school system in Primary 4, she had never been provided with any support service at the early stage of schooling in Britain. Despite the language problem, Siu Ha had completed her secondary education and sat for the CSE and GCE (General Certificate of Education) examinations in 1987. Although Siu Ha was quite happy that she had passed the CSE English (Mode 3) which she was not too confident in, she failed in the CSE History (Mode 3), O-level GCE Physics and Mathematics which demand a certain level of English proficiency in order to understand specific concepts[13].

The failure of Lai Ying and Siu Ha at school shows that the educational problems confronting older immigrant Chinese children are more serious. Before these children emigrate to Britain, they have a few years of education in Hong Kong where schooling begins at six and Chinese is the medium of instruction in most primary schools. When they join the schooling system in Britain, they are placed at a level according to their age. In Britain, schooling starts at five. It means that immigrant children from Hong Kong will miss at least one year of education when they continue their studies in Britain. If no compensatory education is provided, such a gap can be exacerbated by the fact that the language of instruction in British schools is English. In addition to the language handicap and the lack of appropriate support for non/limited English-speaking children at school, the declining economy in Britain has discouraged some Chinese children in Britain to set up any ambitious objectives in their studies.

In Britain unemployment has been a serious social problem. It is not surprising that university graduates may have problems in securing a job. Therefore many school children in Britain are not motivated to work hard or to further their studies in universities. A second year university student who is indigenous British from the Midlands at the interview indicated that many British pupils regard university studies as being too risky when opportunities in the job market are limited. If they are offered a job when they finish secondary education, they prefer working to studying. Two fifth year secondary school British girls without any Chinese background but learning Chinese as an after-school activity had a similar point of view. They asserted that they were not very keen to study in the sixth-form since they were not very interested in university education.

Chinese children in this country study with the British. Their value judgement is quite similar to their British peers. When Lai Ying and Siu Ha were interviewed when they were in their fifth year, they said that they had never thought of entering a university because they were not too confident in their academic work as well as their English ability. Like many other British children, they were quite anxious to be financially independent so that they could do what they want. Social status did not worry them very much as they understood that in a class-conscious society like Britain where covert racism always exists, it is not easy for a non-English speaking average person to climb up the social ladder.

Similar to the point of view of the two Chinese school girls, the experience of two working Chinese girls in their early twenties proves that the younger generation of the Chinese in Britain have become more pragmatic. They no longer believe that there is a correlation between education and social mobility as their parents do.

One of these working girls was Lan Sum who worked at a Chinese community centre as a part-time youth worker. She got five GCE O-level passes and a 'B' in A-level Statistics. After Lan Sum had obtained the Higher National Diploma in Business Studies, she failed to get a job in her field of studies even though her spoken English sounds like that of a native speaker (she got a 'B' in O-level English). At the moment when Lan Sum was interviewed, she only relied on part-time jobs to earn her living. Since she had been unemployed for almost a year despite the fact that she had some professional training and qualifications, she thought of going to Hong Kong to look for job opportunities[14].

Another Chinese working girl was Tsau Yin who was a community worker at a different Chinese community centre. She was one of the founders who set up a Chinese group in one of the boroughs in London. Tsau Yin was very intelligent. By skilfully lobbying the councillors and officers, she obtained funds from the local government to establish a community centre for the Chinese group in a London borough. Although she had only completed secondary education, the full-time job she had at the centre offered her a salary which was higher than people with a university degree. While Tsau Yin was on the job, she thought of obtaining professional training at a higher education institution. However, she realised that if she gave up her present job to further her studies, the completion of the professional training might not guarantee her a job with better pay. Later Tsau Yin resigned from her job at the Chinese community centre. She was offered some other jobs by people whom she knew. One of which was to work in an insurance company where she could possibly earn about £20,000 a year, quite an attractive income to someone with an average educational background[15].

The inference from the two case studies is that the situation in Britain is very different from that in Hong Kong. Chinese people in Britain are minority only. They have to struggle very hard for survival. Chinese parents always hope that their children can get out of the 'ghetto' by obtaining more education. However, the racist reality, examples of the educated unemployed and the success of the less educated in British society has discouraged the younger generation of Chinese from furthering their studies after compulsory schooling. What they are more concerned about is getting a job, possibly not in the catering business, which will help them to earn a living.

In conclusion, many of the Chinese children in Britain fail to meet the expectations of their parents and teachers — the majority of Chinese children are unable to speak the Chinese language. Some of them underachieve at school and some have lost interest in their studies. A few groups of Chinese children refuse to integrate with children of other races. All these problems have an impact on the development of well-being of Chinese children in Britain. Many Chinese parents in Britain think that by teaching the Chinese language to their children in Britain, some of these problems could be eliminated. To what extent are problems of Chinese children solved? Are there other alternatives to cope with Chinese pupils' problems?

Notes to Chapter 4

1. The eight dialects which were officially agreed at the Technical Conference of the Standardization of Modern Chinese held in Peking in 1955 were Putonghua (Mandarin), Wu, Yue (Cantonese), Xiang, Hakka, Gan, Northern and Southern Min.
2. Anglo-Chinese schools are schools where English is supposed to be the medium of instruction for all subjects except Chinese language and Chinese history.
3. The data are based on classroom observations and interviews with the subjects during a seven-month period while the author was a teacher of the after-school Chinese class of the school.
4. The information was given by an ESL teacher who was in charge of the organisation of language classes of the school.
5. The data are based on observations and interviews with the group of Chinese pupils at a Chinese community centre in London.
6. In examples 1 and 2 information was given by the subjects on different occasions after the author had come to know them in an after-school Chinese class.
7. Source of information: Question 9 in Section 2 of Questionnaire A.
8. Source of information: Question 10 in Section 2 of Questionnaire A.
9. Source of information: Question 1 in Section 2 of Questionnaire A.
10. Source of information: Question 2 in Section 2 of Questionnaire A.
11. The information was obtained by classroom observations and interviews with the subject, his family and teachers at his Chinese and nursery schools.
12. The facts were revealed to the author by the subject herself at several interviews.
13. The facts were revealed to the author by the subject herself at several interviews.
14. The information was obtained by interviews with the youth worker at a Chinese community centre in London.
15. The information was collected on a friendship basis over a two-year period.

5 Mother Tongue Teaching in the Chinese Community

The case studies in the previous chapter have demonstrated that some Chinese children in Britain do have problems in living in two cultures. They cannot reconcile the values which they acquire in the British society with what is expected by their parents. Since the ethnic minority culture gained no support in the British education system before the adoption of the 1977 EEC Directive, the Chinese community had put in a lot of effort to establish Chinese supplementary schools/classes to provide Chinese language/culture education to help Chinese children to adjust themselves to the two cultural environments — the Chinese family and the British society in which they live.

While the number of Chinese children is increasing in Britain, there is a growing demand for Chinese language/culture education by Chinese parents. In order to meet the demand, changes have taken place in the development of Chinese supplementary schools/classes.

Development of Chinese Supplementary Schools/Classes

The Pre-war Chinese school

The old Chinese immigrants were very conscious of the influence of western culture on their children living in Britain. They were afraid that their children would be seduced by the English life-style and would become hooligans or ruffians. The early immigrants believed that by promoting Chinese culture among Anglo-Chinese children, they would become 'better men and better women'. In the first Chinese class started in 1928 at a restaurant in London, the Chinese language, customs, culture and folklore were taught to Chinese children. Later, with a donation of £500 from Sir Robert Ho Tung, a prominent citizen of Hong Kong, Irene Ho, a daughter of Sir Robert Ho Tung, helped the Chinese class to acquire its school premises in Pennyfields in East London and founded the *Chung Hua* Chinese School which had an enrolment of about 20

Chinese students. The *Chung Hua* Chinese School is usually regarded as the first Chinese supplementary school in London (Jones, D., 1980).

Besides providing an educational service for Chinese children, *Chung Hua* Chinese School acted as an employment agency and a dissemination centre for information about China. Owing to the return of the Chinese teacher to China, the school was closed before the war broke out (Chann, 1982; China Journal, 1935; Jones, D., 1980; Ng, K.C., 1968; Shang, 1984).

After the closure of the *Chung Hua* Chinese School, Chinese classes became stagnant for about two decades. No information on the further development of Chinese supplementary schools/classes was available.

Expansion of Chinese supplementary schools/classes

Late 1960s – early 1970s

Despite the fact that a Cantonese class was resumed by the Overseas Chinese Service in April 1963 (Ng, K.C., 1968), the expansion of Chinese schools/classes did not take place until the late 1960s when there was a significant increase of Chinese children in Britain as a result of immigration and natural growth. While these children are growing up in Britain, Chinese parents are very anxious that these children should maintain their cultural identity and values. Since the traditional practice of sending British-born Chinese children back to Hong Kong to receive Chinese education became impossible after the grandmothers had joined the Chinese families in Britain, the Chinese community had to seek an alternative solution to the problem of providing cultural education for their children in Britain.

Chapter 2 mentions that within the Chinese community, some Chinese benevolent associations had been set up by Chinese immigrants of whom the majority were related to one another in terms of clanship or lineage (Collins, 1957; Ng, K.C., 1968; Shang, 1984). When the education provision in the New Territories was inadequate, these clan societies used to take up the responsibility of providing education for children in their own village (Baker, 1964). As sending Chinese children back to Hong Kong to receive Chinese education became difficult after Chinese families had re-united in Britain, more Chinese supplementary schools/classes had been established by Chinese benevolent associations to provide Chinese language/culture education for Chinese children in Britain. The relative increase in the number of Chinese supplementary schools/classes in the late 1960s marked a new era of the development of self-help education within the Chinese community.

Based on the information given by a former student of the London Kung Ho Association Chinese School, this section tries to use the organisation of that particular school to illustrate how the self-help education provided by the Chinese community solves Chinese children's problems in Britain.

Before the Kung Ho Association Chinese School came into existence in 1968, the London Kung Ho Association was originally a social club set up in 1947 by a group of seamen and catering workers. Its aim was 'to provide a gathering place for members to spend their leisure time' (London Kung Ho Association, 1985:26–27). As a result of the influx of immigrants from Hong Kong in the 1960s, its membership had been increased and activities were expanded. Wives of the members also met at the Association. In 1966 these women formed a Women's Club attached to the Association (*ibid.*). The first Chinese class was initiated by these women of whom some had been deprived of education in the traditional Confucian society.

According to the informant who is the daughter of one of the founders of the London Kung Ho Association Women's Club, there were two Chinese families who met quite regularly on Saturdays and Sundays for tea at the Association which was located in a basement in Chinatown in Soho. Chinese children were around while mothers were having tea and chatting. The mothers were inspired to establish a Chinese class where they took turns to teach Chinese basics to their children at a ping-pong (table-tennis) table in the basement. As far as Mr Cheung, the headteacher, could recall, the Chinese class of the London Kung Ho Association only started with about six or seven children.

Due to the political background of the school, apart from learning the Chinese language, Chinese pupils were inculcated Chairman Mao's political ideology through the 'red book'. Later the curriculum was expanded when more voluntary teachers joined the school. In addition to the Chinese language, the geography and history of China, calligraphy and Mandarin had formed part of the curriculum.

At that time, children went to the Chinese school two days a week — Saturday and Sunday. They had formal classroom teaching in the morning. In the afternoon they joined various extra-curricular-activities such as singing, dancing, orchestra and table-tennis organised by the 'free-club' of the school. Since the celebration of traditional festivals is quite significant in Chinese culture, the school believes it important for children of Chinese origin in Britain to be educated this way. Pupils of the Chinese school were taken to join Chinese New Year parties organised by other Chinese communities in some major cities in Britain. Although Chinese pupils in that school were provided a variety of educational cultural activities, the Chinese class was completely free. It was only at a later stage that a £10 tuition fee per year was charged in order to meet the running costs of the school.

After the establishment of the first Chinese class by the London Kung Ho Association, the Chinese community has become more conscious of the increasing demand for mother tongue education while the number of Chinese children is increasing. According to the nation-wide Chinese school survey carried out in 1979 by the Chinese Chamber of Commerce (UK) (1980), four more Chinese classes had been founded by various groups between the late 1960s and the early 1970s. All these Chinese classes are self-financing. The day-to-day running of the school relies mainly on the contributions of Chinese parents and membership subscriptions. Similar to the London Kung Ho Chinese Class, none of these schools has any proper school premises to carry out classroom activities. Classes are held in the headquarters of the association concerned, church halls or chapels (Chinese Chamber of Commerce (UK), 1980; NCC, 1979).

Late 1970s – early 1980s

After the reunion of husbands and wives in the late 1960s and the early 1970s, more Chinese children have been born in the UK. By the late 1970s, many of the British-born Chinese children had reached school age. Chinese parents understand that once their children go to British schools and start learning English, they will tend to forget the Chinese language which they learn at home. In order to help these Chinese children to maintain the Chinese language while they are educated in British schools, Chinese parents want to send them to Chinese supplementary schools as soon as their children reach the Chinese school admission age — 5 or 6 years. Such a phenomenon of sending children to Chinese classes at an early age is different from the situation in the past. Consequently Chinese supplementary schools usually have a fairly long waiting list, especially for classes at beginners' level. One of these schools claimed that the number of applicants on their waiting list can be as large as 30 to 50 each year.

Although there has been a significant increase in the demand for

Chinese language education, the lack of space for holding Chinese classes has prevented some small-scale Chinese supplementary schools from accepting all the applicants. In order to solve the problem, more Chinese supplementary schools/classes have to be established. Initiatives have been taken by Chinese parents, community leaders and Chinese associations to establish more Chinese classes. According to Chann's (1984) paper on 'The Silent Minority' which was presented at the National Conference on Chinese families in Britain on 26 November 1982, of the 56 private Chinese classes that the Hong Kong Government Office (London) was associated with, 71% (40) were established between the late 1970s and early 1980s. Chann's statistics are close to findings of the Chinese School Survey conducted by the Chinese Chamber of Commerce (UK) in 1979. The results of the survey indicate that 74% (23) of the 31 Chinese classes in Britain were founded between 1975 and 1979 (Chinese Chamber of Commerce (UK), 1980). Compared with the seven schools being established between 1968 and 1974 in Britain[1], the number of Chinese classes set up within the last few years had at least tripled those being established at an early stage. The rate of expansion of Chinese classes since the late 1970s is much faster than before.

Besides the increase in the number of Chinese supplementary schools/classes, changes have been made in the organisation of some Chinese classes in order to meet the needs of the changing clientele and the aspirations of Chinese parents in Britain. By the use of the IBE (International Bureau of Education) taxonomy[2] (Holmes, 1979), the present organisation of Chinese classes is analysed.

Organisation of Chinese Supplementary Schools/Classes

With the support of some LEAs and the Hong Kong Government Office (London), together with the initiatives taken by some enthusiastic Chinese teachers who want to improve Chinese language education within the Chinese community, some Chinese supplementary schools/classes have already been modified or innovated in order to make Chinese education more effective and relevant. As many of the changes are quite recent and they only take place in individual schools only, not much about the new practices of Chinese supplementary schools has been recorded. The investigation of the present organisation of Chinese classes has to rely on the information provided by organisers/headteachers of 13 Chinese schools[3] and 25 teachers at interviews as well as the author's teaching experience and classroom observation at a Chinese school in

Chinatown for four years. Some statistical data in relation to the study were obtained by questionnaires filled in by headteachers/organisers of seven Chinese supplementary schools. Findings are as follows.

Aims

Despite the fact that most of the Chinese supplementary schools are run differently, the aims they set for the school are quite similar to one another. Except a few schools, the aims of the school are not stated anywhere but are mutually understood by the staff of the school. Among the seven Chinese supplementary schools which returned the questionnaire[4], five consider that the following are the most important objectives which their school would like to achieve.

(i)   To provide Chinese language education for overseas Chinese.
(ii) To encourage young overseas Chinese to have an awareness of Chinese culture.
(iii) To help to bridge the communication gap between Chinese parents and their children by the provision of Chinese language education for Chinese children[5].

The common objectives of the Chinese language education of the five schools indicate that Chinese education in Britain places a strong emphasis on the cultural aspect, especially in terms of lanugage. Other educational and psychological needs of Chinese children have been ignored.

Administration

As there is an absence of a central agency to provide guidelines for the day-to-day running of Chinese supplementary schools, the administration of these schools is quite decentralised. Individual schools set up their own system of administration. Regardless of the variations, the administration of Chinese supplementary schools/classes can be divided into three levels by referring to Parsons' (1958) formal organisation model: (1) the public interest group, (2) the managerial group and (3) the technical group.

(1) The public interest group

There are three main types of Chinese association running Chinese supplementary schools/classes in Britain namely:

(i) Chinese associations or groups which have commercial interests, similar trade orientations and clanmanship.

(ii) Christian denominations which include mainly the Anglican and non-conformist groups.

(iii) Newly formed groups which are attached to Chinese community centres and aided by direct grants from Local Councils (Tsow, 1983).

The public interest group of Chinese supplementary schools in fact is the executive committee of the organisation/association supporting the school. Members of the executive committee are elected annually. Since the majority of people on the committee are laymen who have no direct contact with the school, the power to formulate policies of the school is usually delegated to the headteacher or the education sub-committee of the school. The executive committee (public interest group) acts as a 'watch-dog' only.

(2) The managerial group

While most of the schools are expanding, it is unlikely that Chinese supplementary schools can rely solely on their headteacher, who works on a part-time voluntary basis, to formulate all school policies on his/her own. Schools which are affiliated with churches or Chinese organisations/associations usually form an education sub-committee, or a managerial group in Parsons' terms, to handle such matters as the appointment of teachers, the selection of textbooks and the drawing up of the school calendar. The headteacher is usually the ex-officio member of the managerial group. The teaching staff in the managerial group are appointed by the headteacher or the school organisers. The appointment is normally based on the teacher's seniority or performance at school.

Among the seven Chinese schools, three had formed a managerial group in addition to the public interest group. Even though the other four schools had not established any formal managerial groups such as education sub-committees, two schools indicated that matters concerning the school were usually decided jointly between the headteacher and the teaching staff[6].

In order to obtain ideas from teachers to help to improve the management of the school, the managerial group of some Chinese supplementary schools usually try to arrange meetings with their teachers at least once a term. Since the majority of schools do not have their own school office and the school premises are allowed for use for a limited time for holding Chinese classes only, such kind of meetings are usually held on informal occasions at teachers' homes or at a Chinese restaurant. While teachers are enjoying the meal, school matters will be discussed at the same time. Some policies formulated by the managerial group in fact are based on ideas collected in those informal staff meetings.

(3)   The technical group

This group in Chinese supplementary schools usually refers to the part-time voluntary teachers appointed from all walks of life. Their main duty at school is teaching the Chinese language. Some of them may be given extra responsibilities such as helping to look after the school library or organising after-school activities.

Owing to the voluntary nature of the service contributed by Chinese teachers, many of the extra duties of teachers cannot be made obligatory. However, the commitment and the enthusiasm of some Chinese teachers to their teaching job has motivated them to do extra work. In addition to the teaching of the Chinese language during school hours, some of the Chinese teachers provide counselling for students during recess time or after school to help some Chinese pupils to solve their emotional and academic problems. Some teachers even pay family visits to students who seem to have problems within the family. The initiatives taken by Chinese teachers to solve the psychological problems is a kind of duty which cannot be easily fulfilled by English-speaking teachers at state schools.

Finance

Unlike the situation in the past where most of the Chinese supplementary schools had to rely solely on the support of the organisation or association founding the school, additional financial assistance ranging from £1,000 to £2,000 per year has been obtained by Chinese supplementary schools in London from the Hong Kong Government Office (London) since the late 1970s. At the same time, the LEAs contribute about £750–£1,500 per year to help to meet the current expenditure of Chinese supplementary schools/classes[7]. Besides the financial assistance, some LEAs have permitted the free use of their school premises for the holding of Chinese classes. Of the seven schools, five reported that they were using LEA school premises[8]. Except one school, four schools claimed that they did not need to pay any rents[9]. In addition to the two major sources of income, some schools are able to obtain a substantial amount of money from the donations of individual parents, tuition fees or membership subscriptions of the associations. Five schools claimed that the money they obtained from various sources was just sufficient to meet the expenditure of the school. Two schools said that the money was not enough[10].

Because of limited finance, the majority of Chinese supplementary schools have to charge tuition fees. Six out of seven schools charged a tuition fee within the range of £10 to £30 per annum[11]. According to the explanation given by headteachers, the tuition fees charged are to help to meet the costs of photocopying and the purchase of exercise books only. The Chinese tuition remains virtually free to Chinese children. Although some schools have noticed that some Chinese parents have been taking advantage of Chinese classes by treating them as inexpensive nurseries, they still welcome all children joining Chinese classes regardless of the non-educational motives of some Chinese parents.

Class organisation

Chinese supplementary schools are independent of the British education system. As there are no central agencies to co-ordinate the running of Chinese schools, the organisation of Chinese supplementary schools/classes varies, depending on the school's knowledge of the education system in Hong Kong, their openness to change, the preference of Chinese parents, the children's ability as well as the nature of the premises used for teaching.

In London one Chinese supplementary school has acquired its own school premises since 1977[12]. The majority of Chinese classes are held in private houses, centres and church halls (GB. P. H. of C., HAC, 1985; Tsow, 1984). The list of Chinese schools compiled by the Hong Kong Government Office (London) (1985) shows that 8 out of the 16 Chinese supplementary schools in London were using 11 of the LEA school premises[13]. The lack of own school premises and the rents charged by some organisations for the use of their premises have restricted the school hours of Chinese classes. Chinese parents' occupational background, their working hours and the supply of teachers are important factors to consider when deciding the duration of Chinese classes. The majority of Chinese classes are held at the weekend on Saturday and Sunday. Most Chinese supplementary schools have about an average of two hours for each class. A few will last for three hours [14].

Although Chinese classes are short, many Chinese parents are quite satisfied. In interviews with 25 Chinese parents, except for a few parents who wanted to have some more Chinese classes arranged in the evening during the week, most of them preferred having classes at the weekend only because they wanted their children to give priority to their English school work. On the other hand, interviews with 40 Chinese students indicated that 71% (27) of the respondents' fathers and 38% (15) of their mothers worked in the catering business. Many of these parents had to work in the evening between 5.00 p.m. and 12 midnight. It would be impossible for parents to take their children to Chinese classes during the week.

According to Tsow's (1984) survey, about 75% of the parents said that either one or both of the parents would accompany their children to the Chinese class. Eighteen (35%) out of the 51 children in this research said that they had to rely on their parents to drive them to school because public transport was inconvenient in the place where they lived. In fact, many of the pupils do not live close to Chinese supplementary schools. Tsow's (1984) study shows that 39% of her subjects had to travel more than five miles in order to attend Chinese supplementary schools in London. 19% claimed that it took them more than half an hour to get to school. Among the sample of 430 Chinese children in this survey, 43% (185) had to spend about an hour on their journey to get to Chinese school[15]. The findings indicate that although Chinese classes are short and are held once at the weekend only, such an arrangement of Chinese classes has minimised Chinese parents' trouble of taking their children to Chinese classes during the week.

Except for two Chinese supplementary schools which have a slightly different arrangement, most of them start in September and finish in July[16]. Regardless of the variations in the school year, there are usually about 30 to 40 teaching weeks in the academic year. Some parents would like to see the school year extended into the summer holiday. Since the LEA school premises are closed during the summer and teachers prefer to take holidays at that time, it is difficult to satisfy the expectations of Chinese parents.

A Chinese supplementary school in London had organised a summer school on an experimental basis for their own pupils in 1986. Instead of teaching the Chinese language, a variety of activities such as video showing, calligraphy and Chinese chess were arranged. Even though the summer school was free, students' support and participation was quite disappointing. Besides students' lack of interest in the summer school, the recruitment of the project staff was another problem because not many of their own teaching staff were willing to work in the holiday. Based on the experience of that school, it seems that organising summer schools for Chinese children is a speculation of the needs of only very few Chinese parents and their children. Many of the Chinese parents are quite satisfied with the present activities of Chinese supplementary schools within the academic year.

Class sequencing

Since the majority of Chinese supplementary schools have adopted Chinese textbooks which are designed for primary school pupils in Hong Kong, many of these schools have structured their classes like those in Hong Kong. In order to complete the whole cycle of basic Chinese education in Britain, four out of the seven schools pointed out that it will take at least eight years, i.e. two years in kindergarten and six years in primary[17].

Instead of adopting the traditional Hong Kong system, three schools claimed that they had created a grade level system of their own[18]. Two Chinese supplementary schools had divided the basic Chinese education into twelve grade levels. Another Chinese supplementary school had adopted an eight grade-level system[19]. Because of the differences in the method of structuring classes at Chinese supplementary schools, four of these schools claimed that theoretically it takes a minimum of ten years to finish the primary cycle of Chinese language education in Britain. In the other two schools, twelve years are required. The only Chinese supplementary school which had exactly the same primary school structure as that in Hong Kong required a minimum of eight years to finish the basic Chinese education [20]. According to Chinese supplementary school headteachers, the reason for extending the primary cycle of the Chinese education in Britain is mainly because of the lack of a language environment for the use of Chinese and the limited time of each class. Consequently children's progress in learning is much slower than their counterparts in Hong Kong. They require a relatively longer time to complete the basic Chinese education which normally takes six years in Hong Kong.

Curriculum

Medium of instruction

Although a considerable number of Chinese in Britain speak Hakka, the lingua franca within the Chinese community is Cantonese. Of the 25 Chinese teachers interviewed, except one who spoke Mandarin much better than Cantonese, the majority of the teachers spoke Cantonese as their mother tongue. Under these circumstances, Cantonese has been adopted by the majority of Chinese supplementary schools in London as the medium of instruction. Of the 13 Chinese supplementary schools visited in London, 12 of them had confirmed that they used Cantonese as the medium of instruction.

Among the Chinese in Britain, there are a small proportion of Chinese from Taiwan, Singapore and Malaysia where Mandarin is taught at school. Many Chinese parents from these countries are Mandarin-speaking. They therefore expect their children to be taught in Mandarin. In order to meet the needs of these parents, two Chinese supplementary schools in London, being founded by Mandarin-speaking parents, use Mandarin as the medium of instruction[21].

According to the headteacher of one of the Mandarin-medium schools, some of their pupils were Cantonese-speaking. They were expected to learn the Chinese language taught in Mandarin because their parents thought that it would be more useful to their children's future career if they could speak Mandarin which is more internationally recognised. Their children could learn Cantonese at home from them. Thus, the establishment of a few Mandarin-medium Chinese supplementary schools has helped to meet the various expectations of Chinese parents in Britain.

Although Chinese teachers are supposed to use either Cantonese or Mandarin as a medium of instruction, 73% (316) of the 432 Chinese pupils in the sample indicated that some English had been used in their Chinese class[22]. According to the explanation given by Chinese teachers at interviews, the reason for using English in addition to Cantonese or Mandarin is to meet the needs of pupils and achieve efficiency in teaching the Chinese language to children in Britain. The need of English for comprehension purpose had been confirmed by 69% (294) of 424 Chinese pupils studying at Chinese supplementary schools in London[23].

Content

It has been mentioned in Chapter 3 that because of the lack of understanding of the Chinese culture by some Chinese children in Britain, conflicts between Chinese parents and their children are inevitable. Chinese parents 'feel strongly that only through a knowledge of the language, and thereby the history and literature, can the children have a true understanding of their parents' attitudes, standards and values' (GB. P. H. of C. HAC, 1985, Vol. 2: xli). In order to meet Chinese parents' expectations and eliminate conflicts between Chinese parents and their children, the curriculum content, as pointed out by Tsow (1984) and one of the speakers at a teachers' seminar held on 25 October 1986[24], has focused on the development of Chinese children's listening, reading, spoken and writing skills in Chinese.

Since there is no particular syllabus governing the curriculum content, teaching is based on what is provided in the textbooks. Generally speaking, it is quite impossible for Chinese supplementary schools to finish the two volumes of the Chinese language textbook within a year. The policy adopted by most of the Chinese teachers is to select topics related to the glamorous history, the great inventions of China, the major Chinese festivals and customs, Confucius' ideas of filial piety, popular classical poems and some sight-seeing places in Hong Kong. By including a variety of topics in the curriculum, Chinese schools hope that Chinese pupils will form a positive image of their cultural identity and be able to understand their parents' expectations.

Many Chinese mothers, probably some fathers too, have only reached primary level education. Some of the Chinese parents are illiterate in both Chinese and English. They hope that if their children know both Chinese and English, they will help to write Chinese letters to Hong Kong and contribute their bilingual skills to their parents' catering business. On the other hand, translation is one of the linguistic skills to be tested in the GCE O-level Chinese examination which some students in senior level classes would like to attempt. In order to meet the needs of Chinese parents and prepare Chinese pupils for the GCE O-level Chinese examination, most Chinese supplementary schools put a fairly strong emphasis on letter-writing and translation when students reach Primary three or four. If there are texts concerning letter-writing, they will never be missed.

As translation in Hong Kong is considered as an advanced and professional skill, primary school children in Hong Kong are not expected to learn any translation. As a result, there is nothing in primary school

Chinese textbooks published in Hong Kong that Chinese teachers in Britain can refer to when they teach translation. As the majority of Chinese teachers in Britain are not trained translators, the teaching of translation is simply based on individual teachers' knowledge of the two languages. Before Chinese children in Britain can master the Chinese and English basic skills, the learning of translation from untrained teachers will exert more pressure on Chinese pupils in learning the Chinese language.

In order to solve the problems faced by Chinese pupils in translation, some teachers encourage students to memorise texts. In tests or examinations within the school, teachers try to set translation questions based on the texts taught. In case students find it difficult to express themselves in Chinese, they can rely on what they can remember from texts. Such a method may have helped students to cope with the translation questions in internal examinations, however, questions in the GCE Chinese examination are not based on any one particular textbook. In the GCE O-level Chinese examination papers of June 1983, 1985 and 1986, it was noticed that the two translation passages of 350 words for Chinese and 100 words for English were not from any of the Chinese textbooks which Chinese supplementary schools were using. The memorisation of texts may not be helpful to students in the GCE Chinese examination.

Many Chinese teachers have assumed that Chinese spoken skills can be developed within the family, therefore many Chinese teachers have ignored the development of Chinese spoken skills at school[25]. In fact, the training of Chinese spoken skills has to be strengthened as it has been noticed that quite a few Chinese students in kindergarten and Primary one Chinese classes are unable to speak or understand Cantonese[26].

Besides beginners, some Primary three students in a popular Chinese supplementary school in London also have problems in reading and speaking Chinese (Cantonese). In the final examination in 1985/86, a Cantonese oral test based on the format of the Hong Kong Certificate of Education (HKCEE) English oral examination[27] had been designed by the author and one of her colleagues to test the reading and conversation ability of Primary three students. It was found that many British-born Chinese children who went to Chinese school in Britain had failed to express themselves clearly and fluently in Cantonese when they were asked questions about the pictures given.

The failure of some Chinese pupils to express themselves in fluent

TABLE 5 *Classroom language-related activities to facilitate the learning of Chinese*

Language-related activities	Very often No.	(%)	Frequency Sometimes No.	(%)	Never No.	(%)	Total number of respondents
Videos	4	(1)	27	(7)	382	(93)	413
Tapes*	8	(2)	46	(11)	361	(87)	415
Crossword puzzles	1	(0.2)	32	(8)	379	(92)	412
Riddles	2	(0.5)	95	(23)	315	(77)	412
Role-playing	3	(0.7)	75	(18)	334	(81)	412

Source: Question 24 of Questionnaire A.
    *Tapes with Chinese songs or stories.

Chinese after a few years' Chinese education signals that some Chinese pupils need more training in Chinese spoken skills. If such training is ignored in the curriculum content, the aim of bridging the communication gap between Chinese parents and their children set by Chinese supplementary schools will be difficult to achieve.

Owing to the nature of the Chinese language and the lack of opportunities to use Chinese in the majority society, it is quite difficult for Chinese children in Britain to learn the Chinese language. In order to make Chinese lessons more interesting, singing usually forms part of the curriculum in beginners' classes.

In the upper grade level classes, teachers sometimes adopt an activity approach to stimulate students to learn Chinese by the use of puzzles, riddles and role-playing[28]. Unfortunately such an approach in teaching has not been widely supported. About 80 to 90% of Chinese pupils reported that none of these activities had been carried out in the classroom (Table 5). Consequently only about one quarter of the Chinese

TABLE 6 *Students' comments on Chinese classes*

General remarks	Number of respondents	(%)
Quite interesting	117	(28)
O.K.	261	(61)
Quite boring	48	(11)
Total	426	(100)

Source: Question 25 in Section one of Questionnaire A.

pupils found their Chinese class interesting. About 60% of the pupils were quite indifferent towards Chinese classes (Table 6).

In order to develop reading skills, most teachers follow the traditional method to teach Chinese in Britain. Teachers first introduce new words on the blackboard. While the teacher is reading the text, students will repeat it parrot-fashion. Some teachers may use homophones to help students to memorise the pronounciation of certain words. Such a method is not very effective. More than 90% of 435 Chinese students had created their own romanisation symbols based on English to learn the pronounciation of Chinese[29].

Although many teachers have realised that the student-invented romanisation symbols are not perfect to learn the pronounciation of Chinese, they cannot find any better ways to help Chinese children to learn spoken Cantonese because they were not taught any phonetic systems when they themselves learnt the Chinese language at school. Moreover, they are not trained teachers to teach Chinese as a second language. In order to develop Chinese children's Cantonese reading skills, one Chinese supplementary school in London had tried to teach romanisation to grade four and five students. Results of the experiment are in preparation[30].

Besides teaching various skills of the Chinese language, schools which are affiliated with church denominations have made Bible study a compulsory component of the curriculum. Since these Chinese classes are free and the learning of some religious ideas does no harm to children, Chinese parents usually have no objection to the learning of the Bible by their children in the Chinese class. Teachers of those two Chinese schools said that through the Bible, students could learn more new vocabulary. Students' opinions about the incorporation of religious education in the Chinese class vary. Some of them are indifferent. Some of them dislike it but they cannot opt out of religious education if they want to join the Chinese class. Three pupils who had transferred from one of the church-supported Chinese supplementary schools to another Chinese supplementary school pointed out that they found learning the Bible boring and it was a waste of their time in the Chinese class.

In conclusion, although there is very limited time for Chinese classes, Chinese pupils are expected to gain a variety of knowledge at Chinese supplementary school.

Teaching materials

Textbooks used by Chinese supplementary schools in Britain are mainly supplied by the Hong Kong Government Office (London) [31]. The school which adopts Mandarin as the teaching medium uses one more textbook which is an overseas edition published in Taiwan. Since these textbooks are designed for students living in a Chinese culturally orientated society to learn the Chinese language, it has been criticised that the textbooks are not appropriate for the clientele in Britain whose age is much older than those for whom the books are originally designed (DES, 1985; Tsow, 1984). The age difference between the clientele in Britain and those in Hong Kong is shown in Table 7.

In order to meet the needs of Chinese children in Britain and supplement the inadequacies of Chinese textbooks, six out of the seven Chinese supplementary schools claimed that their teachers had helped to produce teaching materials for use at different grade levels. Teaching aids such as tapes and word cards were available at some of these schools (Table 8).

Some of the Chinese educational videos in fact can be borrowed from the Hong Kong Government Office (London) and public libraries. At a Chinese supplementary school in north London, it was discovered that a considerable amount of the reading materials and audio-visual aids such as tapes with songs and stories in Chinese were on a long-term loan to the school from a nearby public library.

Although it seems that teaching aids of various types are available

TABLE 7 *Age differences between Chinese children in London and those in Hong Kong attending primary level education*

Primary level	Age range attending each level		Age differences (in years)
	in Hong Kong	in London	
1	6–7	7–13	1–6
2	7–8	9–15	2–7
3	8–9	10–13	2–4
4	9–10	12–18	3–8
5	10–11	12–23	2–12
6	11–12	14	3

Source: Findings from the interviews with 43 Chinese pupils attending Chinese classes at different grade levels in Chinese schools in London.

TABLE 8 *Availability of teaching aids/materials at different grade levels in Chinese schools*

Teaching aids/ materials	Number of schools with teaching aids available at different grade levels				
	Pre-primary (Grades 1–2)	P1–2 (G3–4)	P3–4 (G5–6)	P5–6 (G7–8)	Secondary (G8–12)
Chinese tapes	3	3	2	2	0
Word cards	5	2	0	0	0
Story books	3	4	4	3	2
Self-produced aids*	6	4	3	3	1
Other textbooks†	0	2	1	1	0

Source: Results of Question 29 of Questionnaire B.
Key:
*: Teaching aids produced by individual teachers.
†: Textbooks other than those supplied by the Hong Kong Government Office (London).
P: Primary
G: Grade.

at most of the Chinese supplementary schools, they are not frequently used by teachers. 93% (382) of 393 Chinese students complained that they had never been shown any Chinese videos in class. 87% (361) of 415 Chinese respondents said that they had not been given Chinese educational tapes to listen[32].

The reason for not fully utilising the audio-visual aids is that the time for each class is too limited. Since there is usually some form of assessment at the end of each term or school year, teachers tend to spend most of the time on teaching the textbook to prepare students for tests or examinations. Another reason is mainly a matter of individual teachers' confidence in the use of audio-visual aids in lanugage teaching. Many of the Chinese teachers believe that the traditional rote-learning method is the most effective way to learn the Chinese language. They would avoid the use of audio-visual aids in teaching the Chinese language.

With regard to the subject matter of Chinese textbooks, opinions of teachers vary. Some teachers think that topics such as the night scene of Hong Kong and the Peak are too Hong Kong orientated and too remote. Students would find it difficult to associate what they learn at Chinese school with their daily life in Britain. Some teachers insist that the Hong Kong orientated texts should be taught as Hong Kong is the native country of many of the Chinese children in Britain. It has been noticed by teachers that some Chinese pupils are able to visit their home country once or twice a year. Although some of them do not have any chance to see their native land, teachers feel teaching something about Hong Kong will widen students' general knowledge.

Examinations

Among the 13 Chinese supplementary schools, only two had post-primary Chinese classes preparing students for the GCE O-level Chinese examination[33]. The rest of the schools only had internal termly or yearly examinations. Because of the absence of syllabus, the majority of Chinese teachers select their own topics of interest to teach. Therefore it would be very difficult to set any uniform examinations or tests for each grade level. Criteria for assessment vary. Under these circumstances, students having completed a certain grade level in different classes in the same school does not necessarily mean that they have reached the same standard of Chinese. The lack of uniform assessment usually leads to conflicts between teachers. Teachers often complain that there are weak students who should not have been promoted to their class as they have not reached the standard.

Since June 1986, the first CSE Chinese paper has been set by the London Regional Examining Board with consultation from two Chinese supplementary school headteachers in London. Similar to the GCE O-level Chinese paper, there is a section on essay-writing in the CSE Chinese paper. The number of words required is 60 to 80 which is less than that required in the GCE O-level Chinese examination. Instead of being tested on the conventional translation skills as in the GCE O-level Chinese examination, students in the CSE examination are given jumbled sentences in English and are asked to re-arrange them in a logical order in Chinese. Besides translation, students have to sit for an oral examination and a listening test. Since the CSE Chinese examination content is not quite related to the curriculum of Chinese supplementary schools, not many Chinese supplementary schools adopt the CSE examination as a yardstick to assess their pupils even though there is an absence of an appropriate assessment instrument. Of the seven Chinese supplementary schools, only one would give priority to preparing Chinese children for the GCE/CSE Chinese language examination by regarding it as the second aim of the school. Others only considered such a task as the last or the second to last aim among all the objectives of the school[34].

Extra-curricular activities

Many of the Chinese teachers have realised that some Chinese children's intention of attending Chinese school is to make friends only. If the school premises can be used after class and teachers are available, extra-curricular activities will be arranged for pupils. Unfortunately the time for the use of the school premises is restricted to the teaching hours only and most of the teachers cannot commit themselves to the organisation of extra-curricula to meet the specific needs of some Chinese children. Of the 13 Chinese supplementary schools, only three schools were able to arrange extra-curricular activities such as singing, dancing and games after school or before the Chinese class starts.

In recent years, because of the establishment of some Chinese community centres which have recognised the socialising needs of Chinese children, some of these centres are open at the weekend. Usually children like to drop in at these centres before or after Chinese class. Besides meeting their friends, children can watch Chinese videos and play table-tennis, chess or computer games. Thus these Chinese community centres seem to be playing a complementary role in helping to solve Chinese children's problems which Chinese supplementary schools are unable to do because of physical and human constraints.

Besides weekly activities, there are some annual culturally orientated activities such as the Chinese New Year and Mid-autumn Festival celebration parties which the majority of Chinese supplementary schools will never miss. By organising parties to celebrate these festivals and having the participation of Chinese parents, organisers of Chinese supplementary schools think that they will help to promote Chinese culture as well as bridging the gap between Chinese parents and their children. Moreover, teachers can take the opportunity to have a better understanding of Chinese parents' expectations of the school. In addition to festival celebrations, outdoor activities such as school picnics are organised when the weather is warm. Parents are often invited to join the picnics as the major aim of such an activity is to improve the relationship and communication between students, parents and teachers.

Teacher education and supply

Despite the fact that about 94% (113) of the sample of 120 teachers were unqualified teachers (Table 9), their educational background, age and enthusiasm have given them confidence in carrying out various educational tasks at Chinese supplementary schools.

TABLE 9 *Teacher training qualifications (TTQ) of teachers at seven Chinese schools in London*

School number	with TTQ recognised*	Number of teachers with TTQ not recognised	Other professsions	Total
1	2	9	10	21
2	2	1	19	22
3	2	2	9	13
4	0	1	19	20
5	0	0	15	15
6	0	0	22	22
7	1	0	6	7
Total	7	13	100	120

Source: Questions 34 and 35 of Questionnaire B.
*Qualification recognised in the UK.

Of the 120 Chinese teachers in the sample, 37% (45) were students from Hong Kong[35] who were pursuing university or higher education in the UK. Twenty-three of the teachers were parents with children studying in the Chinese school where they taught[36]. The rest of the Chinese teachers were UK citizens working in various professions. Regardless of their occupational background, almost all Chinese language teachers had completed secondary education (Table 10). The majority of them had their general/basic education (primary and secondary) in Hong Kong.

Except teaching methodology, teachers' knowledge of the Chinese language should be adequate for them to teach Chinese at primary school level. Since many of the teachers were brought up and educated in Hong Kong, they have better knowledge of the type of cultural values that Chinese parents in Britain want their childen to maintain — to succeed in education and respect parents.

After having experienced life in Britain, many of the Chinese teachers are able to diagnose some of the cultural conflicts faced by Chinese pupils in Britain. Such knowledge in fact has helped many Chinese teachers to fulfil their responsibilities and eliminate some of the 'culture shock' problems of their pupils. As mentioned in the section on the 'technical group', some of these teachers have taken initiatives to counsel students and visit parents at home. These jobs could be difficult for English-speaking teachers at British state schools to carry out.

Besides having knowledge of the two cultures, the young ages of

TABLE 10 *Educational attainment of the teachers in seven Chinese schools in London*

School number	Secondary	Number of teachers Post-secondary without a degree	Post-secondary with a degree	Not known	Total
1	8	4	1	8	21
2	—	18	4	—	22
3	—	6	6	1	13
4	7	—	13	—	20
5	*	*	*	*	15
6	5	7	10	—	22
7	3	3	1	—	7
Total	23	38	35	9	120

Source: Question 36 of Questionnaire B.
  * The headteacher did not state the number but claimed that all their teachers have at least completed post-secondary education or higher.

the Chinese teachers have proven an advantage in carrying out their educational mission in Chinese supplementary schools. Of the one-hundred teachers at seven Chinese supplementary schools, about 45% were between 20 and 25 years or under (Table 11). Therefore many of the Chinese pupils find their Chinese teachers friendly and easy to approach when they have problems.

TABLE 11 *Age of teachers in some Chinese schools in London*

School number	Number of teachers in the following age-range 20–25 or under	26–30	31–35	35+	Not known	Total
1	14	1	2	4	—	21
2	12	5	2	—	3	22
3	—	7	6	—	—	13
4	*	*	*	*	*	*
5	3	3	5	4	—	15
6	14	1	6	1	—	22
7	2	—	—	5	—	7
Total	45	17	21	14	3	100

Source: Question 40 of Questionnaire B.
  * Details of the age of teachers at School No. 4 were not available as the question had not been answered.

Despite the fact that Chinese teachers perform various tasks at Chinese supplementary schools, the majority of them do not have salaries. Six out of the seven Chinese supplementary schools reimbursed the travelling expenses of their teachers every month [37]. Some teachers with a monthly travel ticket waived the reimbursement because they regard teaching as a community service. Being a member of the Chinese community in Britain, some of the Chinese teachers think that they are obliged to contribute some service in terms of education which is in need in the community.

Owing to the commitment of teachers to their teaching job and the voluntary nature of the educational service of Chinese supplementary schools, officially rewarding Chinese teachers with a fixed rate of salary is not a common practice among Chinese supplementary schools. As a result, many of these schools have problems in the supply of teachers. It was found that about one-third of the teaching force of the seven Chinese supplementary schools had to rely on overseas Chinese students studying in the UK[38]. The mobility of these teachers is quite high. When teachers finish their studies in the UK, many of them will give up their teaching job and return home. Setting up a salary scheme probably will help to attract some Chinese–UK citizens to join the teaching force. Unfortunately the financial situation of most of the Chinese supplementary schools cannot allow such a practice.

In order to solve the problem of teacher supply, six of the seven Chinese supplementary schools preferred to recruit their teachers through the recommendations of their staff instead of appointing people who respond to their advertisement directly [39]. The schools thought that such a method of recruitment would probably eliminate the problem of the mobility of teachers by taking advantage of some personal relationship between the new and old staff.

As the recruitment of teachers is so restricted to personal relationship that some Chinese supplementary schools do not have enough teachers at the beginning of the school year. The solution to the problem is that either the headteacher helps with the teaching or classes are combined together until a new teacher is appointed. If the school adopts the second solution, teaching will be quite difficult because the teacher cannot give much attention to individual students if the class is big. It has been mentioned that Chinese pupils in Britain have various problems which need to be solved in a cultural environment in which they feel more comfortable and familiar like that of Chinese supplementary schools. The shortage of teachers leading to the lack of attention given to individual students would probably aggravate the problems of Chinese pupils.

Conclusion

Despite all sorts of problems, Chinese supplementary schools have been trying to make use of their limited resources to provide a place where Chinese children can learn some Chinese to solve their communication problems with their parents. At Chinese school, children can also make friends with peers of the same ethnic origin so as to eliminate some of their emotional problems. Owing to the lack of finance and expertise, Chinese language education within the Chinese community has never been able to run effectively to meet the needs of Chinese children in Britain.

After the adoption of the 1977 EEC Directive, Chinese language education was gradually incorporated into some ILEA schools. There has been an assumption that if Chinese is taught during school hours by qualified teachers in the maintained sector, the quality of Chinese education will be improved (Chann, 1982). The following chapter examines how the short-comings of the Chinese language education provision in the Chinese community is complemented when Chinese is taught in British state schools.

Notes to Chapter 5

1. Source of information: Question 1 in Questionnaire B.
2. The IBE taxonomy refers to such components as administration, finance, organisation and structure, curriculum, and teacher education and supply which are usually used to analyse a school system (Holmes, 1979).
3. The selection of the 13 Chinese schools for the investigation was mainly based on the recommendation of the senior officer at the Chinese Community Relations Section of the Hong Kong Government Office (London). These schools are organised by various groups of people. Among them, two schools are run by churches, one by a clanship association, one by professional people, four by parents' groups, one by a local Chinese association, one by a local Chinese community centre, three by people engaging in various business. These schools were established at different stages. Five of the schools are located in central London. The rest are scattered around the north and south-east of the City of London. Among the 13 schools, only one of them officially uses Mandarin as a medium of instruction.
4. The questionnaire was distributed to 12 schools, only 7 could be collected. The failure to collect the questionnaire from the other 5 Chinese supplementary schools did not lead to a complete loss of data as some of these school headteachers had been interviewed. The main purpose of sending the questionnaire to the headteachers was to test the reliability of the information provided at interviews and obtain statistics which some of the headteachers failed to provide at interviews.

5. Source of information: Question 4 in Questionnaire B.
6. Source of information: Question 5 in Questionnaire B.
7. Source of information: Question 8 in Questionnaire B.
8. Source of information: Question 9 in Questionnaire B.
9. Source of information: Question 10 in Questionnaire B.
10. Source of information: Question 12 in Questionnaire B.
11. Source of information: Questions 6 & 7 in Questionnaire B.
12. The information is based on interviews with Chinese school headteachers, materials provided in the annual journal of the Chinese Chamber of Commerce (UK) (1980) and responses to Question 9 in Questionnaire B. When the research was completed, another Chinese school in London had also acquired its own premises in the late 1980s.
13. One school was using two of the LEAs' school premises and another one was using three. Therefore in total 11 school premises were lent to 8 Chinese schools to run their classes (Hong Kong Government Office (London), 1985).
14. Source of information: Question 21 in Questionnaire B and interviews with Chinese supplementary school headteachers.
15. Source of information: Question 8 in Section 1 of Questionnaire A.
16. Source of information: Question 23 in Questionnaire B.
17. Source of information: Question 16 in Questionnaire B.
18. Source of inforamtion: Question 13 in Questionnaire B.
19. Source of information: Question 15 in Questionnaire B.
20. Source of information: Question 16 in Questionnaire B.
21. The author was only able to visit one of the two Mandarin-medium schools. The information of the use of Mandarin as a medium of instruction in two Chinese supplementary schools was given by some of the Chinese supplementary school headteachers at interviews.
22. Source of information: Question 20 in Questionnaire A.
23. Source of information: Question 22 in Questionnaire A.
24. The Chinese teachers' seminar was organised by three well-established Chinese schools in London on an experimental basis. Therefore basically the participants were mainly teachers from the three Chinese schools. According to the organisers of the seminar, the main purpose of the seminar was to find out the effectiveness of such a small-scale seminar organised by Chinese schools themselves compared with that of the nation-wide seminar organised by the Hong Kong Government Office (London). A report of the seminar in Chinese had been prepared by the author and is available at the Harrow Chinese School, the London Kung Ho Association Chinese School and the Oversease Chinese Education Centre.
25. The information is based on the talk given by one of the guest speakers at a Chinese teachers' seminar held on 25 October 1986 in London.
26. The information is based on interviews with Chinese teachers and pupils in beginners' classes as well as the author's experience in teaching lower primary Chinese classes as a supply teacher.
27. In 1982 and 1983 the author was one of the English oral examiners of the HKCEE. The format of the English oral examination was that candidates were required to read a short English passage and hold an English conversation with two oral examiners. The theme of the conversation could be based on a picture given in the examination or anything related to the daily life of students. In the Chinese oral examination designed by the author in

collaboration with one of her colleagues, students were given a very short Chinese passage on a huge picture card to read. After reading, the pupils were asked a few questions related to the picture given.

28. Source of information: Question 24 in Section 1 of Questionnaire A.
29. Source of information: Question 19 in Section 1 of Questionnaire A.
30. The data were obtained at a Chinese teachers training seminar organised by the Hong Kong Government Office (London) on 6 January 1986 in London.
31. Source of information: Question 25 in Questionnaire B and interviews with headteachers of 13 Chinese supplementary schools.
32. Source of information: Question 24 in Section 1 of Questionnaire A.
33. Source of information: Question 14 in Questionnaire B and interviews with Chinese supplementary school headteachers.
34. Source of information: Question 4 in Questionnaire B.
35. Source of information: Question 32 in Questionnaire B.
36. Source of information: Question 33 in Questionnaire B.
37. Source of information: Question 38 in Questionnaire B.
38. Source of information: Question 32 in Questionnaire B.
39. Source of information: Question 37 in Questionnaire B.

6 Chinese Language Education in British State Schools

Compared with speakers of other community languages in British schools, Chinese (Cantonese)-speaking pupils are relatively few. In the 22 secondary schools and one sixth-form centre in Ealing, Manchester, the ILEA and Walsall visited by the HMI (Her Majesty's Inspectorate) in the spring of 1982, only 41 Cantonese-speaking pupils were found to be the prospective clientele of the state school-based Chinese language class out of a total of 1,294 foreign language speakers (Table 12) (DES, 1984).

Within the ILEA, the four Language Censuses showed that there were only 5 to 6% Chinese-speaking pupils out of an average total of 47,000 language minority speakers. The proportion of Chinese-speaking pupils was far below other language minority pupils such as Bengali, Turkish, Greek and Gujerati (Table 13) (ILEA Research & Statistics, 1979 & 1982; Kysel, 1983 & 1985).

Despite the relatively low number, the distribution of Chinese pupils within the 10 administrative Divisions (see Map 7) of the ILEA is quite scattered. Table 14 shows that except in Divisions 5 (Tower Hamlets)

TABLE 12 *The take-up of minority languages at 22 secondary schools and one sixth-form centre*

Languages	Estimated number of speakers who could have opted	Number opting
Punjabi	950	71
Italian	69	30
Bengali	150	38
Greek	54	12
Cantonese	41	7
Turkish	30	3

Source: DES (1984:14).

TABLE 13 *Percentage of some major language minority pupils in the ILEA*

Language groups	Percentage in Language Census Years			
	1978	1981	1983	1985
Bengali	8.2	12.0	18.1	22.0
Gujerati	6.6	7.5	7.2	6.8
Turkish	10.0	9.8	8.6	7.7
Greek	10.6	8.6	6.8	5.4
Chinese	4.8	5.0	5.6	6.3

Sources: ILEA Research & Statistics (1979), Table 1, page
       number not known.
       ILEA Research & Statistics (1982, Figure 1:10).
       Kysel, F. (1983, Figure 1:7).
       Kysel, F. (1985, Figure 1:7).

TABLE 14 *Number of school-based Chinese classes in ILEA as in July 1985*

	Divisions										Total
	1	2	3	4	5	6	7	8	9	10	
Primary	—	1	—	—	4	—	1	—	2	—	9
Secondary	—	4	1	—	1	1	1	1	2	—	10

Source: ILEA (1986, Table 1:17).

and 2 (Westminster and Camden), schools in the rest of the Divisions either have no school-based Chinese classes, or one only, or a maximum of two Chinese classes (ILEA, 1986). The absence or paucity of Chinese classes within the ILEA individual Divisions implies that there are very few Chinese pupils in those administrative areas. It would be difficult to justify the setting up of Chinese classes in individual schools. The teaching of Chinese in some of the ILEA schools is only a fairly recent effort started in the early 1980s (ILEA, 1986).

Despite the fact that the ILEA has a fair amount of statistics on their language minority pupils (DES, 1984), no information about the specific ILEA schools teaching the Chinese language could be obtained from the Information Office at the County Hall. Through contacts with Chinese pupils at a Chinese supplementary school in London, a few ILEA schools were discovered teaching the Chinese language. Letters had been written to some schools to request observation of their school-based Chinese classes. No replies were received from those schools until the time when the second part of the fieldwork in the USA was due to start. Attempts had been made to contact and interview the ILEA Bilingual Inspector on various occasions about Chinese language teaching in ILEA schools. The response from the Inspector was quite disappointing and uncooperative.

Time was a major constraint of this research. Since there had been difficulties in gaining access to school-based Chinese classes, it was finally decided that the study of Chinese language education in the maintained sector would confine itself to literature, interviews with Chinese pupils and educators in this country, together with the author's teaching experience in two after-school Chinese classes at two ILEA secondary schools for seven months.

Organisation of State School-Based Chinese Classes

Aims

Despite the supportive aim being stated in the Bullock Report (DES, 1975) that schools should 'help to maintain and deepen [the language minority pupils'] knowledge of their mother tongue' (p. 294), the complex linguistic situation in state schools, the traditional preference for learning the 'high status' European languages and the lack of support from the central government has made it difficult to achieve the aim of community languages education.

According to the language censuses conducted by the ILEA in the early 1980s (ILEA Research & Statistics, 1982; Kysel, 1983 & 1985), there were more than 100 languages spoken by pupils within ILEA schools. Among such a large number of languages, 13[1] were spoken by about 80% of the Authority's pupils from various language minority groups (Kysel, 1985). The findings imply that there is a possibility that a large number of languages can be found within individual ILEA schools.

According to an ESL teacher of a secondary school in the ILEA, 48 languages had been identified in that particular school. While the timetable was crowded with all the core courses and various examination subjects, the school would find it very difficult to accommodate all minority languages in the timetable if every linguistic group made a demand for the learning of their mother tongue at school.

Even though the teaching of minority languages can be incorporated into the school curriculum, there are problems in the supply of teachers.

For instance, if the school with 48 languages spoken by their pupils wants to give equal recognition to all the languages, it will mean that 48 language teachers have to be employed. Since there are certain criteria[2] to monitor the application for funds from Section 11 of the Local Government Act 1966 for the employment of additional teachers to meet the special needs of their Commonwealth immigrant school population (DES, 1971a; NCC, 1984; NUT, 1978), it is unlikely that all community language teachers required by one particular school can be supported by the grants of Section 11. Because of the uncertainty of funds for the employment of sufficient and qualified teachers, the aim of mother tongue teaching stated in the Bullock Report may not necessarily be regarded by all schools as a high priority.

Besides the technical and practical problems such as timetabling and staffing, language-minority pupils' choice of preference for second language learning has some implications on the aims of mother tongue teaching at school. According to the report of the HMI's (DES, 1984) visits to 22 secondary schools and one sixth-form centre, it was found that even though 11 minority languages were offered at school, the number of pupils opting for their language was small compared to the number of pupils speaking those languages as mother tongues.

Among the 41 prospective Chinese-speaking consumers of the Chinese language course at school, only 7 had opted for it (Table 12) (*ibid.*). Of the 216 Chinese pupils in the sample of this research, about one-third would opt for French as a second language to study at school even though Chinese was offered[3]. The minority pupils' opting out of mother tongue education in their own school either implies that minority children are quite satisfied with the mother tongue education provision at supplementary schools or they do not see the need of maintaining their own language.

Findings of the ILEA's language censuses have proved that many of the schools within the Authority's administration are composed of many racial groups. There are various problems in the arrangement of mother tongue classes for individual groups at school. Mother tongue education at school can only aim at the development of

> mutual respect and tolerance among different cultural groups rather than of allowing pupils from particular ethnic minorities to study their own culture in a systematic and exclusive way (McLean, 1983:188).

In other words, schools would like to see that mother tongue education will help to achieve social integration of all children at school. While resources are limited, it will be beyond the ability of the school to help to maintain the mother-tongue skills of minority language pupils by organising language classes exclusively for them.

Organisation and structure

Despite the fact that Chinese pupils are increasing in individual schools in the ILEA, their number is not large enough to convince the Local Authority schools to organise Chinese classes from kindergarten and upwards, like the structure adopted by most of the Chinese supplementary schools. On the other hand, the aims of mother tongue education provision in state schools are different from those of Chinese supplementary schools. Consequently the general organisational pattern and structure of Chinese classes within the Chinese community cannot be adopted by state schools.

Owing to the shortage of Chinese teachers, the limited number of Chinese students at each grade level in individual state schools and the congested situation of the timetable in state schools, Chinese language education is only available for pupils at certain grade level(s) only as an option to be taught during school hours. According to the ILEA's (1986) Review of Languages Education, mother tongue education provision at primary school level is more of a supportive service helping children who lack the knowledge of English to understand concepts learnt through English. The teaching of mother tongues to develop oral and literacy skills is available for older children from specific linguistic groups being withdrawn from their classes to learn their mother tongue. At secondary level, community languages are normally available as a fourth year option and a few schools are introducing Chinese in the first or second year. As part of a policy of cultural awareness, one school had attempted to teach Chinese as a community language to both Chinese and non-Chinese speakers from the second to the fifth year.

The ILEA's languages education report further points out that if schools fail to have enough students of their own to make up a viable group, the community language class is likely to be held after school. Unfortunately the report has not stated whether any of the state school-based Chinese classes had been held after school. Findings of this research are that Chinese classes had been organised by two ILEA schools after school hours. The ILEA made no intervention into the organisation of these two after-school Chinese classes.

At primary school level, Chinese language learning is also available during school hours. As the Chinese language skills of individual children vary, pupils are divided into groups according to their level of competence in Chinese. The groups have different times for their Chinese lesson[4].

In the after-school Chinese classes held at the two ILEA secondary schools, pupils were divided into groups according to their level of competence in Chinese. Since the class was held once a week and the duration of the class was one and a half hours to two hours, all groups remained in the classroom throughout the lesson and waited for their turn to have tuition from the teacher[5].

Even though Chinese teachers at state schools use the same criteria commonly used by Chinese supplementary schools to allocate pupils to different groups, it is very unlikely that state schools can have as many groups or classes as those at Chinese supplementary schools to meet individual students' needs. However, by having a homogeneous age group attending the school-based Chinese classes restricted to certain grade levels, teachers find it easier to prepare teaching materials and develop methodology to teach the Chinese language than their counterparts at Chinese supplementary schools who may have a class of students with an age spread of several years. An example drawn from Table 7 shows that among Primary 3 pupils studying at Chinese supplementary schools, their age may range from 12 to 18. Such a big age gap among students studying at the same grade level is unlikely to happen in schools in the maintained sector.

Although the Chinese language has been incorporated into the mainstream school curriculum in some of the ILEA's primary and secondary schools, there is an absence of continual and smooth transfer of students from one level of Chinese class to another within the system. If Chinese is introduced in the lower primary or junior secondary level as an option, the school cannot guarantee that a higher level of Chinese will be available when students are promoted to a higher grade level[6]. The ILEA's (1986) report on languages education states that at present community languages are often available as a fourth year option. It may not mean that pupils will have opportunities to study the Chinese language systematically at school between primary and the third year in secondary school.

If Chinese is abruptly introduced as an option in the upper secondary level, there will be a problem of deciding what level of Chinese should the course be geared to. Should it be elementary, intermediate or advanced? If elementary level Chinese is only introduced until the community language options are available in the fourth year, will Chinese parents be patient enough to wait for such an opportunity? If a higher level of Chinese is taught, does it mean that pupils have to go elsewhere to prepare themselves for Chinese education at their own school? The restrictions on the organisation of Chinese classes in maintained schools implies that Chinese supplementary schools will probably have to play a role to provide Chinese education to help to fill up all the gaps in Chinese language teaching in British state schools.

Curriculum

Medium of instruction

Unlike Chinese supplementary schools where children are exclusively Chinese, pupils attending Chinese classes at state schools may come from various cultural backgrounds. Therefore the medium of instruction varies, depending on the composition of the Chinese class. If the class is exclusively Chinese who speak Cantonese as a home language, the teaching medium will basically be Cantonese and occasionally with some English to help those who are not fluent in Cantonese. However, if the group is made up of pupils who speak various mother tongues and do not have any background of Chinese, English has to be used for giving instructions.

Content

The cultural background of the clientele has some influence on the design of the curriculum content. If students come from a Chinese cultural background and are able to use Chinese to hold a simple conversation or understand Chinese, the content will be designed to maintain and develop the Chinese linguistic skills of children. Since the Chinese language is available in the CSE examination, the examination syllabus has to a certain extent governed the design of the curriculum content of Chinese language education in some secondary schools.

As the relevance of the imported Chinese textbooks has been criticised by many Chinese language teachers, these books are not highly recommended to maintained schools for teaching the Chinese languge. Instead, Chinese teachers appointed by the ILEA are required to spend some of their time on preparing teaching materials from various sources (ILEA, 1986). Therefore the content of Chinese language teaching is not predetermined by any particular overseas published Chinese textbook.

Non-Chinese speaking pupils also have the right to join the state school-based Chinese classes. The development of Chinese spoken skills therefore automatically forms a major component of the content of Chinese education in British state schools.

In one of the after-school Chinese classes, an experiment had been tried out on two fifth-year English-speaking girls without any background of the Chinese language by teaching them phonetic symbols to romanise Cantonese. After about 20 minutes' explanation, the two English-speaking girls were able to distinguish the six basic tones[7] in Cantonese and read some Chinese on their own with the help of the phonetic symbols.

The same phonetic system was taught to two Chinese children who were in the first and second year in a secondary school. One of them had all her education in Britain and the other one had a few years' education in Hong Kong before she came to Britain. Probably because of the age difference, they required a slightly longer time to understand the tones and the use of phonetic symbols.

By observing the progress of pupils in the classroom for seven months, it was noticed that the set of phonetic symbols and tones are very useful to non-/limited Cantonese-speaking children to learn the pronunciation of Cantonese. If the use of phonetic symbols can be widely promoted among Chinese supplementary schools to teach spoken Cantonese, children's problems in oral reading can be eliminated.

Teacher education and supply

While Britain has been exploring ways of incorporating community languages into the curriculum, no initial training of teachers of community languages was available until the mid 1980s. Since overseas teacher training qualifications are generally not recognised in Britain, the majority of teachers of Chinese in Local Authority schools are unqualified. Their title of appointment is instructors only (ILEA, 1986).

Unlike teachers at Chinese supplementary schools who regard teaching as a community service, instructors employed by the ILEA to teach community languages, including Chinese, in Local Authority schools are required to pursue training courses during the term of employment to obtain the professional qualifications recognised in the UK. In order to meet the immediate needs of untrained or inexperienced teachers of community languages, in-service training in the form of workshops are usually organised by the ILEA, teachers' centres and educational institutions throughout the school year. In addition to in-service training, initial training to provide teachers with professional skills in community language teaching has been established at the University of London Institute of Education (Levine, 1987) and Avery Hill College by the mid 1980s (ILEA, 1986). In order to attract more people to join the community language teaching team and encourage instructors to obtain the PGCE (Post-graduate Certificate in Education) qualification, five instructor posts have been reserved for a special scheme of initial employment and subsequent secondment on full pay for the PGCE secondary training (ILEA, 1986).

Even though initial training is available, prospective bilingual teachers do not seem to be very interested in choosing the teaching of Chinese as one of the professional options during the course of training. In 1986/87 the Insitute of Education University of London received no applications for the training of Chinese language teacher. In the following year a few enrolments were received and arrangement had been made to provide tuition for the pupils registered. Finally the only student who seemed to have decided to choose teaching Chinese as his Further Professional Option suddenly shifted to do computer science and dropped out from the teaching of community languages course. As the response to the professional training of teaching Chinese at school level was not very supportive, the supply of qualified teachers to teach Chinese as a community language in Britain remains to be a problem.

Conclusion

Since there is an absence of national legislation which states clearly how mother tongue/culture education should be provided at school, the state school-based Chinese language/culture classes set up by the ILEA or individual schools themselves are only at an experimental stage — Chinese classes are held during and after school hours. They are available at different grade levels in different schools. In some state schools, Chinese classes are open to Chinese and non-Chinese speaking pupils. Individual state schools or the ILEA are exploring the most effective way to incorporate Chinese language into the mainstream school curriculum.

Because of the availability of grants from Section 11 of the Local Government Act 1966, money from the Local Authorities, expertise from the Local Education Authorities and in individual state schools, state school-based Chinese classes are in a better position in terms of administration, finance, curriculum, teacher education and supply than

Chinese supplementary schools. Owing to the multi-cultural/lingual environment and the relatively low proportion of Chinese pupils in individual state schools, many of the state school-based Chinese classes only aim at promoting language/culture awareness and racial harmony at school.

The aim of the state school-based Chinese classes can neither meet the aspirations of Chinese parents nor the needs of Chinese children who have already had some knowledge of Chinese. As a result, the support of the state school-based Chinese classes by Chinese pupils or parents is quite disappointing. According to the HMI's (DES, 1984) report, only 7 out of the 41 prospective Chinese-speaking pupils opted for the Chinese language at state schools. In the two ILEA secondary schools where Chinese classes were available, the enrolment of Chinese pupils from the very beginning was not satisfactory. Later only two Chinese pupils in each class had regular attendance until the classes were finally dissolved. Such a lack of support of the state school-based Chinese classes from Chinese parents and pupils indicates that Chinese language education in the maintained sector has failed to meet the needs of Chinese pupils.

Evidence has indicated that there are problems in organising Chinese classes in British state schools. The assumption that Chinese might be taught more effectively in state schools has to be questioned. In order to look for more effective language education policies to help Chinese pupils to succeed in the national English-medium education system and at the same time maintain their cultural identity, a cross-country reference is made to the language education provision for Chinese pupils in the United States where social conditions are quite similar to those in Britain.

Notes to Chapter 6

1. The 13 popular minority languages at ILEA schools are Bengali, Turkish, Gujerati, Urdu, Chinese, Spanish, Greek, Punjabi, Arabic, Italian, French, Portugese and Yoruba (Kysel, 1985).
2. One of the criteria for eligibility as set by Section 11 of the Local Government Act 1966 is that the LEAs applying for grants from the Home Office to meet the expenditure incurred on the employment of extra staff necessary to cater for the needs of immigrant children have to prove that within their boundaries, 2% or more of the entire school population are children of Commonwealth immigrants (DES, 1971a; GB. Home Office, 1986; NUT, 1978).
3. Source of information: Question 11 in Section 1 of Questionnaire A.
4. The information is based on an interview with a Chinese language teacher teaching at a state primary school.
5. The information is based on the author's teaching experience in the after-school Chinese classes in two secondary schools.

6. The information is based on interviews with a part-time Chinese language teacher teaching at a state primary school and an ESL teacher who was responsible for organising language classes at a secondary school.
7. There are in total 9 tones in Cantonese but 6 of them are commonly used (Lau, 1972).
8. The information was supplied by a member of the working party on the establishment of the Further Professional Option 'Teaching a Community Language' in the PGCE course at the Institute of Education University of London.

Part III:
Education Provision for Chinese Children in the USA

7 Problems of Chinese–American Pupils in San Francisco and New York City

San Francisco is the oldest Chinese community in the USA. Since 1970 New York City has become the largest Chinese community in the country. Therefore the two cities have been selected as the bases of the study of Chinese–American pupils' problems.

Problem Analysis of Chinese–American Pupils

Change in the natural environment

Increase of Chinese children in the USA

Similar to the situation in Britain, changes in the immigration policies of the USA in the 1960s has had some effects on the number of Chinese children in the USA. According to the statistics compiled by the US Department of Justice, Immigration and Naturalization Service 1961–73, about one-quarter to one-third of the Chinese female immigrants in that period were in the 20 to 29 year age group (Sung, 1976). Compared with the Chinese male immigrants in the same age group, the number of female immigrants had almost doubled or tripled that of the males. Since many of the female immigrants came to the USA either to join their husbands or marry Chinese bachelors there, more and more Chinese children had been born in the USA. By making reference to the US Department of Health, Education and Welfare, National Center for Health Statistics (1946–69), there was an average of about 6,000 Chinese born in the USA each year of the 1960s, compared to the annual live births of about 5,000 in the 1950s (Table 15).

Besides natural growth, immigration also contributed to the increase of Chinese children in the USA. With reference to the US Department

TABLE 15 *Live births of the Chinese in the United States, 1950–1968*

Year	Number of live births
1950	5,029
1951	4,870
1952	4,742
1953	4,592
1954	4,396
1955	4,429
1956	4,690
1957	4,666
1958	4,706
1959	5,024
1960	5,846
1961	6,172
1962	5,780
1963	6,048
1964	4,498
1965	5,808
1966	5,668
1967	5,798
1968	6,270

Source: US Department of Health, Education and Welfare, National Center for Health Statistics, 1950–68 (in Sung, 1976:23).

of Justice, Immigration and Naturalization Service (1962–73), of the total Chinese immigrants to the USA in the early 1960s about a quarter were children under 19. After the passage of the Immigration and Nationality Act of 1965, the admission of Chinese dependent children (under 19) soared to between 30 and 36% of the total Chinese immigrants in the late 1960s (Table 16).

In the late 1960s the average annual number of dependent Chinese children immigrants in the USA was about 6,600. In the early 1970s it was about 5,000 (*ibid.*). By adding these averages of the dependent Chinese immigrant children to the annual Chinese live births, the size of the total Chinese dependent children in the USA was at least doubled.

TABLE 16 *Chinese dependent children admitted to the USA 1962–1973*

Year	Number	Percentage	Total immigrants
1962	1,111	23.8	4,669
1963	1,312	24.4	5,370
1964	1,406	24.9	5,648
1965	1,282	26.9	4,769
1966	6,476	36.8	17,608
1967	8,007	31.9	25,096
1968	4,941	30.1	16,434
1969	7,189	34.4	20,893
1970	5,051	28.1	17,956
1971	4,252	24.1	17,622
1972	5,691	26.2	21,730
1973	5,548	25.6	21,656

Source: US Department of Justice, Immigration and Naturalization Service, Annual Reports. Washington, DC, 1962–73, Table 9 (in Sung, 1976:6).

Increase of Chinese children in American schools

Unlike the Chinese in Britain, about 15,000 of the Chinese entering the USA between 1962 and 1965 were refugees from China (Wang, L.C., 1971). In the late 1970s there was an influx of 'boat people' from Vietnam (Brand, 1987; Woo, 1985). Their intention of coming to the USA was to look for refuge and opportunities. They were quite prepared to make permanent settlement in the USA. Besides refugees, there were professionals from Hong Kong, Taiwan and various parts of south-east Asia who wanted to look for opportunities and set up their new homes in the USA (Brand, 1987; Tsang, 1982). Since the United Stated was viewed by the Chinese as a land of opportunities and freedom, various groups of Chinese immigrants, together with Chinese residents who had reunited with their families from abroad, were quite happy to transplant their roots to the USA. Like Chinese in Britain, American-born or immigrant children of Chinese immigrants in the USA had gradually joined the American education system.

As illustrated in Chapter 2, Chinese–Americans are highly urbanised and their concentration in Chinatowns in San Francisco and New York City is much higher than Chinese in London. As a result, there is a relatively high concentration of Chinese pupils in schools in the Chinatown area in both San Francisco and New York City.

The survey of the New York City Board of Education (in Sung, 1979) revealed that School Districts 2 (in Chinatown in the Lower East Side of Manhattan), 24 and 25 (in the Satellite Chinatown of Queens) (see Map 8), which are similar to the situation in ILEA in London, had accommodated the largest number of Oriental pupils[1] in New York City between 1970 and 1976. The enrolment of Oriental pupils in the three School Districts has been increasing since 1970 (Table 17). The proportion of the Chinese population in some of the schools in these school districts is far more significant than in London.

From a study of Chinese pupils in some schools in Chinatowns in New York City, Sung (1979) discovered that in one Chinatown elementary school, the Chinese constituted about three quarters of the school population. In an elementary school in the Satellite Chinatown, 20% of the student enrolment were Oriental. At junior high level[2], one school in Chinatown had a record of 70% of the school population were Orientals. The paired junior high school in Queens showed that its Oriental student population had been increased from 3% in 1971 to 12% in 1976. At high school level[3], one school in Chinatown accommodated about 900 Chinese pupils (23%) out of its total enrolment of 3,800 in 1976, which showed a rise from the 8% in 1965. One Satellite Community high school claimed that their Oriental school population had risen from 3% in 1971 to 10% in 1976.

Although surveys similar to Sung's (1979) are not available in San Francisco, statistics compiled by the San Francisco Unified School District showed that of the 115,457 students in schools within the District in 1969–1970, 14.4% were Chinese (Chin, 1972).

Visits to some schools in San Francisco and New York City in the spring of 1987 discovered that Chinese pupils in two elementary schools (one in each city) ranged from 70 to 95% of the school population. Two junior high schools (one in each city) indicated that about one-third to one half of the total school population were of Chinese origin. An article from a local Chinese newspaper (The World Journal, 1985) in New York City asserted that Chinese pupils of one high school in Chinatown in New York City had been increased to 35%. A paired high school had been visited in San Francisco. No statistics on Chinese pupils of that school were available. Through classroom observation, it was estimated that Chinese pupils in that school might have constituted about one-third to one half of the total school population.

MAP 8 *New York City School Districts*
Source: New York City, Department of City Planning (in Sung, B.L., 1979:45).

Compared with the size of Chinese pupils in British state schools in London, the number of Chinese pupils in individual American public schools in Chinatowns is more significant. In London except a few primary schools which can be comparable with the American counterparts, the number of Chinese pupils in individual British state schools in London is relatively small. Evidence can be referred to Table 13 when the

TABLE 17 *Oriental pupil enrolment in school districts in Chinatowns in New York City, 1970–1976*

District and level	1970	1971	1972	1973	1974	1975	1976
District 2	6,092	6,342	6,600	6,803	6,868	6,669	7,054
Elementary	3,386	3,435	3,435	3,432	3,410	3,330	3,638
JHS/Interm.	1,233	1,249	1,363	1,367	1,357	1,446	1,520
Acad.Hi & Vo.	1,479	1,658	1,802	2,004	2,101	1,893	1,896
District 24	910	1,080	1,303	1,548	1,792	1,953	2,505
Elementary	498	592	677	771	856	889	1,230
JHS/Interm.	197	216	295	373	524	448	616
Acad.Hi & Vo.	215	272	331	404	412	586	659
District 25	1,022	1,147	1,322	1,412	1,680	1,876	2,108
Elementary	736	749	871	917	1,120	1,235	1,501
JHS/Interm.	212	232	237	267	309	354	439
Acad.Hi & Vo.	74	166	214	228	251	287	168

Source: New York City Board of Education, Annual Pupil Ethnic Census, Tables 7 & 8 (in Sung, 1979:47–51).
JHS/Interm.: Junior High School/Intermediate School.
Acad. Hi & Vo.: Academic High School and Vocational School.

proportion of Chinese pupils is compared with other language minority pupils in ILEA schools.

'No-Change' in mental states

Aspirations of Chinese parents in the USA

Despite the fact that Chinese in the USA range from recent immigrants to the sixth generation (Chan and Tsang, 1983) and that their socio-economic background is more diversified than those in Britain, aspirations of Chinese–American parents are quite similar to those of the Chinese in Britain. Many Chinese–American parents believe that education is the gateway to success for their children (Fan, 1981; Wong, B., 1982). Besides pushing their children to study hard (Fan, 1981), Chinese–American parents think that competence in the English language is crucial to academic success and subsequently to future career (Guthrie, 1985).

Chinese–American parents' expectation of their children's success in the mainstream English-medium education had been reflected in the annual parents' conference in New York. In the Ninth Annual City-Wide Chinese Parents Conference organised by the New York City Board of Education on 7 May 1987, the majority of Chinese parents requested the school to provide more English tutoring for their children. They understand that their children would have tremendous difficulties in competing with the majority children at school and later in the job market as English is not the mother tongue of their children.

Despite the fact that 14% of the Chinese–Americans claimed English as their mother tongue (US Department of Commerce, Bureau of the Census, 1971), statistics by the late 1970s indicated that the majority (83%)[5] of the Chinese in the United States live in homes where Chinese is spoken (in Chan and Tsang, 1983). Such a phenomenon implies that the communication barrier between Chinese parents in Britain and their British-born children is also found among Chinese in the United States. Thus some of the Chinese-American parents, especially those who are non-English speaking, are very anxious that their American-born Chinese children should have some knowledge of the Chinese language, customs and traditions so that tension between generations can be eliminated (Fan, 1981). Even though some educated American-born Chinese parents are fluent in English and have no problems in communicating with their children, they hope to expose their children to the cultural heritage which they themselves can no longer impart (Guthrie, 1985; Sung, 1979). Although the professional educated new immigrant Chinese are attracted by the affluence of the American society with high technology, efficiency, freedom, democracy and material comforts, they encourage their children to go to Chinese supplementary schools after school hours because these parents prefer the Chinese mode of some of the family relationships (Wong, B., 1982).

In conclusion, both the non-English speaking and the educated English speaking Chinese–American parents want their children to have some knowledge of the Chinese language and maintain some of the traditional cultural values so that they can live in harmony with their children. In addition to the maintenance of culture, Chinese–American parents are more anxious that their children will succeed in the American English-medium education. These aspirations are quite similar to those of Chinese parents in Britain.

Problems of Chinese–American Pupils

Achievement in mainstream education

Although Chinese bilingual education has been available for Chinese children in American public schools since the year after the passage of the Elementary and Secondary Education Act (ESEA) of 1968 (also known as the Bilingual Education Act of 1968), the curriculum in American public schools is still English orientated. Children coming from families where English is not spoken, like those from Chinese families, will certainly have problems in the American English-medium education if they have not mastered the basic English skills. According to a survey conducted by the San Francisco Unified School District (SFUSD), about 2,800 Chinese students in public schools in San Francisco needed help in English in order to function adequately in school (Wang, L.C., 1971). Failure to provide appropriate support for these children has led to underachievement and dropping out from school among some Chinese children, particularly the Chinese teenage immigrants (Chin, 1972; Sung, 1979).

Maintenance of cultural identity and values

Despite the fact that the proportion of Chinese pupils in some American public schools in Chinatown has reached about 90%, Chinese pupils in the United States are confronted with problems in maintaining the Chinese cultural identity and values once they are transferred from one level of schooling to another or being discharged from the bilingual programme to join the mainstream/regular classes where they will be studying with the majority children who come from different cultural backgrounds.

Cultural values such as success in education and respect for authority, which are normally taught in Chinese families, are less significant in the American context. Since Chinese children are educated in American schools, they would find values of their family incompatible with those of the wider society. In order to be accepted by the majority society, some Chinese children may abandon values which are of second nature to them. The involuntary loss of traditional values not only causes pain and anguish to Chinese children but also to their parents and the wider family (Sung, 1979).

Conclusion

Similar to the situation in Britain, Chinese pupils in American public schools are increasing. Since many of the Chinese parents in the USA believe that success in education will lead to social and economic advancement and that harmony in the family can be achieved through the maintenance of some of the Chinese traditional cultural values, they want their children to do well in the American English-medium education and at the same time be given Chinese education.

Evidence has been given in this chapter that many Chinese–American pupils are not proficient in English. After having been exposed to American culture, some of the Chinese–American pupils have acquired another set of cultural values. Their attitude towards schooling and the elders may not be accepted by their parents. At school Chinese pupils' maintenance of 'Chineseness' or traditional cultural values may be laughed at by their peers. These culturally related problems, together with the limited English proficiency, have affected some Chinese pupils' performance at school. Various educational initiatives therefore have been taken by the Chinese community to solve the problems of Chinese children in the USA.

Notes to Chapter 7

1. 'Oriental' and 'Asian-American' have been used interchangeably by schools and the Board of Education before the new immigrant groups (e.g. Koreans, Vietnamese, Filipinos and East Indians) constitute large numbers to the Asian population. According to the 1970 Census, the proportion of Chinese were roughly five-sixths (70,000) of the total (95,000) Asian population. It implies that Chinese would constitute a considerable number among the Oriental pupil enrolment in schools in New York City (Sung, 1979). Although the figures quoted in Table 17 refer to Oriental pupils only, it gives an idea of the growth of Chinese pupils in certain school districts in New York City.
2. Junior high schools are also known as intermediate schools in New York City or middle schools in San Francisco. They usually provide education from Grades 7 to 9. According to an interview with a school district officer in New York City, some intermediate schools in New York City have incorporated Grade 6 in the school.
4. High school is the last stage of compulsory schooling which starts at Grade 10 and finishes at Grade 12.
5. The statistics were obtained from the US Department of Health, Education and Welfare, National Center For Education Statistics (1979).

8 Education Initiatives of the Chinese in the United States

Despite the fact that Chinese in Britain have put a lot of effort into providing Chinese language education for their children in Britain, there are signs that many Chinese children do not perform satisfactorily in the mainstream education in Britain. It seems that the Chinese community in Britain have to extend their educational initiatives in order to meet the needs of Chinese pupils in Britain.

Unlike the situation in Britain, the educational provision by Chinese–Americans is more extensive. Besides Chinese language education, tutoring classes to help Chinese pupils to cope with English school work have been established in Chinese communities in San Francisco and New York City. These educational initiatives probably will meet the needs of Chinese pupils better.

Chinese Language/Culture Education

Aims

Originally Chinese schools[1] in the United States were established to provide general education for Chinese children who were deprived of public education as a result of the *de jure* segregation in the period of 1860–1947[2] (Chin, 1972; Fan, 1981; Low, 1982). Another mission of Chinese schools was to prepare Chinese–Americans for civil service examinations in China (Fan, 1981). Since the abolition of the discriminative segregation policies in the USA, the roles played by Chinese schools have become more diversified. Like Chinese supplementary schools in London, Chinese schools in the USA consider the teaching of the Chinese language, customs, traditions and history as the major aims of Chinese education (Chinese Central High School[3], 1986; Chinese Confucius Temple of Los Angeles[4], 1984; Jung, 1972; Liu, 1975; Peimei News,

1986; St. Mary's Chinese School, 1986). As many of the Chinese parents in the USA have to work until very late in the evening, another purpose served by Chinese supplementary schools is to provide a learning and social environment for Chinese children to keep them off the streets after school.

Administration

Since Chinese supplementary schools in the United States receive no financial support from either the state or the local government, similar to Chinese supplementary schools in London, Chinese supplementary schools in San Francisco and New York City are independent of the State Boards of Education or the Local School Districts. These schools are managed by various groups of people who set up the school. People who are involved in the management of Chinese supplementary schools can be divided into three major groups: (1) the public interest group, (2) the managerial group and (3) the technical group.

(1)   The public interest group

This group have made financial contributions to the setting up of the school. Unlike the situation in London where district/family associations, churches and parents' groups are major sources of finance of the school, Chinese political parties and the 'Kuomintang' (the Nationalist Party of the Republic of China [Taiwan]) plays quite a significant role in supporting Chinese supplementary schools in the USA (Fan, 1981; Fong, 1971; Jung, 1972; the Southern California Council of Chinese Schools, 1986). An Executive Committee or a Board of Directors is usually formed to represent the interests of the people. If the school is supported by various district or family associations, the number of Directors on the Board can be as many as 60[5] so that interests of contributors or groups can be equally represented. Conflicts among individual associations can be avoided.

The Association of Northern California Chinese Schools and the Southern California Council of Chinese Schools have also formed their own Executive Committee to represent the interests of their member schools. Although the two associations are composed of 26 and 68 member schools respectively, the total members on the Executive Committee are 12 in the Association of Northern California Chinese Schools and 7 in the Southern California Council of Chinese Schools. Without interfering the administration of individual member schools, the major function of the Executive Committee of the schools' council is to look after individual schools' interests and co-ordinate their member schools (The Association of Northern California Chinese Schools, 1985; the Southern California Council of Chinese Schools, 1986).

(2)   The managerial group

The managerial groups of Chinese supplementary schools in the two American cities are relatively small. In schools where the finance of the school relies mostly on the tuition fees, the principal is the 'sole manager' of the school who is assisted by a secretary. The principal's main duty at the Chinese supplementary school is to deal with the day-to-day running of the school and possibly the appointment of teachers if he/she is delegated the power by the Executive Committee or the Board of Directors of the school. If the school is affluent, the managerial group will consist of one or two deputy heads to help to maintain a high academic standard and discipline within the school.

Of the 11 Chinese supplementary schools visited, one school in New York City mentioned that of their 60 teachers, ten were delegated some administrative responsibilities. The involvement of teachers in the school management was less popular among other Chinese supplementary schools[6].

(3)   The technical group

Since Chinese supplementary schools in the two American Chinese communities have a longer history, they have reached a certain degree of division of labour within the school. The technical group, which consists of teachers mainly, are not much involved in policy-making of the school. The main duty of the teachers is to implement policies of the school only.

It has been mentioned that the public interest group of some well-established Chinese supplementary schools is composed of people with various interests. Intra-group conflicts and politics are inevitable. In order to secure a teaching job and avoid trouble, some teachers at Chinese supplementary schools are quite willing to follow rules or implement policies in a rigid manner. For instance, when there are inter-school competitions such as calligraphy, choral-speaking or speech competition in festival time, particularly during the 'tsing ning tsik' (the Youth Festival)[7], teachers will follow exactly instructions given by the school and spend their Chinese lesson to prepare students for competitions. In fact, many teachers worry that they do not have enough time to finish the Chinese education syllabus designed by the school.

In terms of assessment, the New York Chinese School have developed a set of criteria for passing and deferring students in their School Supplement (New York Chinese School, 1983b). Since policies have been stated clearly, teachers have less opportunities to input their own ideas without consulting the school authority in advance.

In London Chinese supplementary schools can have certain expectations of their teachers in terms of their initiatives to organise various activities or competitions to stimulate learning. Some Chinese schools in London have also developed criteria for the assessment of students, but the criteria are for teachers' reference only. Chinese supplementary schools in London try to avoid imposing all policies on their teachers as any pressure from school may lead to negative results such as the resignation of teachers. On the other hand, Chinese supplementary schools in London understand that Chinese language education run by the Chinese community is only regarded as a form of supplementary education. There are quite a lot of constraints on the promotion of Chinese education among the Chinese in Britain. If no flexibility is allowed, it will be difficult for the school to obtain the co-operation and assistance of the technical group to help to achieve the aims of the school. In conclusion, owing to the complexity of the background of Chinese supplementary schools in the USA, the degree of autonomy given to the technical group in carrying out their teaching duties varies from school to school.

Finance

In New York City and San Francisco, the 11 Chinese supplementary schools have their own budget to meet the monthly expenditure such as rents and salaries of the custodian and teachers. Unlike London where Chinese supplementary schools can apply to their Local Education Authority and the Hong Kong Government Office (London) for grants, Chinese supplementary schools in New York City and San Francisco receive no financial support from either the Local School District or from any of the Chinese embassies/representatives. In order to meet the expenditure of the school, most of the Chinese supplementary schools in San Francisco and New York City have to rely on contributions from Chinese associations, especially from the district/family associations and tuition fees. If the school is strongly supported by their own sponsor(s), the school fee can be as little as US$3.50 per month as in one Chinese school in San Francisco Chinatown run by a family association. The majority of Chinese supplementary schools in San Francisco and New York City charge between US$8.00 and US$10.00 per month for the Chinese tuition[8]. None of these Chinese suppelmentary schools provide Chinese education completely free like a few Chinese supplementary schools in London.

Organisation and structure

As in London, access to the use of school premises is a major factor governing the organisation and structure of Chinese classes in San Francisco and New York City. Of the 11 Chinese supplementary schools in New York City and San Francisco, eight schools have their own school premises. Classes of these schools therefore can be held throughout the week. From Monday to Friday, classes are held between 3.00 p.m. and 7.00 p.m. with an average of about two hours per session. If two sessions are arranged during the time interval, junior classes will be held in the first session whereas senior classes will be in the latter[9]. Students registered for the weekday session have to attend Chinese classes daily. Their class will not finish until evening. Such an organisation of classes has met the needs of some working parents as Chinese children attending Chinese classes will be kept off the streets after public school while parents are working until late in the evening (Liu, 1975).

Chinese children who live in suburbs or outside Chinatown would find it inconvenient to attend Chinese classes in Chinatown during the week. In order to meet their needs, some Chinese classes are held throughout Saturdays and Sundays in two sessions by using the Local School District school premises.

Among the old Chinese immigrants in the USA, some of them were intellectuals and students from the upper class of the Chinese society (Wong, B., 1982; Wright, 1979). Their educational background and knowledge of the Chinese language is much better than many other Chinese in the USA except that they do not speak English well. Because of the availability of teachers with a higher level of competence in Chinese, classes of junior high or senior high school levels[10] can be offered at some of the popular Chinese supplementary schools in San Francisco and New York City. Among the 11 Chinese schools in San Francisco and New York City, three schools had classes from kindergarten to junior high school level. Two schools provided senior high school level Chinese classes. The other six schools only had classes from kindergarten to primary six.

Except one school in New York City which required their students to spend two years in each grade level in lower primary classes (Primary 1–3), the other ten schools simply followed exactly the teaching schedule in Taiwan or in Hong Kong where it takes one year to complete each grade level. If students attend Chinese classes daily, the Chinese class structure based on the Taiwan or Hong Kong model would not put much pressure on children in learning the Chinese language in terms of progress. Students living outside Chinatowns attend Chinese classes at the weekend only. If they are required to complete one grade level of Chinese within a year, they will have serious learning problems as their counterparts in Britain. In order to meet the needs of Chinese children in the USA, the progress of learning has to be slowed down. It was noticed that a Chinese school in New York Chinatown had tried to extend the time to complete a certain grade at lower primary level so that students could have ample time to build up a good foundation of Chinese.

Similar to the school calendar of Chinese supplementary schools in London, the academic year of the majority of Chinese supplementary schools in San Francisco and New York City is divided into two semesters: the fall semester (August/September — December/January) and the spring semester (January/February — June/July). There is usually an average of 20 teaching weeks per semester and 40 throughout the year[11].

Although the academic year of Chinese supplementary schools in San Francisco and New York City finishes in June/July, many of these schools, particularly those with their own school premises, organise programmes for Chinese children in the summer holiday. The objective is to make use of the holiday to help children to improve and polish the Chinese language skills of children. In London it is not common for Chinese classes to be held in the summer. Therefore children who have not been performing satisfactorily in Chinese schools in London during the year have less chances to improve their Chinese competence in the holiday under the supervision of their teacher. When a new academic year starts, weaker students who have been promoted to a higher grade level will have tremendous difficulties in following lessons.

Many Chinese women in San Francisco and New York City go to work (Kuo, C.L., 1977). The majority of Chinese parents in Chinatown usually work until very late in the evening (Liu, 1975). When children have long holidays, they will either be left alone at home or wandering about the streets. Besides providing an opportunity for children to improve the Chinese language skills, the organisation of Chinese classes in the summer by Chinese supplementary schools in the two American cities helps to eliminate some of the social problems by providing a healthy environment for Chinese children to get together.

Curriculum

Medium of instruction

As Cantonese is now the lingua franca in Chinatowns in both San Francisco and New York City, the majority of Chinese supplementary schools in the two American cities have adopted Cantonese as the medium of instruction. Owing to the recent influx of professional people from Taiwan into the American Chinese communities (Guthrie, 1985) and some parents' preference for the learning of the official language of both the Nationalist and Communist China (The New York Times, 1971), seven out of the twelve Chinese supplementary schools had some Chinese classes taught in Mandarin. In one of these schools, though Mandarin-medium classes were not available, Mandarin was taught as a subject in Grade 5 (Chinese Central High School, 1986). The availability of some Mandarin-medium classes within a school not only satisfies the aspirations of the minority Mandarin-speaking parents but also provides a solution to the debate on which Chinese dialect should be used as a medium of instruction in Chinese schools (*ibid.*).

Besides Cantonese and Mandarin, some English is used in Chinese classes, particularly in kindergarten and in lower primary classes where there are more American-born Chinese children whose mother tongue has been dominated by English[12]. The younger generation speak English mostly when they talk to one another. In order to facilitate learning and meet the needs of the English-speaking Chinese–American children, some English is used by bilingual Chinese teachers to teach the Chinese language and give classroom instructions.

The use of English to supplement Cantonese or Mandarin is not as common as in Chinese supplementary schools in London. Among the Chinese language teachers in San Francisco and New York City, there were a substantial number of teachers who come from Taiwan or mainland China where English is not widely taught. Therefore, not many of them can speak English well. On the other hand, a few well established Chinese supplementary schools in San Francisco and New York City officially do not encourage the use of English in the classroom. Consequently, the learning progress of some Chinese pupils who are less proficient in Chinese is hindered. In a grade 6 Chinese class, it was found that the teacher had used a lot of examples in Cantonese in order to explain a Chinese phrase '期待 [kei doy] (to expect). Among the whole class of 25 children, about half of them were American-born and all children in the class went to American public schools. If the teacher had used an English word 'expecting' to explain '期待 [kei doy], the class would have run more smoothly. Such an inability or failure to use English by Chinese teachers does not appeal to the American-born Chinese parents. As some of them have experienced the pain in learning the Chinese language solely through the medium of Chinese, they prefer their children to be taught by a bilingual Chinese teacher at Chinese supplementary schools (Fong, 1971).

Content

Compared with Chinese supplementary schools in London, the curriculum content of Chinese education at Chinese supplementary schools in San Francisco and New York City is more diversified. As there is a communication barrier between some Chinese parents and their children, the majority of Chinese–American parents want their children to be exposed to Chinese culture through the learning of the Chinese language. Chinese language education in the two American cities therefore focuses on the development of the four basic linguistic skills: listening, reading, speaking and writing (Cheng, K.T., 1986; Jung, 1972; the Peimei News, 1986).

In order to develop an ethnic pride among Chinese children and help them to understand some of the Chinese cultural values, such subjects as calligraphy, history, geography, social studies and letter-writing are commonly taught in many of the Chinese supplementary schools in the USA (Cheng, K.T., 1986, Chu, 1987; Fan, 1981; Jung, 1972; Liu, 1975). Among the various subjects, Chinese history is emphasised (Tom, 1941; Wong, K.T. [not dated]) as it is believed that history will

> give the children a clear picture of what China stands for and has accomplished, and to arouse their appreciation of the Chinese ancient culture and its recent development. Such knowledge helps the children to see their parents' viewpoint and to respect their own race (Tom, 1941: 560).

In schools where Chinese is taught at a secondary school level standard, Chinese literature written in classical Chinese forms part of the Chinese curriculum. Translation from classical Chinese into Modern Standard Chinese is another skill which is introduced to pupils who have reached secondary level standard of Chinese (Central High School, 1986; Fan, 1981). No English skills are required in this form of translation. Therefore, Chinese education in San Francisco and New York City is purely a training of Chinese linguistic skills and an appreciation of Chinese literature. A child's English proficiency will not directly affect his/her performance in Chinese tests or examinations. In London translation in the GCE or CSE Chinese examination means translating Modern Standard Chinese into English and vice versa. Many Chinese pupils fail in the Chinese examination mainly because of their incompetence in the English language.

In order to make Chinese education more interesting for beginners, as most Chinese schools in London do, singing is taught during school hours to children in kindergarten and lower primary classes.

Besides singing, a Chinese supplementary school in Diamond Heights in San Francisco had made an attempt to make the curriculum content more pragmatic and relevant to Chinese children in the United States. Instead of confining the learning of Chinese to the school environment, pupils of that particular school had been taken out to a Chinatown grocery store where they were taught various types of Chinese food and vegetables. In the classroom, students had been explained the ingredients of tea pastries and the diction to be used to order pastries at a Chinese restaurant. The activity approach to teaching the Chinese language not only makes Chinese classes more interesting but also enables students to see the practical values of learning the Chinese language. As a result, many children enjoyed learning Chinese in that school (Fong, 1971).

The diversified nature of the curriculum content of Chinese education at Chinese supplementary schools in San Francisco and New York City can be considered as one of the major factors which has contributed to the rising status of the Chinese language in the American education system. In the last five or six years, American universities/colleges have already recognised the credits that Chinese children obtained from some Chinese supplementary schools as equivalent to credits in a foreign language which is a pre-requisite for admission to a university (Cheng, K.T., 1986; Fu-Mo, 1986). The New York Chinese School in New York Chinatown is one of these schools where credits obtained by their high school graduates attending Chinese classes daily are recognised by some American colleges (Liu, 1975). In Britain, unless students pass the CSE or GCE Chinese examination, credits obtained from Chinese supplementary schools are not recognised by any British universities.

Teaching materials

Since the Hong Kong Government does not have any representatives in San Francisco and New York City, the Department of the Overseas Affairs of the Republic of China has been the sole supplier of Chinese textbooks to Chinese supplementary schools in the United States (Jung, 1972). Except one school which uses Chinese textbooks published in Hong Kong, the majority of Chinese supplementary schools in New York Chinatown use teaching materials published in Taiwan. Similar to the problem faced by Chinese supplementary schools in London, the Taiwan Chinese textbooks are too Taiwan orientated, difficult and political. By making reference to a fourth grade social studies Chinese textbook, Fan (1981) points out that two-thirds of the texts are over-dosed with the National Chinese politics such as the meaning of the national flag and verses of the national anthem. Because of these weaknesses, one school in New York City and one in San Francisco have produced their own textbooks and supplementary materials for teaching the Chinese language (The Cumberland Presbyterian Chinese School, not dated; the New York Best Chinese School, 1984).

Regardless of the political elements and the remoteness of the social context of the texts, the Chinese language textbook '*Hwa Yu*' seems to have solved Chinese children's problems in learning to read Mandarin. Alongside the Chinese characters within the texts, ideographic phonetic symbols used in Taiwan are given. Since the phonetic symbols must be taught in the first few weeks when children begin to learn Chinese (The New York Best Chinese School, 1984), pupils are able to read Chinese characters on their own with the help of phonetic symbols. However, if Chinese classes are conducted in Cantonese as in most of the Chinese supplementary schools, the Mandarin phonetic symbols alongside the Chinese characters will not help to solve the reading problem. Similar to the learning method adopted by Chinese children in London, many of the Chinese pupils in a grade one Chinese class in New York City used English to phoneticise Chinese characters[13].

Except one school in Oakland, many of the Chinese supplementary schools in the USA do not use local Chinese teaching materials published by the Evaluation, Dissemination and Assessment Center (EDAC)[14] they find the texts too easy. In fact, some schools are ignorant of the availability of locally published Chinese teaching materials.

Examinations

Although there are many state-wide and city-wide tests at different levels of schooling in the American education system, there are no such examinations as the GCE or CSE where children's Chinese competence can be measured by a national yardstick. Internal examinations and tests set by individual schools are used to assess the Chinese proficiency of children learning the Chinese language in the USA.

Extra-curricular activities

Similar to the practice of Chinese supplementary schools in London, Chinese supplementary schools in San Francisco and New York City realise that some of their aims can be achieved through extra-curricular activities. Some Chinese supplementary schools in the two American cities have their own school premises and two of them even have their own gymnasium. With the assistance of such central agencies as the Southern California Council of Chinese Schools, the Association of Northern California Chinese Schools and the Department of the Overseas Affairs of the Republic of China, joint school athletic meets and competitions have been organised in addition to the formal classroom Chinese teaching.

In order to inculcate Chinese customs and traditions in Chinese children in the USA, the celebration of the Chinese New Year is one of the major events of Chinese supplementary schools in the USA (Fan, 1981). Since the Confucian concept of filial piety is a cultural value that Chinese parents expect their children to maintain, many Chinese supplementary schools in the USA put a lot of effort in the celebration of Mother's Day. Parents, especially mothers, are invited to join the celebration.

Besides Mother's Day celebration, such extra-curricular activities as the annual inter-school athletic meet organised by the Association of Northern California Chinese Schools (1985) and the Southern California Council of Chinese Schools (1986) also invite parents to participate so as to improve the relationship between Chinese parents and their children.

Historically the Chinese in America had maintained a very good relationship with the Republic of China. Despite the fact that some pro-communist groups had made their debuts in the Chinese community since the Communist take-over of China in 1949, many early immigrants and old organisations such as the Chinese Six Companies are advocates of the Republic of China. As some of the Chinese supplementary schools are supported by the 'Kuomintang' or pro-Kuomintang district/family associations, they believe that by developing a sense of nationalism among the younger generation, Chinese children will gradually be able to identify themselves with their home-country — the Republic of China. Therefore the celebration of the National Day (10 October) of the Republic of China has become one of the two major extra-curricular activities among Chinese supplementary schools in San Francisco and New York City (Fan, 1981). On the National Day of the Republic of China, there are usually parades by students of Chinese supplementary schools in Chinatown (Chinese Central High School, 1986).

Besides the celebration of the National Day of Taiwan, the celebration of the Youth Festival is regarded by Chinese schools in the USA as an important event which will inculcate nationalism among Chinese young people. In the Festival, a series of activities such as inter-Chinese school competitions in calligraphy, essay-writing, speech, volley-ball, basket-ball are arranged (Chinese Central High School, 1986).

Because of parental pressure on Chinese children to succeed at school (Yao, 1979), conflicts in value standards of Chinese parents and their children (Liu, 1975; Tom, 1941; Yao, 1983), the lack of attention from parents (Liu, 1975) and children's frustration caused by the language barrier at school (Tucker, 1972), many of the Chinese supplementary schools realise that they ought to provide some social activities to fill the loneliness and develop a sense of self-esteem among Chinese children. Activities of a recreational nature have also been organised for pupils after Chinese classes. In the two Chinese schools where a gymnasium is available, Chinese pupils can stay behind at school after class to play volley-ball, basketball or have drum corps practice in the gymnasium. Other Chinese schools might have culturally related activities such as Chinese martial arts, dancing and painting available for their pupils.

Teacher education and supply

According to Fan's (1981) research on the educational background of 59 Chinese teachers at six Chinese schools in San Francisco and one publication of the New York Best Chinese School (1984), the majority of teachers at Chinese supplementary schools in the USA are from Taiwan, China and Hong Kong where they received their college/university education or teacher training. It was claimed by some principals that a few of their teachers had obtained a degree in the Chinese language and had many years of teaching experience in their own country. Like the situation in Britain, the overseas teacher training qualifications obtained by Chinese teachers are not recognised in the USA. These teachers are regarded as untrained teachers.

Besides the lack of teacher training qualifications, many of the teachers at Chinese supplementary schools in the USA have not reached a satisfactory standard of English proficiency (Fan, 1981). These teachers are unable to obtain well paid jobs to meet the high costs of living in the USA. Their main purpose of teaching at Chinese supplementary schools is to earn a living (Fong, 1972). Therefore it is difficult to know whether some of these teachers are willing to look into some of the emotional problems of Chinese pupils in the USA as their counterparts in London do.

In terms of age, teachers in Chinese supplementary schools in the two American cities are much older than those in London. According to Fan (1981), many of the Chinese teachers in six of the Chinese schools in San Francisco where his research was conducted were near or beyond retirement. The results of his questionnaire showed that the average age of the teachers was 54 years. In London, the results of the survey indicated that about half of the sample were between 20 and 25 years.

Owing to the age difference, the traditional viewpoints upheld by old Chinese teachers (Fong, 1972), the older generation's ignorance of the needs of Chinese children in the USA (Fu-Mo, 1986) and the communication barrier between English-speaking Chinese children and Chinese-speaking Chinese teachers, the teacher–pupil relationship at Chinese supplementary schools in the USA is not as good as that in London. In order to stop a naughty student from making trouble in class, a Chinese teacher had to negotiate with the child by agreeing to pass him with a good grade in the examination (Fong, 1972). An old Chinese teacher had been laughed at by a twelve year old student at a Chinese restaurant for his ignorance of English and the low-paid teaching job in the Chinese school (Fan, 1981). These examples of humiliation and disrespect for teachers seldom happen in London.

Based on the two examples and the general background of Chinese teachers, it is less likely that Chinese pupils at Chinese supplementary schools in the two American cities would develop a good relationship with their Chinese teachers to the extent that they could talk about their personal problems with their teachers at Chinese school like some of their London counterparts do. In other words, the aim of providing pastoral care to Chinese pupils through Chinese supplementary schools cannot be easily achieved in the USA.

Although Chinese supplementary schools fail to have well qualified teachers to help them to achieve their aims, the offer of a salary to their teachers has eliminated the problems in the supply of teachers which many Chinese supplementary schools in London have at the beginning of the school year. A principal of a Chinese school in New York City emphasised that their school usually has a long list of applicants for the teaching posts at the school. Since supply is more than the demand, the school is very selective about the appointment of its teachers.

Tutoring Classes of Mainstream English-Medium Curriculum

Aims

Although Chinese parents expect their children to maintain their cultural identity by attending Chinese classes, they ultimately want their children to succeed in the mainstream education so that their children can compete with the English-speaking majority in the labour market. While the curriculum of the maintained schools remains to be English-orientated, one's command of the English language is crucial to his/her performance at school. According to the San Francisco Chinese Community Citizens' Survey and Fact Finding Committee (1969), among the Chinese immigrants arriving in San Francisco in the late 1960s, at least 20% were school-age children who had no previous exposure to the English language. Such a record implies that there is a certain proportion of Chinese children in the USA who will require a lot of training in the English language in order to cope with their studies at school. Although bilingual education programmes are available in some public schools in New York City and San Francisco to help to solve the English language problems of Chinese children, Chinese parents are not too confident that the needs of their children can be fully met in American public schools. Therefore, in addition to Chinese language/culture classes, tutoring classes to help Chinese pupils in their mainstream school work have been set up within the Chinese community by various groups or organisations. The Chinese community hope that the tutoring classes will help Chinese pupils to improve their performance in American public schools.

Administration and finance

Based on the nature of the educational services provided, the organisations or groups running tutoring classes are of two main categories:

(1) private educational establishments and (2) community services organisations.

Private educational establishments to Chinese supplementary schools which offer tutoring service in addition to the Chinese education provision. Since tutoring classes are one of the services rendered by Chinese supplementary schools, they are under the same administration as their own Chinese school. Even though the major concern of tutoring classes is the mainstream school curriculum, tutoring classes do not have any interference from the State Boards of Education or the Local School Districts.

Similar to the finances of Chinese classes, tutoring classes have to rely on tuition fees and contributions from the groups or organisations running the Chinese supplementary school. If the tutoring service is considered as part of the Chinese class, the tuition fees will be included in the Chinese class school fees. If the tutoring class is a separate course, records show that the average tuition charges in 1987 were between US$2.00 and US$3.00 per hour (New York Ming Yuan Chinese School in New York City, 1987; YWCA in San Francisco, 1987). A Chinese newspaper article (The World Journal, 1985) reported that the tutoring classes run by the Chinese American Parents and Teachers Association of Southern California was free except an annual fee of US$5.00 was charged to cover the miscellaneous expenses.

Besides educational institutions, tutoring classes as part of the immigrant or youth programmes or day care service are run by Chinese community services organisations such as the Immigrant Social Service, Inc. (New York), the Chinatown Planning Council (New York) and the Community Educational Services (San Francisco) which are funded by the local government or business corporations (Chinatown Planning Council, 1985; Community Educational Services, not dated). Therefore, some of these tutoring classes only charge fees at a minimal level.

Similar to the administration of Chinese supplementary schools, some of these community services organisations are managed by a Board of Directors who act as a public interest group. Among these Directors, many of them are well-educated professionals. At the managerial level, the staff is usually headed by a Director who usually possesses expertise in his/her job in terms of experience and training. Among the technical group, there are trained and untrained staff who are college students or people from various professions who help to promote the educational service either on a voluntary basis or as paid workers[15] (ibid).

Organisation and structure

If the tutoring classes are administered by Chinese supplementary schools, they are usually held within the Chinese school premises. If classes are run by community services organisations, tutoring classes are held on school premises of the Local School District.

As tutoring classes aim at giving supervision to mainstream school work of Chinese children, the majority of tutoring classes are held after school between 3.00 p.m. and 6.00 p.m.. Each class lasts for about two to three hours. Students usually attend tutoring classes twice a week (The World Journal, 1985; YWCA, 1987). Some classes, especially those which form part of the Chinese class programme, are run daily. When pupils come for the Chinese class where the tutoring of English school work forms part of the programme, they are given about an hour to do their homework from American public school before the Chinese class starts. The duration of the tutoring classes at the Day Care Center of the Chinatown Planning Council is three hours. Pupils can go there every day to seek assistance in their school work (The Chinatown Planning Council, 1985).

Some institutions organise special tutoring classes during the summer holiday as part of the summer programme (New York Ming Yuan Chinese School, 1987; New York Best Chinese School, 1984; YWCA, 1987). The duration of each class ranges from two to four hours and the full programme lasts for about seven to eight weeks. One of these summer tutoring programmes in New York indicated that their tutoring classes were held daily. The other programme in San Francisco only had classes three days a week (New York Ming Yuan Chinese School, 1987; YWCA, 1987).

Based on students' grade level in American public schools or their performance in an admission test set by the organisation running the tutoring class, students are allocated to different classes. Each class is supervised by one or two tutors, depending on the size of the class, the age of the pupils and the availability of staff. The size of each tutoring class varies from an average of about ten to twenty pupils or more.

Curriculum

Medium of instruction

As the objective of the tutoring classes is to help Chinese children to cope with their mainstream school work, tutors are proficient in both

English and Chinese. The medium of instruction used by tutors depends on the nature of the tutoring class and the background of the pupils.

If the tutoring class aims at developing the English basic skills of Chinese children, the class will be conducted in English mainly and supplemented by some Cantonese when needed. If the class only provides general supervision on mainstream school work, individual consultation is emphasised. The choice of the medium of instruction in the tutoring class mainly depends on students' confidence in using a particular language.

Content and teaching materials

The content and the teaching materials of tutoring classes depends on the nature and the objectives of the class. If the tutoring class aims at improving Chinese pupils' achievement in a particular subject such as English and mathematics, the content of tutoring will be subject-based. For instance, there are state-wide English language tests to assess the English ability of pupils at different levels of schooling in the USA. In tutoring classes run by the Community Educational Services (San Francisco), students are very often assessed by mock tests prepared by the Executive Director. The aim of these tests, according to the Executive Director, is to see how close their students' English standard is as compared to the state standard. Results of the mock tests will enable the teaching staff to prepare lessons to meet the needs of their pupils. If the tutoring class only provides general school work supervision, no specific content will be set for any particular purpose. However, if the general school work supervision forms part of the day care programme, the content and the teaching materials will be fixed or prepared by the centre director. At a day care centre in New York City where tutoring classes were held, children there were provided snacks to eat at the canteen before the class started. Then students would spend some time doing their assignments under the supervision of a tutor. Besides doing homework, students were taken to the parks nearby to play for a while. Instead of going out, some classes had lessons on making handicrafts. All materials were supplied by the day care centre[16].

Teacher education and supply

The majority of tutors are college/university students or professionals working in various fields. Most of them are Chinese in origin but can speak fluent English and Chinese. Many of the tutors are relatively young. According to the tutors, the teacher–student relationship in tutoring classes was much better than in Chinese classes. Tutors' deep understanding of their pupils was revealed by the fact that they could easily recommend pupils for research interviews in relation to problems of Chinese children in the USA. Regardless of the lack of training, tutors do not seem to have any difficulties in carrying out their classroom duties as they are given supervision and support by their Director. Since tutors do not see themselves as authorities who would demand unreasonable respect from students like some teachers in Chinese supplementary schools, students are more willing to take initiatives to discuss their problems with the bilingual tutors.

In most of the tutoring classes, tutors are paid on an hourly basis. Many college students therefore can treat tutoring as a part-time job to earn some pocket money. The supply of tutors is not a problem to schools which charge fees for joining their tutoring classes. However, in the case of the Community Educational Services (San Francisco) where the organisation could only afford paying two part-time co-ordinators of their tutoring classes, the recruitment of tutors has to rely on personal contacts and individuals' interest in teaching or community service[17].

Conclusion

In order to meet the needs of Chinese pupils and the aspirations of Chinese parents in the USA, both the Chinese language and English school work tutoring classes are provided by Chinese communities in San Francisco and New York City.

Since the Chinese communities in the two American cities were set up much earlier than those in London, more Chinese associations have been established and give donations to Chinese supplementary schools in San Francisco and New York City. As a result, some of these schools have been able to acquire their own school premises and organise various forms of educational activities to eliminate some of the educational and emotional problems of Chinese pupils while these children are struggling for survival in the American society and acceptance by the two cultures in which they live.

Despite the relevance of some of the education provision within the Chinese communities in San Francisco and New York City, the shortage of trained Chinese bilingual teachers has become an obstacle in achieving the objectives of Chinese education in the USA.

Notes to Chapter 8

1. Many of the Chinese schools established in the late nineteenth century were known as 'kwans' (館). Most of the 'kwans' were homes of teachers where twenty to thirty pupils could be accommodated for the learning of Chinese.
2. According to Chapter 329, Section 8 of the California Statues 1890, Negroes, Mongolians (referring to Chinese) and Indians were not allowed to be admitted into public schools (Fan, 1981). Segregated schools were only outlawed in 1947 (Chin, 1972).
3. The Chinese Central High School is the successor of the Ching School (大清書院) established by the Chinese Imperial Government in 1886 (Chinese Central High School, 1986; Fan, 1981).
4. The original name of the Chinese Confucius Temple of Los Angeles was Chung Wah Chinese School (Chinese Confucius Temple of Los Angeles, 1984).
5. The information was obtained by interviewing a staff member of the New York Chinese School who had served the school for more than twenty years. The Board of Directors of the school is made up of representatives from 60 various Chinese associations (New York Chinese School Graduates Record, 1983a).
6. The information is based on visits and interviews with principals/deputy heads of 11 Chinese supplementary schools (6 in New York City and 5 in San Francisco).
7. The Youth Festival is to commemorate the people who died in the revolution led by Dr. Sun Yat San to overthrow the Manchu government in 1911 (Tang, 1986). In order to develop a national identity among overseas Chinese youth, quite a few Chinese schools, especially the well-established ones in New York City and San Francisco, will organise recreational activities and inter-school competitions as well as drum corps parades in Chinatown during the Festival (Chinese Central High School, 1986).
8. The information of the income and expenditure of Chinese supplementary schools was obtained at interviews with principals and staff of the schools visited. Besides interviews, the record of Chinese supplementary schools in San Francisco at the YWCA at 965 Clay Street, San Francisco has provided some data on the tuition fees charged by six Chinese supplementary schools in San Francisco Chinatown.
9. The information was obtained by interviewing Chinese school principals and by referring to the record of Chinese supplementary schools in San Francisco at the YWCA (San Francisco) and in the New York Chinese School Supplement (New York Chinese School, 1983b).
10. According to a teacher, the majority of Chinese supplementary schools in the USA use Taiwan Chinese language textbooks which are designed for the twelve-year basic education (6 years' primary and 6 years' secondary). As a result, Chinese supplementary schools in San Francisco and New York City have structured their classes by following the Taiwan education system. Schools using the American terminology regard Grades 1 to 6 as primary, grades 7 to 9 as junior high and 10 to 12 as senior high. Others simply use 'primary' and 'secondary' in front of a number to indicate the grade level, i.e. primary 1 to 6 and secondary 1 to 6.
11. The information on the duration of the academic year is based on interviews

with principals of the Chinese supplementary schools visited in New York City and San Francisco, as well as on the publications of individual schools (New York Ming Yuan Chinese School, 1987; New York Best Chinese School, 1975–1984; New York Chinese School, 1983b).

12. The phonomenon is supported by a show of hands in a grade 1 Chinese class. Of the 40 pupils in the class, more than half were born in the USA.

13. The data are based on the observation of a grade 1 Chinese class and an interview with the teacher of the class.

14. The information was supplied by the staff of the Asian Resource Center in Oakland.

15. The information on the finance and the administration of tutoring classes is based on interviews with heads and personnel of the organisations/units involved in the educational service.

16. The information is based on classroom observations of tutoring classes run by a day care centre of the Chinatown Planning Council (New York), the Immigrant Social Service, Inc. (New York) and the Community Educational Services (San Francisco).

17. The information was obtained by interviewing Ms. Dorothy Chen, the Executive Director of the Community Educational Services (San Francisco).

9 Chinese Bilingual-Bicultural Education Programmes in American Public Schools

Bilingual education in the USA was initiated by the state of Ohio where instruction in German and English in some schools in Cincinnati were permitted as early as 1840 (Andersson, 1972; Andersson and Boyer, 1976). The Chinese–English bilingual education only made its debut in American public schools in 1962. After the passage of the national and state legislation in the late 1960s (Tsu, 1978), it was given more recognition by the national and local government.

Evolution of Federal/State Funded Chinese Bilingual-Bicultural Education Programmes

In contrast with the situation in Britain, all bilingual-bicultural education policies within American public schools are grounded on some federal and/or state legislation. Failure to comply with the law to provide appropriate education ensuring equal opportunity to public education by individual schools or school districts is regarded as a legal offence. Although Chinese bilingual-bicultural education programmes in American public schools are relatively new and less popular when compared with the German, French and Spanish bilingual education programmes, they are developed on a similar legal basis which is elaborated as follows.

The National Defense Education Act (NDEA) 1958

When the NDEA was passed, its original concern was to raise standards of such subjects as science and modern languages. The Act had already been ignored in the new epoch of bilingual-bicultural education in the USA. However, it played a siginificant role in the

132

incorporation of Chinese language instruction in public schools in California in the 1960s.

According to the NDEA, Chinese was one of the six critical languages which should be given priority in the foreign language development programme. Subsequently, the first summer foreign language institute for the training of Chinese language teachers was held in California in 1961 under the auspices of NDEA. Besides providing support to initiate teacher training for Chinese language teachers, the NDEA had granted its first and the only Chinese instructional material development project to an institution in California. Because of the support of the NDEA to the Chinese language instruction, five public schools in California were able to offer Chinese language instruction at school in 1961 (Advisory Committee for Chinese Language Instruction in California Public Schools, 1962). In the same year, a Chinese language instruction programme was also pioneered at Seward Park High School in New York City (Tsu, 1977 & 1978).

Title VI of the Civil Rights Act 1964

Although the Civil Rights Act of 1964 is more concerned about rights as a whole, it was the first major federal law to have exerted pressure on Local School Districts receiving federal assistance to ensure equal access of national-origin minority children to public education (Ambert and Melendez, 1985; Teitelbaum and Hiller, 1977). According to the law,

> no person in the United States shall, on the ground of race, color, or national origin, be excluded from participation in, be denied the benefits of, or be subjected to discrimination under any program or activity receiving Federal financial assistance (in Ambert and Melendez, 1985:28).

In accordance with the Act, a memorandum was issued by the Department of Health, Education and Welfare (HEW) on May 25, 1970 to define the HEW's policies in relation to the responsibilities of the School Districts to provide equal education opportunity for children with limited English Proficiency (LEP) from ethnic minority groups. Among the major areas of concern, the memorandum emphasises that schools simply providing identical materials and instructions to all students have not ensured equal education opportunity. There should be specialised instruction or programmes designed by the School Districts for children experiencing English language difficulties (Ambert and Melendez, 1985). Since the memorandum did not specify the content of the specialised programmes, bilingual education failed to gain the support of all schools in the USA. However, Title VI of the Civil Rights Act 1964 has provided a legal ground for the ruling of the Supreme Court case Lau v. Nichols in 1974 which has become a precedent for many court cases regarding bilingual education in the USA.

Equal Education Opportunity Act 1974

The Act is based on the Supreme Court ruling of Lau v. Nichols 1974. In the Lau case, Nichols representing the Board of Education of San Francisco Unified School District was sued by a Chinese parent Lau and a group of about 1,800 non-English speaking Chinese students for the denial of equal educational opportunities as a result of the School District's failure to provide English-language instruction or other adequate instructional procedures (Alexander and Nava, 1978; Ambert and Melendez, 1985; Baker and DeKanter, 1983; Tsu, 1977; Parker, 1978; Tsang, 1982). Based on Title VI of the Civil Rights Act 1964, the Supreme Court was in favour of the plaintiffs and declared that

> . . . there is no equality of treatment merely by providing students with the same facilities, textbooks, teachers, and curriculum; for students who do not understand English are effectively foreclosed from any meaningful education (Ambert and Melendez, 1985:33).

After the court decisions, the 1974 Equal Education Opportunity Act put the Lau v. Nichols ruling into the federal legislation which requires all School Districts to provide service to meet the special needs of LES/NES (limited English-speaking/non-English speaking) students. In other words, School Districts are obliged to take affirmative steps to provide special English service and the employment of teachers with appropriate language facilities to help students to overcome the language barrier in the process of learning (Alexander and Nava, 1976; Ambert and Melendez, 1985; Parker, 1978; Teitelbaum and Hiller, 1977, Wagner, 1981). Not only has the foundation of bilingual education been laid, the educational responsibilities of the School Districts for the non-English speaking pupils has also been clarified by the Equal Education Opportunity Act 1974.

The Bilingual Education Act 1968

The Bilingual Education Act of 1968, being incorporated into the Elementary and Secondary Education Act (ESEA) and becoming Title VII of the ESEA, is the most significant federal law which leads to the flourishing of bilingual education in the United States (Andersson, 1972; Tsu, 1977). Section 702 of the Act states clearly the federal government's support of bilingual education as follows:

> In recognition of the special educational needs of the large numbers of children of limited English-speaking ability in the United States, Congress hereby declares it to be the policy of the United States to provide financial assistance to local educational agencies to develop and carry out new and imaginative elementary and secondary school programs designed to meet these special educational needs (20 U.S.C. 880b) (in Ambert and Melendez, 1985:19–30).

In accordance with the Act, federal funds will be allocated for the planning and development of bilingual education programmes; the training of personnel such as teachers, supervisors, counsellors, aides and support staff involved in bilingual education; and the implementation and maintenance of the programme (Ambert and Melendez, 1985; Tsang, 1982; Wagner, 1981). It was only a year after the passage of the Bilingual Education Act that a pilot Chinese Bilingual Project funded by the Office of Education in the US Department of Health, Education and Welfare, was launched at Commodore Stockton Elementary School in San Francisco (Almquist, 1979; Yu, 1976). At high school level, the first federal funded bilingual education programme for Chinese children was implemented at Seward Park High School in 1975 (Irizarry, 1980; Sung, 1979), a year after the 1974 Amendment was made to the Act.

Owing to the initial success of the two pilot projects, 50 more Chinese bilingual programmes had been developed in the United States by the late 1970s (Tsu, 1977). In addition to the Chinese bilingual-bicultural education programmes at the two pioneering schools, P.S. (Public School) 1, P.S. 2, I.S. (Intermediate School) 131 and I.S. 56 in New York City; the Chinese Education Center, Benjamin Franklin Middle School and Newcomer High School in San Francisco have developed their own Chinese bilingual-bicultural programmes supported by federal and state money[1].

Chinese Bilingual-Bicultural Education Programmes in Public Schools in New York City and San Francisco

New York City and San Francisco not only have the highest concentration of the Chinese population in the USA but also pioneer the Chinese bilingual projects. Therefore public schools within or adjacent to New York and San Francisco Chinatowns where Chinese bilingual-bicultural education programmes are available have been chosen for the study. Chinese bilingual-bicultural education programmes at 3 elementary schools (2 in New York City and 1 in San Francisco), 2 junior high schools (1 in each city) and 2 high schools (1 in each city) had been examined. Classroom observations and interviews with teachers and principals had been conducted. Findings are reported as follows.

Aims and Objectives

It has been mentioned in Chapter 7 that Chinese children in the United States usually have two major problems: (1) the use of a foreign language (English) in learning and (2) the unsatisfactory performance at school as a result of culture shock. The major aim of the Chinese bilingual-bicultural education programmes is to ensure equal eduational opportunities by the effective use of the native language of LES pupils to help them to achieve competence in English. This is to make sure that LES pupils will not fall behind in mathematics and other subjects while they are learning English (Chan and Tsang, 1983; Epstein, 1977; Hernandez-Chavez, 1978; Lum, 1971; Ovando, 1983; Parker, 1978; Ramirez, 1985; Spolsky, 1978). Another aim is, to the extent necessary, to provide an opportunity for LES pupils to learn their native language and demonstrate the school's appreciation of the child's culture. Since the aims of bilingual education programmes are stated in the Bilingual Education Act, schools have to demonstrate that their programmes are designed in such a manner to meet the national objectives.

Although the objectives of bilingual education in Britain can be found in official reports such as the Bullock Report (DES, 1975) and the 1977 Green Paper (DES, 1977), they are not backed up by any national legislation. As a result, individual LEAs and schools providing mother tongue education for Chinese pupils do not have common objectives. Some schools expect that the mother tongue education course will help language-minority children to maintain their mother tongue. Some schools simply want their pupils to be aware of the presence of other cultures and languages at school.

Administration

Similar to the situation in Britain, the administration of bilingual-bicultural education programmes is quite decentralised. Individual School Districts or schools establish their own programmes to meet the needs of Chinese pupils. Although the administration of the bilingual education programmes is decentralised, there is legislation which states clearly how bilingual education should be monitored. Generally speaking, Chinese bilingual education programmes in the USA are administered by three levels of personnel, namely: (1) the public interest group, (2) the managerial group and (3) the technical group.

(1) The public interest group

Public interest is highly recognised in the administration of bilingual-bicultural education in the USA. According to the 1974 Amendment of the Bilingual Education Act, applications for federal funds for the development of bilingual education programmes are required to have consultation with parents of the potential bilingual programme students prior to the submission of the application. In the process of planning, implementation and evaluation of bilingual programmes, applicants are required to form committees composed of parents and secondary school students to participate (Ambert and Melendez, 1985).

In compliance with the legal requirement, a Chinese bilingual-bicultural education programme known as Project CHAMP (The Chinese Achievement and Mastery Program) at Seward Park High School reports that the parents' advisory committee had held four meetings to inform Chinese parents about the planning, components and goals of the project in 1985–1986. Being part of the Project an annual Project CHAMP parents' meeting was included (Office of Educational Assessment [O.E.A.] Bilingual Education Evaluation Unit, 1986).

Besides the academic components of the Chinese bilingual pro-grammes, Chinese parents are informed of all sorts of services available for their children at school through the annual city-wide Chinese parents' conference organised by the New York Chinese Bilingual Educators Committee. In the Ninth Meeting which was held on 17 May 1987, education authorities such as principals and teachers of public schools, officials of the Office of Bilingual Education New York State Education Department and the Bureau of Bilingual Education New York State

Education Department as well as community leaders were invited. Some of these authorities were required to participate in workshops designed for Chinese parents. In one of the workshops, Chinese parents were consulted by the Program Specialist of the Office of Bilingual Education New York City Board of Eduation about the educational services that parents expect to have in public schools. Such a direct consultation with parents by government offficials indicates that a certain degree of public interest has been taken into consideration in designing Chinese bilingual-bicultural education programmes.

In Britain there is no legal requirement of parental involvement in the formulation of school policies in regard to the provision of special educational or support service for language minority children. A secondary school in London which was going to set up an after school Chinese class tried to get Chinese parents informed about the school activities by inviting Chinese parents to meet the Chinese teacher before the class started. Finally only one parent attended the meeting. According to some teachers of that school, Chinese parents are usually not very interested in teacher–parent meetings because of the language barrier. Due to the inadequate interpretation service available at the LEAs and the absence of a city-wide Chinese parents' conference similar to that in New York City, it has been quite difficult for state schools in Britain to get to know Chinese parents' expectations of the education of their children.

(2)   The managerial group

Since Chinese bilingual-bicultural programmes in the USA are funded by federal/state money, the composition of the managerial group is more complex than in British state schools where minority languages education is not directly funded by the national government. Basically the managerial group of Chinese bilingual-bicultural education programmes in the USA consists of two major groups — officials at the state and school levels. The state officials allocate finance to individual schools or School Districts to develop bilingual programmes. In compliance with the Bilingual Education Act, they will keep track on the progress of the federal-funded bilingual programmes by demanding an annual report from the federal-funded recipients (Ambert and Melendez, 1985).

In order to ensure that LEP students are provided with specialised instructions and no discriminatory testing mechanisms are used to evaluate LEP children for placement purposes at school, the Office of Civil Rights (OCR) is authorised to conduct compliance reviews of the School Districts receiving federal funds. A set of guidelines called the Lau Remedies were developed by the Task Force in 1975 to help the OCR to determine whether the School Districts work in accordance with the Lau decision.

At the District level, the bilingual project personnel work closely with the regional Superintendent to ensure that the bilingual project will accommodate the district-wide instructional priorities (Reisner, 1983b). Regional superintendents such as the Chinese Bilingual Coordinator of the Community School District 1, the Director of the Bilingual-Bicultural Programs of the Community School District 2 and the Program Specialist of the Office of Bilingual Education New York City Board of Education are represented by Chinese[2]. Their main duty is to supervise and give assistance to Chinese bilingual-bicultural programmes and ensure that the programmes have met the special needs of LEP/NEP students and comply with the law.

At the school level, the bilingual programme director will be responsible for the administration and the implementation of bilingual education programmes. According to the evaluation report of Project CHAMP (O.E.A. Bilingual Education Evaluation Unit, 1986), the project director's main duties include: supervising staff, reporting and discussing the programme implementation with the school principals, maintaining contact with the assistant principals and chairpersons in charge of various subjects, co-ordinating the programme at each school site and planning staff development and parental involvement activities. She is also required to make regular visits to school sites implementing the same programme (*ibid.*).

Within the ILEA, except the two bilingual inspectors, who were appointed by the ILEA in the early 1980s to give guidance and advice to schools providing mother tongue education and language support service to language minority children (ILEA, 1986), there is an absence of bilingual expertise in individual schools like that in American public schools where bilingual-bicultural education programmes are available.

(3)   The technical group

In order to meet the special educational needs of LEP/NEP children, support service such as counselling and curriculum development is the major concern of the bilingual education programmes. Therefore the technical group being responsible for the implementation of the programme not only consists of bilingual teachers to carry out classroom teaching but also counsellors, aides, and support staff providing various service to help to achieve the programme objectives (Ambert and Melendez, 1985; Parker, 1978). At Seward Park High School, the technical group of the Chinese bilingual-bicultural education programme is made up of a bilingual guidance counsellor, two resource specialists, a curriculum specialist, five paraprofessionals[3] (aides) and one bilingual family assistant (O.E.A. Bilingual Education Unit, 1986). All of them share the responsibilities of teaching, curriculum development, translation, student guidance, etc. (Leung, 1977).

In the ILEA, all support service rendered by the technical group of the Chinese bilingual-bicultural programmes in the USA are duties of a single bilingual community language teacher if there is one at the school (ILEA, 1986).

Organisation and Structure

Except giving warning to School Districts that discriminatory mechanisms should not be utilised in the process of assessment and placement of LEP/NEP children, the Bilingual Education Act leaves the design and the organisation of bilingual education programmes to the School Districts. As the needs and background of students in individual schools are different, there are variations in the organisation and structure of bilingual education programmes. Based on the findings of the study of seven Chinese bilingual-bicultural programmes at various public schools in New York City and San Francisco, the main features of the organisation and structure of some Chinese bilingual-bicultural education programmes are summarised as follows.

Similar to the British education system, all children attending American public schools are allocated to a grade level according to their age. If children's home language is not English, their language proficiency will be assessed by some city-wide tests such as the Language Assessment Battery (LAB) in New York City and the Language Assessment Scale (LAS) in San Francisco (San Francisco School District, n.d.). If a student scores below the 21st percentile in the LAB and 36th percentile in the LAS, he/she will be classified as LEP student who will be entitled to receive bilingual education (*ibid.*). The language proficiency of students is indicated by numbered levels such 1, 2, 3 etc. Classes at each grade level are labelled differently to reflect the language proficiency of the pupils in a particular class. The programme of each class is governed by a specific bilingual educational model.

In an elementary school in New York City, the school uses 1, 2 and 3 to represent the various bilingual education models implemented in each class. If a student is allocated to a class following the bilingual model represented by 1, he is one of those LEP students whose score in the LAB is below the 21st percentile. If a student is in a class adopting the transitional bilingual education model represented by 2, his English standard is better than those in 1. Students in the mixed bilingual classes represented by 3 are quite fluent in the English language. In a junior high school, there are two classes of different standards for various subjects at each grade level to meet the needs of their students.   In a high school, the organisation of bilingual classes is quite similar to that in the junior high school. The main difference is that students in the high school have their own programme to follow. For instance, if a student is allocated to Grade 10 according to his age, he may be attending courses at different standard levels; English at the lowest level and other subjects at a higher level[4]. As the time factor is crucial to the academic achievement of LEP/NEP students, there is no official lunch hour in that particular high school. Classes are held throughout the day. According to the programme director, some pupils arrive at school early in order to obtain additional tuition from their teachers.

An elementary school in San Francisco Chinatown, being designed particularly to serve the LEP/NEP Chinese newcomers, has adopted an all-year round teaching schedule to cope with the problems of the in-take of newcomers throughout the year. As explained by the principal of the school, not all classes start and finish at the same time in the academic year. Classes starting late will extend their academic year over the summer. The rationale of such a policy is to help the LEP/NEP newcomers to acquire basic English skills within one year so that students can be transferred to regular public schools as soon as possible. If the summer holiday is utilised for teaching newcomers who join the school late, these pupils probably would have a chance to be transferred to regular schools when the normal academic year begins.

Chinese teachers with credentials in bilingual education are limited. In order to cope with the problem of the supply of qualified bilingual Chinese teachers, a joint-class system has been adopted by some American elementary schools where Chinese bilingual-bicultural programmes are available. P.S. 2 in New York City is one of the examples using the joint-class system (Von Maltitz, 1975). Similar practice is also found at the Chinese Education Center in San Francisco Chinatown.

If the joint-class system is adopted, pupils of two consecutive grade levels will be accommodated together in one classroom. Grade 1 will combine with 2, 3 with 4, and 5 with 6. In the classroom, a paraprofessional will help one group of pupils while the bilingual teacher is teaching another group of students of a different grade. Some paraprofessionals are required to come in to the school to give assistance on certain days only. If the paraprofessional is not available, students of a certain grade will be assigned written work to do while students of another grade are having tuition from the teacher.

In classes where students are fairly homogeneous in terms of grade-level, paraprofessionals will be required to give support service to newcomers or students whose language ability is weaker when compared with others in the same class. Since paraprofessionals are bilingual, they play quite an important role in helping LEP/NEP children to eliminate some of their frustrations in a new learning environment where all classroom instructions are given in a foreign language.

In London Chinese-speaking children may obtain support service on a one-to-one basis from ESL teachers. If such support service cannot be arranged, they can seek help from teachers who provide assistance for all non-English speaking pupils in the classroom. Unless the ESL or the language support teacher can speak Chinese, all kinds of assistance in the classroom is normally given in English. Teenage immigrant children who are severely handicapped by the English language when they first join the British education system, like those mentioned in the case studies in Chapter 4, will not benefit from support given in English.

Finance

Since bilingual-bicultural education for LEP/NEP children in the USA is supported by both federal and state legislation, federal and state money have become the major sources of finance of the bilingual-bicultural education programmes.

According to O'Malley (1982), Parker (1978) and Alexander and Nava (1976), the major sources of federal support for bilingual instruction come from the following legislation:

(i)   ESEA Title VII (Bilingual Education)
(ii) ESEA Title I (Compensatory Education)
(iii) The Emergency School Aid Act (ESAA) Title VII.

In addition to federal money, state support is crucial to the implementation of bilingual education. However, the support varies widely from state to state, depending on the numbers of LES/NES school pupils (Parker, 1978). In California where a Chinese bilingual programme was piloted, the finance of the bilingual education programmes came from the following sources:

   (i) the Bilingual Education Act of 1972 (California StateLaw) Chapter 1258, Statutes of 1972 (AB 2284),
  (ii) the Educationally Disadvantaged Youth Program (EDY), Chapter 1406, Statues of 1970 (SB 90),
 (iii) the Early Childhood Education Act, Chapter 1147, Statues of 1972 (SB 1302) (Alexander and Nava, 1976) and
 (iv) the Economic Impact Aid/Limited English Proficient (EIA/LEP) funds (SFUSD, n.d.).

About 50 Chinese bilingual programmes in the USA in the late 1970s were financed in a similar manner (Tsu, 1977). The money obtained from various sources is mainly used for the employment of bilingual teachers, the development of curriculum, the training of staff, the establishment of resource centres and the organisation of activities to obtain community involvement (Alexander and Nava, 1976; Ambert and Melendez, 1985; Parker, 1978; Von Maltitz, 1975).

Curriculum

Although various models have been designed by American public schools to implement bilingual education, schools have to follow the curriculum of the bilingual education programmes defined by the Bilingual Education Act 1978 which says that

> there is instruction given in, and study of English and, to the extent necessary to allow a child to achieve competence in the English language, the native language of the children of limited English proficiency, and such instruction is given with appreciation for cultural heritage of such children, and of other children in American society . . . (Public Law 95–561, 1978:3)

In order to comply with the law, the curriculum content of Chinese bilingual education in American public schools consists of two basic components: (1) the English language acquisition and (2) the native language instruction.

(1) The English language acquisition

The Bilingual Education Act of 1978 states clearly that the objective of the bilingual-bicultural programmes is to

> assist children of limited English proficiency to improve their English language skills, and the participation of other children in the program must be for the principal purpose of contributing to the achievement of that objective (*ibid.*).

The teaching of the English language therefore predominates in the bilingual-bicultural education programmes. The major feature which distinguishes the English language instruction in the bilingual education in the USA from that in Britain is the ability of ESL teachers to use two languages — the target language (English) and children's home language (Chinese).

For the purpose of placement, all non-English speaking children in San Francisco and New York City have to undergo some form of assessment of their English proficiency. ESL classes are therefore structured in various standard levels, as revealed by Project CHAMP in New York (O.E.A. Bilingual Education Unit, 1986) and the Bilingual-Bicultural Teacher Aides of the California State Department of Education (1984), to meet the needs of individual students.

In Seward Park High School and a middle school in New York where students' score in the language assessment is minimal, some of the ESL teachers are trilingual Chinese who know English, Cantonese and Mandarin. When there are signs of doubts or queries raised by students, Chinese explanation can be given simultaneously by the ESL teacher. According to the ESL teacher, the use of some Chinese for explanation purposes in class has facilitated learning. As the language barrier has been overcome by the use of two languages in the classroom, Chinese pupils have been encouraged to have their English problems solved in class instead of taking their problems home to seek assistance elsewhere. Teaching has become more efficient as teachers no longer waste time on repeating the English explanation which can be easily understood by pupils when Chinese is used.

At elementary level, instead of allocating students to specific ESL classes of different grade levels, students are assigned to self-contained classrooms under the supervision of a single-classroom teacher who is responsible for almost all instruction. Although most of the self-contained classroom teachers are bilingual, not many of them are trained ESL teachers. Therefore the English language development is carried out by team teaching. Before the class have their English lesson with the qualified English-speaking ESL teacher, the bilingual teacher will give some preliminary instruction in areas related to grammar. After having such a preparation, students will find it easier to follow instructions given by the non-Chinese speaking ESL teacher.   Although the Bilingual Education Implementation Manual of the SFUSD (not dated) emphasises that English should be used as the language of instruction at all times to develop the basic skills of English, the use of some Chinese is inevitable for the purpose of meeting the needs of newcomers.

(2)   The native language component

The native language component refers to two instructional formats: (a) the native language content instruction and (b) the native language arts instruction (SFUSD, n.d.).

(a)   The native language content instruction

The native language content instruction is similar to the transitional bilingual education instruction model defined by Fishman and Lovas (1970). In such a model, classroom instructions are given in the native language (Chinese) of LEP students so as to help them to learn basic skills at elementary level and non-elective coursework (e.g. mathematics, social studies, sciences) at secondary level while students are learning English (SFUSA, n.d.). The extent to which Chinese is used depends on the availability of bilingual teachers, paraprofessionals, Chinese teaching materials and the language competence of pupils. At elementary level, the use of the native language in the classroom is more uniform as instructions are given by one single bilingual teacher in a self-contained classroom. The teacher can switch to any language he/she thinks appropriate and relevant to the situation.

At secondary level, the native language instruction in Chinese bilingual education programmes varies from school to school. Based on classroom observations and interviews with teachers and school administrators at two high schools and two middle schools, three approaches in the native language content instruction can be identified:

(i) Bilingual instruction is given by one single teacher.
(ii) The bilingual teacher is assisted by a bilingual paraprofessional who will pull out NES/LES newcomers or students whose English

proficiency is not good enough to study with the majority students in the class. More Chinese will be used by the paraprofessional in giving instructions to these students.

(iii) The English-speaking subject teacher is assisted by a bilingual paraprofessional. As observed in a science lesson at a high school, the two major roles played by the paraprofessional are translation and interpretation. After a concept is explained by the subject teacher in English, the paraprofessional will interpret it into Cantonese. When notes are given on the blackboard, they will be translated into written Chinese. In other words, all written and oral classroom instructions will be immediately translated into Chinese with the help of the paraprofessional.

(b)   The native language arts instruction

The content of native language arts instruction in Chinese bilingual education programmes in American public schools is quite similar to mother tongue maintenance/community languages education in British schools. Since the Bilingual Education Act of 1978 requires all bilingual education programmes to demonstrate an appreciation of the cultural heritage of the non-English speaking children, native language arts instruction is provided during school hours. In an elementary school in New York City, teachers are officially required to spend 45 minutes a day on teaching the Chinese language. In practice, most of the teachers will ignore the native language arts instruction if their students are NEP/LEP. Instead of giving native language arts instruction, teachers will use the lesson to teach the English language hoping that their students will join regular classes as soon as possible.

Despite the fact that the Chinese language has been included in the Chinese bilingual education programmes in some American public schools, there are different approaches to teach the language. Two models of teaching the Chinese language have been adopted by some public schools in New York City: (1) teaching Chinese as a first language model and (2) the two-way bilingual education programme model.

(1)   Teaching Chinese as a first language model

The model has been adopted by Seward Park High School in New York City where six levels of Chinese are offered. Besides the development of reading and writing skills, literature and culture appreciation is taught (O.E.A. Bilingual Education Evaluation Unit, 1986).

In a level 6 Chinese class, classical Chinese was taught in Mandarin by a teacher from Taiwan. Compared with the standard of Chinese taught at schools in Hong Kong, level 6 Chinese at Seward Park High School is somehow equivalent to senior secondary level Chinese in Hong Kong. A show of hands in class indicated that the whole class of 34 pupils were immigrants from either China or Hong Kong where they had received some Chinese language education before they came to the USA. As Mandarin is used in schools in China, the majority of the students who were from China had no problems in following Mandarin instructions. Cantonese-speaking students from Hong Kong did not have much problem as they were allowed to communicate with their Chinese teacher in Cantonese. On the other hand, their Mandarin problem can be eliminated as the texts are printed in the traditional Chinese script which is the form of written Chinese used in Hong Kong. Therefore, using Mandarin as the teaching medium in level 6 Chinese has not hindered Chinese pupils from maintaining and developing their first language skills.

(2) The two-way bilingual education programme model

As defined by Tsu (1977), the two-way bilingual education programme model involves two groups of pupils who learn in their own and other's language. Such a language teaching model had been adopted by P.S. 2 in New York where three groups of pupils were involved — Chinese, Puerto Ricans and Anglos (Von Maltitz, 1975). P.S. 1 in New York City also follows the same model to teach Chinese. Their target students are the English proficient Chinese immigrants or American-born Chinese children. A few pupils are of non-Chinese background. As the clientele of the two-way bilingual education programme model are much younger and they join the American system almost at the beginning of their school age, the purposes served by the two-way bilingual programme model, as defined by Tsu (1977) are:

(i) re-learning of Chinese by Chinese children who come to the USA between the age of 5 and 8;

(ii) developing a sense of Chinese identity among the American-born Chinese children; and

(iii) enriching non-Chinese speaking children's linguistic competence by learning the majority school mates' language in addition to their mother tongue.

Besides these purposes, another objective of the two-way bilingual education model is to broaden 'the understanding of children about languages and cultural heritages other than their own' (Public Law 95–561:3). Since pupils joining the two-way bilingual education programme have no or very little knowledge of Chinese, the Chinese language is taught as a foreign language with an emphasis on the development of spoken skills. Both English and Cantonese are used interchangeably in order to meet the needs of pupils.

Teaching Materials

Some funds for the implementation of the Bilingual Education Act have been allocated for the establishment of regional resource centres to develop teaching materials in various languages for the bilingual-bicultural programmes (Ambert and Melendez, 1985; Parker, 1978). Centres such as the Asian American Bilingual Center of the Berkeley Unified School District in Berkeley, the Asian Bilingual Curriculum Development Center at Seton Hall University in New Jersey, the Asian Language Programs (KEYS [Knowledge of English Yields Success] Project) of the Los Angeles City Unified School District (National Education Association of the United States, 1984) have developed various English–Chinese bilingual resources[5]. In addition to the effort made by these centres to develop Chinese materials, the ESEA Title VII Chinese bilingual pilot programmes in San Francisco Unified School District and CHAMP at Seward Park High School have taken initiatives to develop various teaching materials with the help of their curriculum development staff of the bilingual education team (O.E.A. Bilingual Education Evaluation Unit, 1986; Chinese Bilingual Pilot Program, ESEA Title VII, SFUSD, n.d.)

Although Chinese teaching materials have been developed with the support of federal and/or state funds, resources available for the Chinese bilingual education programmes are inadequate. Compared with the resources in other languages such as Spanish and French, Chinese materials are relatively few (Parker, 1978). When compared with the Chinese teaching materials in Britain, Chinese curricular and cultural materials developed and published in the USA are far more plentiful.

Teacher Education and Supply

While bilingual education has been expanding after the passage of the Bilingual Education Act, the supply of qualified bilingual personnel is inadequate to meet the demand. Therefore federal funds have been granted for

provic providing preservice training designed to prepare persons to participate in bilingual education programs as teachers, teacher-aides, or other ancillary education personnel such as counselors, and in-service training development programs designed to enable such persons to continue to improve their qualifications while participating in such programs (P.L 90–247, Jan 2, 1968, Sec.7.4 (b)) (in Ambert and Melendez, 1985:271).

After the Bilingual Education Act was amended in 1974, bilingual teacher training continues to be supported by federal funds. The Amendment stipulates that 15% of each bilingual education grant should be used for bilingual staff development. Because of the availability of federal money, universities have been able to set up undergraduate and graduate bilingual teacher training programmes (Ambert and Melendez, 1985; Parker, 1978). Besides setting up training programmes to train bilingual teachers and personnel, 500 fellowships were allocated in 1975/76 by the Office of Education to train teacher trainers. 30 out of the 500 fellowships were specifically for Chinese and Japanese (Tsu, 1977).

Besides universities, in-service training of bilingual teachers have been organised by individual schools and School Districts. The training is usually in the form of workshops or seminars which aim at getting bilingual personnel more familiar with the Chinese language (Cantonese and Mandarin), Chinese culture and heritage, etc. (O.E.A. Bilingual Education Unit, 1986; SFUSD, n.d.).

Because of the availability of bilingual-teacher training programmes, 29 states had laid down special certification requirements of teachers in bilingual programmes by 1982. In addition to the 'standard' or 'regular' certification requirements set up by the state, individual states require 'bilingual endorsement' which varies from state to state. In some states, bilingual endorsement means the requirement of evidence of teacher's capacity in English and the target language. Other states require training in the culture of students and knowledge of the bilingual-instructional methods.Such states as New York and New Jersey require 24 semester hours of work in bilingual education. In a master's programme, approximately half of the total semester hours (30–36 semester hours) have to be in bilingual education (Ambert and Melendez, 1985; Reisner, 1983a).

Besides the requirements for certification set by individual states, the Center for Applied Linguistics (CAL) in 1974 developed a set of guidelines[6] which define the eight skills of bilingual teachers for the preparation and. the certification of teachers in bilingual .education programmes. These guidelines are referred to by some other states during the process of certification of bilingual teachers. The eight skills listed in the Guidelines are:

(i) Proficiency in English and in the home language of children participating in the bilingual program.

(ii) Knowledge of the basic concepts of linguistics, including the nature of bilingualism.

(iii) Ability to promote awareness and understanding of students' cultural backgrounds and the cultural backgrounds of others.

(iv) Ability to use appropriate instructional methods to assist students in achieving their full academic potential in the home language and culture and in English.

(v) Ability to use, adapt, develop, and evaluate instructional materials.

(vi) Ability to conduct comprehensive assessments of students' achievement and growth.

(vii) Knowledge of techniques for promoting parent and community involvement.

(viii) Practical teaching experience in a bilingual-bicultural classroom (Reisner, 1983a:177).

In Britain no national criteria have been set up for the certification of bilingual teachers. Theoretically bilingual teachers or community languages teachers are expected to obtain the PGCE qualification in order to be qualified to teach in maintained schools in Britain. While a few higher education institutions such as the Institute of Education University of London were trying to incorporate relevant courses into the PGCE training programme to meet the needs of prospective bilingual teachers, the development of bilingual personnel depended a lot on the in-service training programmes organised by the LEAs. The ILEA was one of the LEAs which had organised workshops to provide relevant skills for untrained and inexperienced bilingual teachers (ILEA, 1986).

Conclusion

The illustration shows that owing to the support of national legislation, funds are available for the training and hiring of bilingual staff, curriculum development and the implementation of bilingual education for Chinese children in San Francisco and New York City. On the other hand, the Bilingual Education Act states clearly that bilingual education should aim at ensuring equal education opportunities for all children. Even though there are variations in practice, schools and teachers are aware of their responsibility of helping LEP/NEP students to have access to the content of education. By the establishment of Chinese bilingual-bicultural education programmes, frustrations of Chinese pupils as a result of their inability to use the English language will be reduced.

Since the emphasis of bilingual-bicultural education is on the development of English language skills of LEP/NEP students, the teaching of the Chinese language has not been given sufficient attention. In an elementary school where Chinese language learning is available, teachers adopt the enrichment approach to teach Chinese to pupils who are proficient in English. LEP/NEP Chinese pupils are not eligible for joining the Chinese class. Even though English-proficient Chinese pupils are given a chance to 're-learn' their mother tongue, there is no guarantee that they will be given an opportunity to further develop their Chinese skills as the Chinese language course may not be available at higher levels. If it is available, like the one at Seward Park High School, the approach in teaching the Chinese language may not be relevant to the needs of English proficient Chinese pupils who learn Chinese as a forign language. Another problem is the absence of syllabus to govern the continual development of the Chinese language skills of Chinese pupils throughout the whole system.

Notes to Chapter 9

1. The data are based on visits to public schools in Chinese communities in San Francisco and New York City in 1987.
2. The information is based on the observation at the Ninth Annual City-wide Chinese Parents Conference held in New York in 1987.
3. Paraprofessionals, also known as teacher-aides, are teachers who do not have the credentials for the certification of bilingual teachers as required by the state.
4. In 1985/86 there were four levels of English as a Second Language (1 means the lowest level) and six levels of Chinese offered in the Chinese bilingual-bicultural education programme at Seward Park High School (O.E.A. Bilingual Education Evaluation Unit, 1986). In the first year when the bilingual education project was in operation, there were two levels in other subjects such as mathematics, general science, biology and world history (Seward Park High School Bilingual-bicultural Program — Chinese, n.d.).
5. By visiting the New York State Bilingual Multifunctional Support Center at Hunter College of CUNY in New York, the Library of New York City Board of Education Office of Bilingual Education, the Evaluation, Dissemination and Assessment Center at the California State University in Los Angeles, the Asia Resource Center Associates, Inc. in Oakland, California and the Asian Language Programs of the Los Angeles City Unified School District to the Chinese materials developed, it was found that the materials developed include

Chinese language arts for both elementary and high school level, mathematics, economics, social studies and readers focusing on the cultural aspects of Chinese. The majority of these materials are written in both English and Chinese. In some of the materials developed by the Asian Language Programs, romanisation in both Cantonese and Mandarin is provided in the texts.

6. The Guidelines were developed by a panel of 13 bilingual educators and linguists who listed the eight skills which should be given attention to in the training and certification of bilingual teachers (Reisner, 1983a).

10 Recommendations and Conclusions

The inability of Chinese parents to speak English in Britain and their insistence on maintaining their cultural identity has led to the development of Chinese supplementary schools alongside the state education system in Britain. After the adoption of the 1977 EEC Directive, besides the provision of ESL learning, some British state schools either have incorporated Chinese language education into the mainstream curriculum or provide Chinese language instruction as an after school activity. Despite the provision of mother tongue education and language support service, such problems as educational disadvantage, racism at school, language loss and cultural conflict confronting some Chinese pupils in Britain remain unsolved.

Similar educational and psychological problems of Chinese children in New York City and San Francisco have been illustrated in Chapter 7. The provision of bilingual-bicultural education in a more diversified manner in the voluntary and maintained sectors in the two American cities have eliminated some of these problems.

By examining the specific initial conditions in Britain and outcomes of the bilingual-bicultural education policies in New York City and San Francisco, recommendations are made to incorporate some of the American bilingual-bicultural education practices in the London system so as to solve problems of Chinese pupils in London.

Improvement of Educational Provision within the British-Chinese Community

The setting up of Chinese supplementary schools to provide Chinese language education can be seen as an achievement of the Chinese community in Britain in helping to solve some of Chinese children's problems. In order to achieve efficiency and effectiveness of the present educational provision and meet the needs of Chinese children, some of the educational activities within the Chinese \community have to be improved and expanded by making reference to the achievements of the Chinese–Americans in San Francisco and New York City.

Chinese Education in Chinese Supplementary Schools

Administration

(1)   The public interest group
At the public interest level, Chinese supplementary schools in both Britain and the USA have their own Executive Committee or Board of Directors which consists mainly of people who contribute money for the establishment of the school. What is lacking in Britain is a Chinese schools' council which can act as a central agency to co-ordinate or represent interests of all Chinese supplementary schools within a geographical area.

At present the Hong Kong Government Office (London) co-ordinates all Chinese supplementary schools in Britain only in terms of providing textbooks, financial assistance and organising teachers' seminars. Officials of the Office indicated that they have no obligation to provide any forms of assistance for Chinese supplementary schools in Britain as those who benefit from their support are no longer citizens of Hong Kong. They claimed that the welfare and education rights of the Chinese in Britain ought to be looked after by the British government. By 1997 when the sovereignty of Hong Kong is returned to China, it cannot be guaranteed that there will be a representative from Hong Kong to base in London to play a similar supporting role as the Hong Kong Government Office (London) has been doing.

In fact some Chinese supplementary schools in London have realised the difficulties of the Hong Kong Government Office (London) in providing assistance for them. Some initiatives had been taken by some Chinese schools to organise teachers' seminars amongst themselves. If the enthusiastic Chinese supplementary schools try to form a steering group to expand their activities and lobby their Local Education Authority and Council, it would make it possible for Chinese supplementary schools in London to form their own Chinese schools' council or a central body to help to represent interests of Chinese supplementary schools or centralise the limited resources for the achievement of the aims of overseas Chinese education.

(2) The managerial group

The day-to-day running of Chinese supplementary schools in both countries is left to the managerial group headed by the principal/headteacher of the school. The main difference is that in some Chinese supplementary schools in San Francisco and New York City, some members of the managerial group such as the principal and the deputy heads are appointed on a full-time basis. These Chinese supplementary schools are better organised in terms of the communication between different levels of administration, the organisation of student activities and the development of curriculum for the school.

In Britain the majority of Chinese classes are held once a week and each class only lasts for two to three hours. It would be difficult to justify the appointment of full-time managerial staff to work at Chinese supplementary schools.

As the demand for Chinese language education is growing in Britain, classes have been increased within individual Chinese supplementary schools. Consequently the administration of Chinese supplementary schools has become more complicated. In order to improve the management of Chinese supplementary schools in Britain by fully utilising the staff available, the appointment of two senior teaching staff as deputy heads of the school, which had been tried out by a Chinese school in London, seems to be a possible alternative. In cases where the school cannot be notified in advance about teachers' absence, the deputy heads can act as supply teachers so that the headteacher can concentrate on the administration of the the whole school while classes are in progress. If no substitute teaching is required, the deputy heads can assist the headteacher to plan the organisation of the whole school.

(3) The technical group

Owing to the lack of finance for appointing full-time headteachers and the shortage of staff in the managerial group, more teachers are involved in the administration of Chinese schools in Britain than those in San Francisco and New York City. The involvement of teachers in the administration of Chinese supplementary schools in Britain ought to be encouraged as many of the enthusiastic and experienced teachers will contribute innovative ideas to the improvement of teaching and the organisation of Chinese schools.

Because of the voluntary nature of the teaching service, teachers in London Chinese supplementary schools have a higher degree of autonomy in teaching. From the professional point of view, such an autonomy ought to be delegated so that teachers can make teaching flexible to meet the needs of individual students. However, if the autonomy is not properly administered, it will be difficult for schools to plan their administrative policies such as the criteria for the promotion of students from one grade level to another.

Since some teachers are members of the managerial group, technical problems in the implementation of school policies and in teaching can be channelled to the school authority more directly. By taking into consideration the opinions of teachers, a more feasible administrative system can be established.

Finance

Chinese supplementary schools in London have more financial support from various government agencies such as the Local Councils, the LEAs and the Hong Kong Government Office (London) than their American counterparts. However, these financial resources are quite unreliable as it has been anticipated that the Hong Kong Government Office (London) will be dissolved and grants from the ILEA will be discontinued once the ILEA is abolished[1]. In order to ensure that Chinese language education will not be disrupted if financial support can no longer be obtained from relevant government bodies, Chinese supplementary schools in Britain have to be more self-reliant by charging higher tuition fees like most of the Chinese supplementary schools in San Francisco and New York City do. Some schools worry that by raising the tuition fees, some children from poor families will be deprived of their right to Chinese language education. In order to solve such a problem, some Chinese supplementary schools in the USA have established scholarships. Besides providing scholarships, Chinese supplementary schools in Britain can consider establishing a fee-remission scheme.

Organisation and structure

Chinese supplementary schools in both countries tend to organise and structure their classes by following closely either the Taiwan or the Hong Kong education system. Normally it takes at least six years to complete the primary cycle of Chinese education in Taiwan or Hong Kong. In San Francisco and New York City, some Chinese classes are held during the week after school hours. If children go to Chinese classes every day like in the two American cities, the pressure on children to complete the primary cycle of Chinese education in six years will be reduced. In London the majority of Chinese children go to Chinese classes once a week only. When they are pushed to complete the primary cycle of Chinese education within six years by weekly attendance of two to three hours, it is impossible for their Chinese linguistics to be properly developed. In order to improve the quality of Chinese language education among Chinese supplementary schools in London, the Chinese–American model of holding classes after school hours every day is an alternative. Nevertheless, the various conditions in Britain make it difficult to adopt such a policy.

Unlike Chinese–Americans in San Francisco and New York City, not many Chinese in London live in Chinatown. When children go to Chinese supplementary schools in Chinatown in London, the majority of them spend about half an hour to one hour on their journey[2]. If these children attend Chinese classes in Chinatown after school, it will be quite late in the evening by the time they return home. In fact, many Chinese parents want their children to give priority to their studies at British state schools. If their children also attend Chinese classes after school, they will worry that their children would not have time to cope with their English school work.

Although Chinese parents in Britain want their children to go to Chinese supplementary schools to learn Chinese, many of them do not expect their children to have excellent achievement in the Chinese language. They only hope that their children can communicate with them in Chinese and be able to read and write simple Chinese. The most important of all is that their children should show respect for parents in the family and succeed in the mainstream English-medium education. Therefore they think that for their children to attend Chinese classes once a week at the weekend is quite enough.

Even though some Chinese parents are keen to have more Chinese language education for their children during the week, their expectation cannot be easily fulfilled as there are problems in the supply of teachers and the availability of school premises.

Unlike Chinese teachers in the USA who regard teaching in Chinese supplementary schools as a source of income to support their living in the USA, the majority of Chinese teachers in Britain view teaching Chinese at Chinese supplementary schools as a community service. They can only afford some time to teach at the weekend. Among these teachers, many of them are full-time students from Hong Kong who will give priority to their studies during the week. It is less likely that these students will be free to help with Chinese classes during the week.

Besides problems in the supply of teachers, the lack of school premises of Chinese supplementary schools in Britain makes it difficult to organise Chinese classes after school hours. At present many of the Chinese supplementary schools in London are using the LEA school premises to hold classes at the weekend. After school hours, many of these state school premises will be used for various extra-curricular activities. It is unlikely that schools would allow other organisations to hold Chinese classes on their school premises while their internal activities are in progress.

In San Francisco and New York City, Chinese supplementary schools which are able to hold classes after school hours are those which have their own school premises. Many of these Chinese supplementary schools are located in Chinatown where there is a demand for Chinese classes or a 'healthy' environment to keep Chinese children off the streets in Chinatown after school. In order to satisfy the needs of Chinese parents in the two American cities and to fully utilise the school premises, after-school Chinese classes are therefore organised by these Chinese supplementary schools. If Chinese supplementary schools have to use public school premises, their classes are held at the weekend only. The majority of Chinese supplementary schools in London fall into the second category of the Chinese supplementary schools in the USA. If the aspirations of Chinese parents in Britain are to be taken into consideration seriously, it seems that the present arrangement of Chinese classes at the weekend is more appropriate to the situation in Britain.

Curriculum

Medium of instruction

As Cantonese has become the lingua franca within the Chinese communities in San Francisco, New York City and London, the majority of Chinese supplementary schools in the three metropolitan cities have adopted Cantonese as the medium of instruction. Unlike the situation in the two American cities, there are fewer Chinese supplementary schools in London using Mandarin as a teaching medium mainly because of the lack of demand for Mandarin-medium classes and the shortage of Mandarin-speaking teachers in London.

If Mandarin-speaking teachers are available, Chinese supplementary schools in Britain can consider having one or two classes conducted in Mandarin. Parents can select for their children the instruction medium they think appropriate. The reason for recommending such a policy to Chinese supplementary schools in Britain is that among Chinese children attending weekend Chinese classes, some of them do not speak Cantonese at home but other Chinese dialects such as Hakka or Hokkien. It does not make any difference whether the non-Cantonese speaking Chinese children learn Chinese through Cantonese or Mandarin since neither of these teaching media are their mother tongue.

On the other hand, learning Chinese through Mandarin makes it easier to develop spoken skills because romanisation systems such as *pinyin* (phoneticisation) have been developed to help beginners to learn the Mandarin pronounciation. Another advantage of learning Chinese through Mandarin is that learners can write what they speak. If learners are taught in Cantonese, they will have to process their spoken Cantonese into Modern Standard Chinese, which is based on the structure of Mandarin, when they write.

Besides helping non Cantonese-speaking Chinese children to acquire reading and writing skills of the Chinese language, the knowledge of Mandarin will offer more employment opportunities for Chinese children. After China adopted the 'open-door' policy and joined the United Nations, Mandarin, being the national language of China, has been given some international recognition. If Mandarin is added to the linguistic repertoire of the bilingual Chinese children, it is believed that Chinese children will have an advantage when they apply for jobs in organisations which have economic or political relationships with China.

Despite the fact that Chinese is supposed to be the medium of instruction in Chinese supplementary schools, the use of some English for explanation by some bilingual Chinese teachers should not be discouraged. Since English has become a language of learning of most Chinese children in Britain, using some English in Chinese classes will facilitate the learning of Chinese.

Content

The content of Chinese language instruction in Chinese supplementary schools in both Britain and the USA is mainly based on textbooks from either Hong Kong or Taiwan. In order to develop an interest in learning Chinese, many Chinese supplementary schools in London have incorporated singing into the curriculum in lower grade levels. They seem to have ignored other activities which will help to maintain children's interest in learning the Chinese langauge throughout all levels of learning. Taking students out to visit Chinatown by a Chinese school in San Francisco, as mentioned in Chapter 8, is one of the activities that Chinese supplementary schools in London can organise for their pupils. Such an activity is quite educational as some students living outside Chinatown indicate that except buying groceries and having meals at Chinese restaurants in Chinatown, their knowledge of Chinatown or the Chinese community is very limited. How can Chinese parents expect their younger generation to maintain their identity if children have no direct contact with the community where they can learn more about Chinese culture?

Besides the teaching of the Chinese language, several Chinese supplementary schools in San Francisco and New York City have lessons on letter-writing, social studies, calligraphy, history, etc. The teaching of a variety of subjects in Chinese lessons will help to widen Chinese children's knowledge of Chinese culture and make lessons less boring. However, the limited time for Chinese classes in London does not permit the Chinese curriculum to be diversified.

Textbooks

Textbooks used by the majority of Chinese supplementary schools in both countries come from Hong Kong or Taiwan. Although there are Chinese textbooks published by the materials development centres in the USA, these textbooks are not widely adopted by Chinese supplementary schools in the two American cities. The main reason is that many Chinese supplementary schools in San Francisco and New York City are ignorant of the availability of the locally published textbooks. Some of the schools have an impression that the standard level of the Chinese textbooks published in the USA is relatively low compared with those in Hong Kong or Taiwan. Chinese textbooks published in the USA will only be suitable for English-proficient Chinese children who have little or no knowledge of Chinese. As the clientele of Chinese supplementary schools is made up of Chinese children who have received a few years' Chinese education in Hong Kong, Taiwan or China, the set of Chinese textbooks published in the USA therefore are not widely adopted by Chinese supplementary schools in San Francisco and New York City.

Chinese supplementary schools in London also have problems in having appropriate textbooks for their pupils. Since their clientele is composed of immigrant and British-born Chinese children with various levels of linguistic competence, Chinese textbooks published in America, though with English translation and romanisation, will not appeal to Chinese supplementary schools in Britain. On the other hand, some of the texts are too Chinese–American oriented. Facts of the immigration of Chinese people to America and life of Chinese–Americans have formed part of the content. These content components are irrelevant to the situation in Britain. Therefore it is unlikely that Chinese supplementary schools in Britain can adopt Chinese textbooks developed in America for Chinese instruction in Britain.

If in the future money is available for the development of Chinese curricular materials in Britain, Chinese supplementary schools ought to be consulted. Many of the Chinese supplementary schools have been established long before Chinese language instruction is incorporated into the state school curriculum, they should be able to contribute valuable ideas to the curriculum development of the Chinese language.

In the process of designing the content of new Chinese textbooks, Chinese books published in Hong Kong, Taiwan and America can provide a source of reference. The incorporation of some locally-oriented texts from textbooks published overseas (e.g. Hong Kong, Taiwan, USA, etc.) not only gives Chinese children in Britain a better understanding of their mother culture but also widens their knowledge of other varieties of the Chinese culture in societies outside Britain.

Extra-curricular activities

Some Chinese supplementary schools in both Britain and the USA understand that the purpose of some of their pupils of coming to Chinese classes is solely for socialisation into the Chinese cultural norms. The transmission of Chinese culture to overseas Chinese children probably will be more effective through extra-curricular activities than formal classroom teaching. Therefore most of the Chinese supplementary schools in both countries have made an effort to organise extra-curricular or culturally-orientated activities such as school picnics, Christmas and Chinese New Year parties, Chinese martial arts and musical instruments classes in addition to Chinese classes. In some of these activities such as school picnics and major festival celebrations, parents are invited so as to improve their relationship with their children and their communication with the school.

Besides activities within individual Chinese supplementary schools, there are more inter-Chinese school activities such as the annual inter-school athletic meet, essay-writing/calligraphy/choral-speaking competitions in San Francisco and New York City. If a Chinese schools' central agency can be established, or a few Chinese schools try to take the initiative, like the effort made by three Chinese supplementary schools in London to organise a Chinese teachers' seminar in 1986, inter-Chinese school activities can be organised to help to achieve the aims of Chinese education in Britain.

Money for the organisation of inter-Chinese school activities should not be a big problem. It was noticed that the Hong Kong Government Office (London) had been quite generous in sponsoring activities such as outings organised by Chinese community centres and recreational activities organised by Chinese students' groups in London. In the summer of 1986, the summer activities organised by a Chinese supplementary school in London were sponsored by the ILEA. By referring to these precedents, Chinese supplementary schools in London should have good grounds to apply for funds from government agencies for the organisation of inter-Chinese school activities.

If inter-Chinese school activities can be arranged, there will be benefits for Chinese children, parents and Chinese supplementary schools in Britain:

(i) The socialising environment of Chinese children can be expanded. Chinese children will have more opportunities to make friends with children from other Chinese supplementary schools.

(ii) Some of the activities such as essay-writing and choral speaking competitions can help to motivate Chinese children to learn and use the language.

(iii) If Chinese parents are involved in these activities, they will be able to take the opportunity to socialise with other Chinese in Britain as a whole or within their locality. The frustration caused by their restricted social life can be eliminated.

(iv) Through various inter-school activities, Chinese supplementary schools can have a better understanding of what their counterparts are doing. If they want to establish a similar reputation as that of the popular schools, they can know what is expected of the school through some of the inter-Chinese school activities.

In conclusion, if Chinese supplementary schools in Britain can improve the present management of the school, have more contact with other schools through inter-schools activities and make Chinese language instruction more child-centred and activity-orientated, Chinese children will be more willing to attend Chinese classes where they not only learn their mother tongue, but also make friends through various educational and social activities. The 'homely' and lively atmosphere within Chinese supplementary schools will enable Chinese children to find an outlet for their tension.

Training of Chinese language teachers

At present, the training of Chinese language teachers only relies on seminars organised by individual schools or schools' councils as in America and the Hong Kong Government Office (London) or individual schools as in Britain. The main purpose of these seminars is to get teachers together so that they can share one another's experience to improve their teaching skills. (While resources are so limited and teaching at Chinese schools is not the target career of the majority of teachers, such a non-formal teacher training session is one of the solutions to the problem of teacher education.) In fact the training session will be more helpful to inexperienced new teachers if it can be arranged before the academic year starts so that new teachers can learn from their experienced colleagues.

At the moment, Chinese language education provision in British state schools is inadequate. Chinese supplementary schools in Britain still play an important role in satisfying the demand. In order to ensure that children learning Chinese at Chinese supplementary schools are supervised by teachers with professional training, Chinese teachers in the voluntary sector ought to be invited to join training sessions organised by the LEAs.

Supply of Chinese language teachers/bilingual tutors

The supply of teachers remains to be a problem of some Chinese supplementary schools in London as schools rely too much on personal contact for the supply of Chinese language teachers. Since the supply of Chinese school teachers comes mainly from overseas students from Hong Kong, schools with problems in the supply of teachers can consider advertising in university students' newspapers or put up their recruitment advertisements on students' notice-boards at universities or halls of residence. If there are responses to the advertisements, attention should be given to all applications instead of filing them and waiting for recommendations from friends or staff members.

Even though some teachers are willing to work on a voluntary basis, the setting up of a salary scheme like that in Chinese-supplementary schools in the USA will guarantee a more stable supply of teachers. A

Chinese school in London had proved that by reimbursing teachers' travelling expenses, some problems of the supply of teachers had been eliminated.

Bilingual Tutoring Classes

At present the use of Chinese to provide a support service for Chinese children in state schools is not widely available in Britain. Some of the case studies in Chapter 4 have indicated that some Chinese children, especially those who were born overseas, will have problems in understanding English instructions in class when they first join schooling in Britain. If they are not given appropriate support, their performance at school or in public examinations will not reach a satisfactory level.

In order to give assistance to Chinese pupils in their English school work, tutoring classes had been organised by two Chinese supplementary schools in Britain (NCC, 1979 & 1984; QCRC, 1981). One of these schools was the Overseas Chinese Education Centre founded in 1970 in Shepherds Bush (QCRC, 1981). According to one of the founding members, the tutoring service had already ceased. The name of the other school is not known (NCC, 1984). Besides the two schools, the Chinese Association of Tower Hamlets and the Camden Chinese Community Centre have also organised bilingual tutoring classes after school hours for Chinese pupils. In the USA, the Community Educational Services (San Francisco), the Chinatown Planning Council (New York) and some other institutions within the Chinese community provide a similar bilingual tutoring service for Chinese children in San Francisco and New York City in addition to the bilingual education in American public schools.

Since case studies in Chapter 4 have suggested that some Chinese children need bilingual support which at present is not widely available in Britain, bilingual tutoring service ought to be promoted in the Chinese community with the support of the LEAs so that limited English proficient Chinese pupils can have an opportunity to improve their performance at school. As after-school Chinese classes do not appeal to Chinese parents in Britain, bilingual tutoring classes ought to be arranged at the weekend. If there is a clash between the bilingual tutoring and Chinese classes, Chinese parents will have to decide whether they want their children to have cultural maintenance or success in education before they choose the appropriate education for their children.

Bilingual Nursery Schools

Table 18 shows that many Chinese children have a preference for bilingual teachers at pre-primary level, i.e. in nursery schools. As the LEAs are not required by law to provide education for children below the age of 5 (DES, 1983), Chinese communities in Britain probably have to take up the responsibility of providing bilingual nursery education since there is a considerable demand.

Private bilingual nursery education for Chinese children has been offered at Wah Mei Bilingual School in Richmond Area in San Francisco. It has been claimed that the service is quite successful as there are about 300 applicants on the waiting list (Philips, 1984). Chinese–American parents' response and support of private nursery education provided by the Chinese community in San Francisco may give some confidence to the Chinese in Britain in taking up initiatives to set up their own bilingual nursery schools to prepare their children for the English-medium education in the maintained sector.

Based on the LEAs' support of the weekend Chinese classes in the form of finance and free use of Local Authority school premises for holding Chinese classes, and the Local Councils' funding for the establishment of Chinese community centres, there should be some sources for Chinese in Britain to apply for money for the establishment of bilingual nursery schools. Since pre-school education does not form part of formal schooling, bilingual nursery schools for Chinese children can be considered as an ancillary service of Chinese community centres.

TABLE 18 *Preference for bilingual teachers at various levels of schooling*

Level of schooling	Percentage of students preferring bilingual teachers
Pre-primary	52.4
Lower primary	37.9
Upper primary	21.5
Lower secondary	15.9
Upper secondary	14.8

Source: Question 12 in Section 2 of Questionnaire A.

Training of bilingual tutors and nursery teachers

If bilingual tutoring classes and nursery schools are to be set up by the Chinese community, it is very likely that the supply of staff will rely on untrained workers. Methods to train Chinese teachers such as teachers' seminars and joint training schemes with the LEAs should be available to untrained bilingual teachers serving Chinese children in the Chinese community.

Supply of bilingual nursery school teachers

Despite the fact that many Chinese parents work in the catering business, some educated bilingual Chinese mothers help to run or teach at Chinese supplementary schools. Some of them provide crèche services at Chinese community centres. While trained bilingual nursery school teachers are not available, bilingual mothers who are serving the Chinese community in different manners may provide an immediate source of supply of bilingual nursery school teachers.

Improvement of Education Services in British State Schools

Findings of the research have demonstrated that the provision of Chinese language education in British state schools has not addressed the real problems of Chinese pupils. In order to enable Chinese pupils to have equal access to the content of education and eliminate the emotional and psychological problems confronted by them in the process of cultural adjustment, other forms of support service should be available at school in addition to the Chinese language education provision.

Bilingual Instruction and Support Services

Despite the fact that ESL learning and language support service (in English) are available in most British state schools, there are a considerable number of Chinese pupils joining tutoring or additional English classes conducted by bilingual teachers in Chinese community centres. The lack of progress and communication between English-speaking teachers and Chinese pupils implies that there is a demand for Chinese bilingual teachers to help Chinese pupils to cope with their educational and emotional problems in British state schools. Of the 416 Chinese pupils,

64% indicated that when they first joined English-medium schooling in Britain, they could only follow very little or none of the English instruction[3]. Table 18 shows that more than half of the 389 Chinese pupils want to have bilingual support at primary level. The demand for bilingual support is higher at pre-primary stage. This preference for Chinese bilingual teachers by Chinese pupils tends to decrease when pupils move to upper grade levels[4]. Based on findings of the questionnaire and the case studies, Chinese bilingual teachers ought to be appointed in order to eliminate the educational disadvantage of Chinese children.

From the economic point of view, the appointment of Chinese bilingual teachers to serve a small number of Chinese pupils in individual schools can be costly unless Chinese bilingual teachers in individual schools can work across the entire school population. Because of the absence of a Chinese bilingual team which can be found in American public schools, Chinese bilingual teachers in British state schools will be delegated a variety of responsibilities.

Besides providing language support service in the classroom, Chinese bilingual teachers will be responsible for the pastoral care of Chinese children who may be deprived of such care as a result of differences in culture or language barrier. The provision of pastoral care by teachers from a wide range of cultural backgrounds including Chinese is important. This will in the first instance help Chinese children, especially those who begin schooling in Britain but without any knowledge of English, to overcome a lot of their emotional problems during the period of adaptation. On the other hand, a more sensitive pastoral system for all pupils can be developed within the school where Chinese bilingual teachers are involved.

Besides looking after Chinese newcomers, Chinese bilingual teachers may have to give counselling to Chinese bilingual pupils as a central part of their brief. The case studies have indicated that after gradual assimilation by the majority culture and the lack of contact and communication with parents for various reasons, some Chinese pupils will have conflicts with their parents and their mother culture. If bilingual counselling is not available at school, it will be more difficult for Chinese children to obtain bilingual counselling service elsewhere in Britain.

If elementary Chinese education is provided at school, Chinese bilingual teachers will certainly be considered as the 'best' candidate to take up the job. In other words, Chinese bilingual teachers will need to spend time on preparing or developing materials for teaching the Chinese language.

Parents' participation in parent-teacher meetings and effective communication between schools and parents are crucial to the education of children. If Chinese bilingual teachers are available at school to act as translators or interpreters, Chinese parents who do not speak English will be encouraged to participate in some school activities. Schools will be able to have a better understanding of the expectations of Chinese parents and the needs of Chinese children. Eventually education in British state schools can be geared to meeting the needs of Chinese children.

Since the responsibilities of Chinese bilingual teachers are numerous and complex, the appointment of at least one Chinese bilingual teacher to base in a British state school where there are Chinese pupils is needed. In schools where there is a high concentration of Chinese pupils, which may be the case in schools located in Westminster, Camden and Islington, a Chinese bilingual education team like that in some American public schools in New York City and San Francisco ought to be formed.

Chinese Language Education Provision

Owing to the lack of guidance from the DES and an absence of a Chinese examination syllabus, the organisation of Chinese classes varies from school to school. Chinese pupils' opting out of Chinese education in their own school and attending Chinese classes at the weekend indicates that Chinese language education provision in the maintained sector ought to be improved to serve the needs of Chinese children.

In *The National Curriculum 5–16: A Consultative Document* (DES, 1987), it was proposed that a modern foreign language should be included as one of the foundation subjects during compulsory secondary schooling. However, it was not mentioned whether a modern foreign language should be included in the foundation subjects for primary school children. If Chinese becomes one of the modern foreign language options at secondary level, as suggested in Section 36 of *Modern Languages in the School Curriculum: A Statement of Policy* (DES, 1988), it will be more important that the DES should work in collaboration with Chinese supplementary schools in the design of a Chinese syllabus and curriculum. On the other hand, the variety of the Chinese language to be taught in state schools ought to be specified because of the complexity and diversity of the Chinese language as mentioned in Chapter 1.

If a syllabus and a curriculum for secondary level Chinese can be developed, all resources available for Chinese language education in the maintained sector should be channelled into the provision of Chinese language education at secondary level. Chinese supplementary schools should try to link up their primary level Chinese language education provision with that in state secondary schools. If the division of labour between the voluntary and the maintained sectors can be achieved in terms of the provision of Chinese language education, wastage in limited resources can be avoided. Chinese children can spend some of their time joining other activities instead of attending Chinese classes in both the voluntary and public sectors to acquire similar language skills. The Chinese linguistic skills of Chinese children can be developed systematically and progressively when the roles and responsibilities of the voluntary and maintained sectors are clearly defined.

Training of bilingual/Chinese language education teachers

Although training sessions for community languages teachers are available at the ILEA and some higher education institutions such as the Institute of Education University of London, the training of bilingual community languages teachers is at an experimental stage.

In the course of training of bilingual education teachers at master's level at New York University, prospective bilingual education teachers are provided with some general knowledge of the cultural background of language minority pupils in American public schools. If prospective bilingual education teachers cannot pass the languages assessment when they enrol, they will be given training on their linguistic skills in the training course to ensure that they will be competent in using the target languages in bilingual teaching. Despite the fact that Chinese language education forms a component of the Chinese bilingual-bicultural education programmes in the two American cities, there is an absence of training in the teaching methodology of Chinese or other mother tongues as a foreign/second language at school level or for maintenance purpose[5].

If Chinese is to be incorporated into the mainstream curriculum where students are expected to achieve a certain level of linguistic competence which will enable some of the students to sit the GCSE (General Certificate of Secondary Education) Chinese examination, the weaknesses detected in the American bilingual education teacher training model ought to be strengthened when training community languages teachers to teach mother tongues, including Chinese in British schools. In other words, methodology in teaching Chinese as a foreign/second language in an English-speaking environment ought to be developed by bilingual education teacher training institutions. An analysis of British–Chinese pupils' learning difficulties in Chinese would be helpful in this respect. Based on a few term-tests and examinations sat by some primary level pupils in a Chinese supplementary school, common errors have been analysed and incorporated in Appendix 5. Since no similar Chinese error analysis has been done in this country, the error analysis of a sample students would provide a starting point for teacher trainers concerned to carry out further research and develop appropriate teaching methods to teach community languages effectively and efficiently in British state schools.

Chinese bilingual teachers have multiple roles to play in British state schools. In addition to the training of methodology in teaching the Chinese language, prospective Chinese bilingual teachers ought to also be provided knowledge of counselling and child psychology so as to help them to handle the emotional problems of children.

Training of bilingual education teacher trainers

Bilingual-bicultural education provision for language minority pupils in British state schools is a fairly new educational development. The lack of immediate response from higher education institutions to provide bilingual education teacher training has indicated a shortage of teacher trainers. The idea of providing fellowships by the national government to train bilingual teacher trainers, as has been done in the United States, will help to solve the problem of teacher training in bilingual education.

However, the training of prospective bilingual education teacher trainers should not be confined to Britain only. Some ideas of the design of the training programme of bilingual education teacher trainers can be borrowed from the USA. Ms. Gay Wong, the Specialist of the Bilingual Program of the Alhambra School District in Los Angeles pointed out that in recent years, the Alhambra School District has been experimenting in overseas summer training for their bilingual education teachers by organising tours to Hong Kong and China where the majority of Chinese–American pupils come from. Besides sight-seeing, bilingual education teachers study the education system, culture and the language of Hong Kong and China if arrangement can be made. The knowledge that bilingual education teachers acquire through such a study tour will enable bilingual teachers to understand the background of their Chinese pupils better.

The idea of providing cultural education for bilingual education teachers abroad can be modified and incorporated in the design of a training programme for bilingual education teacher trainers in Britain. Since there is an absence of appropriate personnel to train bilingual education teacher trainers in Britain, as a starting point, prospective bilingual education teacher trainers can carry out some research on the target bilingual pupils by visiting their community/supplementary schools and British state schools where they are educated. Visits to both types of educational institutions are crucial as they will enable prospective bilingual education teacher trainers to develop an insight into the various conflicts confronted by language minority pupils in Britain.

After a time interval, probably one academic year, the training site of the prospective bilingual education teacher trainers can be shifted to countries where the target bilingual pupils come from. In order to provide a base convenient for the prospective bilingual education teacher trainers to carry out their cross country research, arrangement for attachment can be made with some teacher training institutions or universities in countries where the prospective bilingual education teacher trainers will be visiting. During the course of training in the native land of the bilingual pupils, besides learning the target culture or language of their bilingual pupils, the prospective bilingual education teacher trainers should focus on comparing and contrasting the education systems and teaching methodology used in the target country and Britain. Such a comparative study is important because many of the academic problems faced by bilingual pupils in British schools are rooted from the gap or differences between the two systems. In order to carry out the comparative study, classroom observation in schools at different levels and attending teacher training seminars should not be omitted from the training programme.

Since bilingual education in the USA has been established much earlier than in Britain, training of bilingual education teachers and teacher trainers is available at some higher education institutions. Part of the training programme for bilingual education teacher trainers in Britain can be extended to the USA at the final stage of the training. After obtaining sufficient information about the conditions in which bilingual students are brought up and educated, prospective teacher trainers in the final stage of their training in the USA should be able to select the type of bilingual education teacher training models which they find in the USA to fit into the British context. It is estimated that the training of bilingual education teacher trainers will probably take two or three years.

Supply of Chinese bilingual teachers

While bilingual education teachers training has not been well developed in Britain, the supply of trained bilingual education teachers in the maintained sector is inadequate. In order to meet the immediate needs of Chinese pupils in British state schools, Chinese bilinguals with teacher training qualifications from Hong Kong should be recruited. Before they obtain the teacher training qualifications in Britain, they can be assigned duties similar to those of the paraprofessionals in American public schools by giving group tuition or translation assistance in the classroom. Outside the classroom, they can help to provide counselling or develop Chinese curricular materials.

Conclusions

The recommendations above have suggested that a lot of joint effort between the maintained and voluntary sectors will be required if initiatives are taken to improve the education of Chinese pupils in Britain. The Chinese community has to seek ways of channelling some of their resources to sensitise their education services to meet the real needs of their children. The British government should give recognition to the needs of Chinese pupils at school by encouraging the appointment of Chinese teachers to the establishment of schools to carry out various duties such as Chinese language teaching, counselling and the provision of pastoral care. Since the 1981 Census indicates that Chinese children being born in Britain are increasing and Chinese pupils in the questionnaire indicate that their failure to understand English instruction is more serious at pre-primary level, there is a need for some attention to be given to the provision of bilingual nursery education for Chinese children. If Chinese pupils' language skills in English and Chinese can be developed properly at an early stage, some of the problems they face in British schools as a result of cultural adjustment and language barrier will be eliminated.

Notes to Chapter 10

1. The ILEA was abolished in 1989 before the book was published.
2. Source of information: Question 8 in Section 1 of Questionnaire A.
3. Source of information: Question 9 in Section 1 of Questionnaire A.
4. Source of information: Question 12 in Section 1 of Questionnaire A.

5. The information was obtained by interviewing two of the staff members running the bilingual education teacher training course at master's level at New York University. The author had also attended two sessions of the training programme.

Appendix 1

Questionnaire A: Research on the Language Education Needs of Chinese Pupils in Britain

Instructions:

Please answer the questions in both Sections 1 and 2 by putting a '√' in the spaces provided.

Section 1: Chinese language education

1. Sex:

    A. Male   _____
    B. Female   _____

2. Age: (Please state)   _____

3. Place of birth:

    A. United Kingdom   _____
    B. Hong Kong   _____
    C. Vietnam   _____
    D. China   _____
    E. Others (Please specify)   _____

    (If you were not born in the UK, please answer Question 4 and continue with the rest of the questions. If you were born in the UK, please continue with Question 5.)

4. If you were NOT born in the UK, at what age did you come to the UK? (Please state)   _____

5. Please *underline* the language(s) that you speak to the following people.

A.   Grandfather — Cantonese Hakka Chiuchow Mand. Viet. Eng.

B.   Grandmother — Cantonese Hakka Chiuchow Mand. Viet. Eng.

C.   Father — Cantonese Hakka Chiuchow Mand. Viet. Eng.

D.   Mother — Cantonese Hakka Chiuchow Mand. Viet. Eng.

E.E. brother(s) — Cantonese Hakka Chiuchow Mand. Viet. Eng.

F.E. sister(s) — Cantonese Hakka Chiuchow Mand. Viet. Eng.

G.Y. brother(s) — Cantonese Hakka Chiuchow Mand. Viet. Eng.

H.Y. sister(s) — Cantonese Hakka Chiuchow Mand. Viet. Eng.

I.   Friends who can speak Chinese and English

     (Please state the language(s))   _____

Key:

Mand.: Mandarin   Viet.: Vietnamese   Eng.: English
E.: Elder   Y.: Younger

(Note: The abbreviations were put in long-hand in the actual questionnaire being sent out.)

6.   Please *underline* the language(s) that the following people speak to you.

A.   Grandfather — Cantonese Hakka Chiuchow Mand. Viet. Eng.

B.   Grandmother — Cantonese Hakka Chiuchow Mand. Viet. Eng.

C.   Father — Cantonese Hakka Chiuchow Mand. Viet. Eng.

D.   Mother — Cantonese Hakka Chiuchow Mand. Viet. Eng.

E.E. brother(s) — Cantonese Hakka Chiuchow Mand. Viet. Eng.

F.E. sister(s) — Cantonese Hakka Chiuchow Mand. Viet. Eng.

G.Y. brother(s) — Cantonese Hakka Chiuchow Mand. Viet. Eng.

H.Y. sister(s) — Cantonese Hakka Chiuchow Mand. Viet. Eng.

I.   Friends who can speak Chinese and English
       (Please state the language(s))   _____

7. At what age did you start Chinese class (The first Chinese school
    in Britain that you went to)? (Please state)   _____ ʻ

8. How much time do you spend on your journey (including transport
    and walk) to go to Chinese school from home (one way)?

    A. Less than half an hour   _____
    B. About an hour   _____
    C. More than an hour   _____

9. Why do you come to the Chinese class?

    (If you have more than one of the following reasons, please use 1,
    2 and 3 to indicate your first *three* rasons. ʻ1ʼ indicates the most
    important reason; ʻ2ʼ indicates less important and ʻ3ʼ indicates the
    least important.)

    A. My parents want me to join Chinese class   _____
    B. Learning the Chinese language is my own interest   _____
    C. I want to go to Chinese school to meet my friends.   _____
    D. Going to Chinese school is better than staying at home at the
       weekend   _____
    E. I must learn the Chinese language in order to communicate with
       my parents.   _____

10. If your English day school organises some activities such as outings
    or ball games for you at the same time when you have your Chinese
    class, what do you prefer to do?

    A. Attend Chinese class.   _____
    B. Join the activities organised by English day school.   _____

11. Assuming that the following languages are offered at your English
    day school, which one do you prefer to study as a second language?
    (Please tick *one* answer only)

    A. Latin   _____
    B. French   _____
    C. German   _____
    D. Chinese   _____

12. What sort of job do you most prefer to do when you finish your
    studies? (Please tick *one* answer only)

A. To be a professional (e.g. accountant, doctor, nurse, engineer, fashion designer, etc.)   _____

B. Doing clerical jobs in a commercial firm (e.g. typist, book-keeper, secretary, clerk, etc.)   _____

C. Working in a Chinese restaurant or 'take-away' shop   _____

D. Working in a Chinese supermarket   _____

E. Others (Please specify)   _____

13. Which of the following countries would you first start looking for your job?

A. UK   _____

B. China   _____

C. Hong Kong   _____

D. Others (Please specify)   _____

14. Which of the following countries would you prefer to settle permanently? (Please tick *one* answer only)

A. UK   _____

B. China   _____

C. Hong Kong
(Note that Hong Kong will become part of China by 1997)

D. Others (Please specify)   _____

15. Do you write to your relatives/friends in Hong Kong or China in Chinese?

A. Very often   _____

B. Sometimes   _____

C. Never   _____

16. How often do you do the following activities in your spare time? (Please put a '√' in the appropriate boxes.)

Activities	Very often	Sometimes	Never
A. Watching Chinese videos			
B. Watching English television			

C. Watching English videos

D. Reading Chinese magazines

E. Reading English magazines

F. Reading Chinese newspaper

G. Reading English newspaper

H. Reading Chinese story books

I. Reading English story books

J. Listening to Chinese songs/music

K. Listening to English songs/music

17. How much time do you spend on doing Chinese homework (including preparation for dictation and revision) per week?

A. Less than an hour   _____

B. About an hour   _____

C. About 2 hours   _____

D. About 3 hours   _____

E. About 4 hours   _____

F. More than 4 hours   _____

18. Have you ever been taught the proper sequence (which line to write first) of writing the lines or strokes of Chinese words?

A. Yes   _____

B. No   _____

19. Do you use English to help to memorise the pronunciation of Chinese words?

A. Very often   ——
B. Sometimes   ——
C. Never   ——

20. What is the language(s) of instruction that your teacher uses in Chinese class?

A. Cantonese only   ——
B. Mandarin (Putonghua) only   ——
C. Mainly Cantonese and some English   ——
D. Mainly Mandarin and some English   ——
E. English mainly and some Cantonese   ——
F. English mainly and some Mandarin   ——
G. Others (Please specify)   ——

21. Which of the combination above (Question 20) would enable you to understand Chinese lesson better? (Please tick *one* answer only)

A. Cantonese only   ——
B. Mandarin (Putonghua) only   ——
C. Mainly Cantonese and some English   ——
D. Mainly Mandarin and some English   ——
E. English mainly and some Cantonese   ——
F. English mainly and some Mandarin   ——
G. Others (Please specify)   ——

22. What language(s) would you prefer your teacher to use in the Chinese lesson:

A. Cantonese only   ——
B. Mandarin (Putonghua) only   ——
C. Cantonese mainly and some English   ——
D. Mandarin mainly and some English   ——
E. English mainly and some Cantonese   ——
F. English mainly and some Mandarin   ——
G. Others (please specify)   ——

23. How do you like the text-book which you are using?

(If you are not using any text-books, think of the text-book which you used before or notes given by your Chinese teacher.)

A. Interesting   _____
B. O.K.   _____
C. Boring   _____

24. Has any of the following activities been carried out in the classroom at your Chinese school?

Activities	Very often	Sometimes	Never
A. Watching videos			
B. Listening to tapes			
C. Cross-word puzzles			
D. Solving riddles			
E. Role-playing			
F. Others (Please state)			

25. How do you find your Chinese class in general?

A. Quite interesting   _____
B. O.K.   _____
C. Quite boring   _____

Section B: English language education

1. What do you think of your standard of English?

A. Good   _____
B. Above average   _____
C. Average   _____
D. Below average   _____
E. Bad   _____

2. Have you ever attended any special English/ESL (English as a

Second Language) class in your English day school or at any language centre?

A. Yes   ____

B. No   ____

(If 'Yes', please continue with Question 3.
If 'No', please continue with Question 6.)

3. How long have you stayed in that English class?

A. Less than half a year   ____

B. About 1 year   ____

C. About $1\frac{1}{2}$ years   ____

D. About 2 years   ____

E. Others (Please specify)   ____

4. To what extent you find that English class helpful?

A. Helpful in developing both oral and written skills   ____

B. More helpful in oral skills than written skills   ____

C. More helpful in written skills than oral skills   ____

D. Not helpful at all   ____

5. What sort of teacher do you expect to have to conduct the special English class in your English day school?

(Please use 1, 2 and 3 to indicate the order of your preference.)

A. Native speaker of English who can speak English only   ____

B. Native speaker of English who can speak both
   English and Chinese   ____

C. Chinese bilingual who can speak both English and
   Chinese   ____

6. If there were English classes organised by the Chinese community, would you attend?

A. Yes   ____

B. No   ____

(If 'Yes', please continue with Question 7.
If 'No', please continue with Question 8.)

7. What sort of teacher do you expect to have to conduct the English tutoring classes organised by the Chinese community?

(Please use 1, 2 and 3 to indicate the order of your preference.)

A. Native speaker of English who can speak English only   _____

B. Native speaker of English who can speak both English and Chinese   _____

C. Chinese bilingual who can speak both English and Chinese   _____

8. At what level did you begin English schooling in the UK?

A. Pre-primary (playgroup/nursery school)   _____

B. Lower primary (infant school/primary 1–3)   _____

C. Upper primary (junior school/primary 4–6)   _____

D. Lower secondary (1st year–3rd year)   _____

E. Upper secondary (4th year and upwards)   _____

9. On the first day when you began English schooling in the UK, how far could you follow teacher(s)' instructions?

A. None   _____

B. A little bit   _____

C. About half   _____

D. More than half   _____

E. I understood almost everything   _____

10. What did you do when you failed to understand classroom instructions?

A. Cried   _____

B. Followed what other children did   _____

C. Kept quiet to wait for the teacher to come   _____

D. Went home to tell mother the communication problems at school   _____

E. Others (Please specify)   _____

11. How long did it take before you could gradually understand general classroom instructions?

A. 1 months   ———
B. 2 months   ———
C. 3 months   ———
D. 4 months   ———
E. 5 months   ———
F. Half a year   ———
G. About a year   ———
H. Others (Please specify)   ———

12. What sort of teacher do you prefer to have to conduct the English lesson in the following stages of schooling at British school?

(Please 'V' the appropriate boxes.)

Nationality and language skills of the teacher		
Chinese speaking English & Chinese	British speaking English & Chinese	British speaking English only
PP		
LP		
UP		
LS		
US		

Key:

PP: Pre-primary LP: Lower-primary UP: Upper-primary LS: Lower-secondary US: Upper-secondary

(Note: The abbreviations were put in long-hand in the actual questionnaire being sent out.)

[THANK   YOU]

Appendix 2

Questionnaire B: Research on Chinese Language Education Provision by the Chinese Community in Britain

Instructions:

Please answer the following questions by putting a '√' in the space provided.

1. When was your school established?
    (Please state the year)   _____

2. How many students did you have when the school was founded?
    (Please insert the number)   _____

3. How many students do you have this year (1986–87)?
    (Please insert the number)   _____

4. What are the aims of your school?

    (If there is more than one aim, please use 1, 2, 3, 4 and 5 to indicate the importance of those aims. '1' means the most important and '5' means the least important.)

    A. To provide Chinese language education for overseas
       Chinese   _____
    B. To encourage young overseas Chinese to have an awareness of
       Chinese culture   _____
    C. To help to bridge the communication gap between Chinese
       parents and their children by the provision of Chinese language
       education   _____
    D. To provide a base for Chinese children to come together so that
       they can identify with one another   _____
    E. To prepare Chinese children for the GCE/CSE Chinese language
       examination   _____
    F. Others (Please specify)   _____

5. Who decides the following school policies?

(Please put a 'V' in the appropriate box.)

School policies	Teachers	H. teacher	Ed. sub-com.	Ex. Com.
A. Appointment of teachers				
B. Teaching medium				
C. Textbooks				
D. School calendar				
E. School hours				
F. Internal examination(s)				
H. School budget				

Key:
H. teacher: Headteacher Ed. sub-com.: Education sub-committee
Ex. Com.: Executive committee of the organisation

(Note: The abbreviations were put in long-hand in the actual questionnaire being sent out.)

6. Does your school charge any tuition fees?

A. Yes   ——
B. No   ——

(If 'Yes', please continue with Question 5.
If 'No', please continue with Question 6.)

7. How much are the tuition fees each term (half a year)?

A. Less than £5   ____
B. £6–£10   ____
C. £11–£15   ____
D. £16–£20   ____
E. More than £20   ____

8. Check the list of financial sources in the following. Then put in the information required by following the instructions.

(a) Put a '√' in the appropriate boxes in the first two columns. 'Yes' means that part of the school finance comes from that particular source. 'No' means that particular source does not provide any financial support for the school.

(b) State in the third column which YEAR that particular source of finance began to form part of the school money.

(c) Indicate the total amount that the school receives from each source.

Financial sources	Yes	No	Year of commencement	Total amount received in 1985/86
A. Local Education Authority				
B. Hong Kong Government Office (London)				
C. Christian church				
D. Tuition fees				
E. Membership subscription				
F. Others (Please state)				

9. What sort of premises is your school using?

    A. Schools belonging to the Local Education Authority   _____
    B. Youth centres belonging to the Local Council   _____
    C. Properties belonging to a religious group   _____
    D. Properties belonging to a non-religious organisation to which the Chinese school is affiliated   _____
    E. Others (Please state)   _____

10. Does your school need to pay any rents for the use of the above premises?

    A. Yes   _____
    B. No   _____

    (If 'Yes', please continue with Question 11.
    If 'No', pleasse continue with Question 12.)

11. How much are the rents per year?
    (Please state)   _____

12. Is the financial support that the school receives from different sources sufficient to meet the yearly expenditure of the school?

    A. More than sufficient   _____
    B. Just sufficient   _____
    C. Not sufficient   _____

13. How are Chinese classes in your school graded?

    A. Following more or less the kindergarten/primary school grade-level system used in kindergartens and primary schools in Hong Kong   _____
    B. The school has developed its own grade-level system (e.g. Grades 1, 2, 3, etc. are used to represent each level of the primary cycle)   _____
    C. Others (Please state)   _____

    (If 'A' is your answer to Question 13, please continue with Question 14. If 'B' is your answer to Question 13, please continue with Question 15.)

14. Which of the following grade-levels are available at your school now?
    (Please put a '√' next to the grade-level available.)

A. Play-group   _____
B. Lower kindergarten   _____
C. Upper kindergarten   _____
D. Primary 1   _____
E. Primary 2   _____
F. Primary 3   _____
G. Primary 4   _____
H. Primary 5   _____
I. Primary 6   _____
J. 1st year (Secondary)   _____
K. 2nd year (Secondary)   _____

15. Which of the following grade-levels are available at your school now?
(Please put a '√' next to the grade-level available.)

A. 1st year   _____
B. 2nd year   _____
C. 3rd year   _____
D. 4th year   _____
E. 5th year   _____
F. 6th year   _____
G. 7th year   _____
H. 8th year   _____
I. 9th year   _____
J. 10th year   _____
K. 11th year   _____
L. 12th year   _____

16. Normally how long does it take to complete the whole cycle of Chinese education in your school?

A. 8 years   _____
B. 9 years   _____
C. 10 years   _____
D. 11 years   _____
E. 12 years   _____
F. Others (Please state)   _____

17. What is the minimum age for admission to your Chinese school?

A. 4 years old   ——

B. 5 years old   ——

C. 6 years old   ——

D. 7 years old   ——

E. Others (Please state)   ——

18.   What is the *normal* number of students in each class?

A. About 10 or less   ——

B. 11–15   ——

C. 16–20   ——

D. 21–25   ——

E. More than 25   ——

19.   Are all classes of your school held at the same time?

A. Yes   ——

B. No   ——

20.   When are the classes of your school held?

(If classes are held at different times, you can tick more than one
answer. If the times are not given, please specify those times in the
space provided in E.)

A. Sunday   10.00 a.m.–1.00 p.m.   ——

B. Sunday   1.00 p.m.–4.00 p.m.   ——

C. Saturday   10.00 a.m.–1.00 p.m.   ——

D. Saturday   1.00 p.m.–4.00 p.m.   ——

E. Others (Please specify)   ——

21.   How long does each class last?

A. Less than 2 hours   ——

B. About 2 hours   ——

C. About 3 hours   ——

D. More than 3 hours   ——

22.   Usually how many teaching weeks are there in your school calendar?

A. Less than 25 weeks   ——

B. 25–30 weeks   ——

C. 31–35 weeks   ——

D. More than 35 weeks   ——

23.   How are these teaching weeks distributed in the year?

A. Early September–early July   _____

B. Early September–mid July   _____

C. Early September–late July   _____

D. Mid September–early July   _____

E. Mid September–mid July   _____

F. Mid September–late July   _____

G. Others (Please state)   _____

24. What is the *major* language of instruction in your school?

A. Cantonese   _____

B. Mandarin (Putonghua)   _____

C. Others (Please specify)   _____

25. Is your school using the text-book supplied by the Hong Kong Government Office (London)?

A. Yes   _____

B. No   _____

(If 'Yes', please continue with Question 28.
If 'No', please continue with Question 26.)

26. If the textbooks used by your school are not supplied by the Hong Kong Government Office (London), where are they published?

A. Taiwan   _____

B. The People's Republic of China   _____

C. Singapore   _____

D. Others (Please specify)   _____

27. Which type of Chinese characters are taught by the majority of the teachers of your school?

A. The complicated form   _____

B. The simplified form   _____

28. How many of your teachers speak the following languages/dialects as their mother tongue?
(Please state the number)

A. Cantonese   _____

B. Mandarin   _____

C. Hakka   _____

D. Others (Please specify)   _____

29. Which of the following teaching aids/materials are fully provided at the level stated?

(Please put a '√' in the appropriate box to indicate its availability.)

Teaching aids/materials	PP (G1–2)	P1–2 (G3–4)	P3–4 (G5–6)	P5–6 (G7–8)	Second. (G8–12)
A. Chinese videos					
B. Chinese tapes (songs/music/language)					
C. Word cards					
D. Story books which students can borrow					
E. Teaching materials produced by teachers					
F. A variety of textbooks by different publishers					
G. GCE/CSE examination syllabuses					
H. GCE/CSE past examination papers					
I. Others (Please specify)					

Key:
PP: Pre-primary Second.: Secondary P: Primary G: Grade

(Note: The abbreviations were put in long-hand in the actual questionnaire being sent out.)

(Please insert *numbers* in the space provided in Questions 30–36.)

30. How many teachers are there in your school?   _____

31. How many of them have the UK citizenship status?   _____

32. How many of the teachers are students from Hong Kong
     studying in the UK?   _____

33. How many of them are 'parent–teachers' (teachers who have
     children studying in the school)?   _____

34. How many of them possess teacher training qualifications
     recognised in the UK?   _____

35. How many of them possess teacher training qualifications
     which do NOT qualify them to teach in the UK?   _____

36. How many of your teachers have completed the following educational
     levels?

     A. Secondary   _____
     B. Post-secondary (without a degree)   _____
     C. Post-secondary (with a degree)   _____

37. How many of your teachers were recruited by the following methods
     in 1985–86?

     (Please use 1, 2 and 3 to indicate the three major sources. '1'
     indicates the most popular way that the teachers join the school.
     '2' is less popular and '3' is the least popular.)

     A. People recommended by the teaching staff   _____
     B. People reply to advertisements in newspapers or community
        centers   _____
     C. People apply directly to the school   _____
     D. People approached by the headteacher   _____
     E. Others (Please specify)   _____

38. How are teachers rewarded for their service?

     A. Teachers are paid an hourly rate   _____
     B. There is a contribution from the school to reimburse teachers'
        travelling expenses   _____
     C. Teachers are completely unpaid in any form   _____
     D. Others (Please specify)   _____

39. How many of your teachers have been working at the school for
     the periods stated?

A. Less than 3 months   ——
B. 3–6 months   ——
C. 6 months–1 year   ——
D. 1 year–2 years   ——
E. More than 2 years   ——

40. How many of your teachers are in each of the following age-range?
     (Please state the *number*)

     A. 20–25   ——
     B. 26–30   ——
     C. 31–35   ——
     D. 35+   ——
     E. Not known   ——

[THANK   YOU]

Appendix 3

Number of Subjects Interviewed

	UK	USA
Chinese school headteachers/organisers	13	13*
State school headteachers/deputy heads	—	9
Chinese language teachers in the voluntary sector	32	9
Bilingual tutors in the voluntary sector	1	5
Teachers in the maintained sector	9	28
Pupils of Chinese origin	75	22
Pupils of non-Chinese origin	3	—
Chinese parents	34	2
Staff of curriculum development/resource centers	—	4
Teacher training staff at universities	2	2
Officials of state school administrative units	1	5
Officials/workers of Chinese organisations	12	5
Researchers of mother tongue teaching projects	2	—

*The number has included headteachers of two Chinese supplementary schools in Los Angeles. One of them was interviewed at a Chinese association in Los Angeles but no visit was made to the school. Therefore the number does not correspond to the figure used in the book.

Appendix 4

Number of Schools/Institutions/Chinese Families Visited

	UK	USA
Chinese supplementary schools	13	12*
State primary schools	—	4[†]
State junior/junior high schools	—	2
State secondary/high schools	2	3[†]
Curriculum development/resource centres	—	3
Universities providing teacher training	1	1
State school administrative units	2	3
Chinese community organisations	5	4
Chinese families	4	1

*The number has excluded a Chinese school in San Francisco which did not permit any surveys to be conducted at the school.
†The number has included one school in Los Angeles but not included in the findings of the research.

Appendix 5

Chinese Linguistic Problems Among Chinese Pupils Attending Part-Time Chinese Classes in Britain

Because of the complex linguistic structure of the Chinese language, Chinese children who learn it as a second/foreign language usually find it quite difficult, despite the fact that Chinese is their mother tongue. By analysing the performance of some Chinese pupils in tests and examinations, it was found that Chinese children who attend mother tongue classes on a part-time basis usually have common linguistic problems which are illustrated as follows.

Reading

Unlike the English alphabet, the Chinese script is non-phonetic (Alitto, 1969; Jeffery, 1949; Wang & Earle, 1972). If a character is formed by a radical only (e.g. |[yʌt⁶] sun), it will give no clue to the pronunciation. The corresponding sound of each character has to be learnt by heart.

Of the 435 Chinese children in the sample, the majority (50 to 60%) never read Chinese newspaper or Chinese fiction[1]. No more than 32% of these pupils would spend an hour on Chinese homework every week[2]. Therefore it will be unlikely that these pupils can remember the pronunciation which is taught within the two- or three-hour Chinese lesson each week. Their difficulties in memorising Chinese pronunciation has been reflected by the inability of Primary two, three and four students to read questions in tests or examinations. If the whole or part of the test/examination paper is not read through at least once by the teacher, many of the pupils will not know what they are asked to do.

Another linguistic feature of the Chinese language which creates problems for Chinese children in reading is tones. Being a tonal language, the Chinese language uses various pitch levels to indicate different lexical items. Changing the tones can alter the meaning (Comrie, 1981; GB. P. H. of C., HAC, 1985; Wang, 1973; Wang & Earle, 1972). Of the nine basic tones of Cantonese, six are commonly used (Lau, 1972). Since Chinese children in Britain do not speak Cantonese as frequently as their Hong Kong counterparts, many of them fail to get the tones correct. Table 19 shows a few common examples of the confusion of tones among some Chinese pupils in a Primary 3 Chinese class in London.

Besides the confusion of tones, Chinese oral reading of Chinese children in Britain has been interfered by English. By referring to the phonetic symbols created by a group of 16 Primary 3 students in a test, it was discovered that many British-born Chinese children have confused the initial consonant cluster [ts] with [ch]. Regardless of the mistakes on the vowels, it was noticed that such words as 秋 [tsau¹] (autumn), 牀 [tsŋn⁴] (bed) and 前 [tsin⁴] (front) beginning with the [ts] consonant cluster have been romanised by pupils by the use of [ch] to represent the initial sound. Since [ch] and [ts] are two complete different sounds, the confusion of them usually lead to the speaking of 'English-Cantonese' by some Chinese children who are brought up and educated in Britain.

Besides [ts], [ŋ] is another problem initial sound. Since [ŋ] never occurs at the beginning of any English words, it is common that most pupils tend to drop the initial [ŋ] sound. Instead of saying 額 [ŋat⁶] (forehead) and 我 [ŋ:³] (I/me), students may simply say [at⁶] and [ɔ:³].

TABLE 19 *Confusion of tones*

	Chinese characters	Pronunciation	Tone number	English meaning
1.	時	[si:]	4	time/hour
	事	[si:]	6	matters
2.	滿	[mu:m]	3	full
	門	[mu:n]	4	door
3.	應	[yiŋ]	1	ought to
	認	[yiŋ]	6	admit/recognise

Note:
The phonetic symbols used for indicating the pronunciation of the Chinese characters in the table are mainly based on those of the International Phonetic Association.

Writing

The writing difficulties confronted by Chinese children in Britain fall into four main categories: (1) the use of strokes, (2) the confusion of homophones, (3) the use of classifiers and (4) the change of Chinese from Cantonese into Modern Standard Chinese (MSC) which is based on the structure of Mandarin.

(1)   The use of strokes

In the Chinese language, there are about 80,000 ideograms (Jeffery, 1949). In order to be able to read a Chinese newspaper, one should have a knowledge of 4,000 to 7,000 Chinese characters which are formed by two basic units — strokes and radicals. There are about twenty distinct strokes in the Chinese language (Wang, 1973) which have been classified by Chang and Chang (1978) into four main categories: (i) lines, (ii) sweeps, (iii) angles and (iv) hooks (Figure 1). The sequence and the

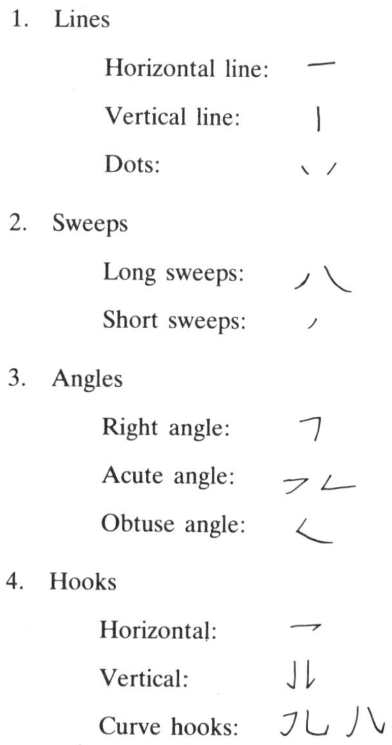

1.   Lines

      Horizontal line: ⟍

      Vertical line: |

      Dots: ╲ ╱

2.   Sweeps

      Long sweeps: ╱ ╲

      Short sweeps: ╱

3.   Angles

      Right angle: ⌐

      Acute angle: ⌐ ∟

      Obtuse angle: ∠

4.   Hooks

      Horizontal: ⌐

      Vertical: ⅃ Ⅼ

      Curve hooks: ⅃Ⅼ ╱\

FIGURE 1 *Basic strokes of Chinese characters*
(Source: Chang, R. and Chang, M.S., 1978:25–26).

geometric position of the strokes are crucial to the formation of a character. If words are simply made up of five or six strokes, students normally do not have problems in producing the ideograms. However, if words are too complicated in terms of the number and the types of strokes involved, pupils will either miss out, add in or confuse some of the strokes forming the words. A collection of pupils' difficulties in the use of strokes to write Chinese characters are given in Tables 20, 21 and 22 under the headings of strokes missing, strokes redundant and strokes confused respectively.

(2)   Confusion of homophones

The previous section has indicated that Chinese children in Britain are quite weak in distinguishing the various tones. As there are a large number of homophones in the Chinese language (Alitto, 1969), Chinese pupils will easily confuse words with similar sounds. Of the 60 wrong words detected from a class of eighteen Primary 3 students sitting an examination in July 1986, 26 mistakes are of such a nature. For instance, instead of writing 新 [sʌn¹] 年 [niŋ⁴] (New Year), a student may write 生 [sʌn¹] 年 [niŋ⁴]. A full list of mistakes under this category detected in the test is given in Table 23.

TABLE 20 *Wrong words — strokes missing*

Chinese script with wrong word underlined				Correct character expected	English meaning
1	歷 [lik⁶]	史 [*]		史 [si:²]	history
2	映 [*]	現 [yin⁶]		映 [yiŋ²]	reflect
3	住 [*]	步 [bo⁶]		進 [tsʌn³]	improve
4	準 [*]	備 [bei⁶]		準 [tsʌn²]	prepare
5	好 [*]	了 [liu³]		好 [hou²]	That is it
6	門 [mu:n⁴]	始 [tsi²]		開 [hɔi]	begin
7	學 [hɔk⁶]	業 [*]		業 [yip⁶]	education
8	電 [diŋ⁶]	景 [ki ²]		影 [yiŋ²]	a film
9	參 [*]	加 [ga:¹]		參 [tsam¹]	participate
10	下 [ha:⁶]	固 [gu:³]		個 [gɔ:³]	next
11	學 [*]	校 [hau⁶]		學 [hɔk⁶]	school

*Pronunciation is not available as there is no such word in the Chinese script.

TABLE 21 *Wrong words — Strokes redundant*

Chinese script with wrong word underlined		Correct character expected	English meaning
1 東 [douŋ¹]	西 [*]	西 [sai¹]	things
2 噴 [*] / 池 [tsi⁴]	水 [soei²]	噴 [pʌn³]	fountain
3 考 [hau²]	試 [si:³]	試 [si:³]	examination
4 禮 [*]	堂 [dɔn⁴]	禮 [lai³]	hall
5 仐 [liŋ⁶]	天 [tin¹]	今 [gʌm¹]	today
6 兵 [biŋ¹] / 球 [kau⁴]	兵 [bʌŋ¹]	乒 [biŋ¹]	table-tennis
7 耐 [*]	心 [sʌm¹]	耐 [nɔi⁶]	patient

*Pronounciation not available as there is no such word in the Chinese script.

(3)   Use of classifiers

Classifiers is a linguistic feature peculiar to Chinese (Wang, 1973; Bruce, 1986). Regardless of the number, all nouns must be preceded by a classifier. For instance, the Chinese equivalent to 'an orange' is 一 [yʌt¹] (one) 個 [gɔ:³] (classifier) 橙 [tsang²] (orange). 'Three books' is written as 三 [sam¹] 本 [bu:n²] (classifier) 書 [sue¹] (books). The main problem with Chinese pupils in Britain in the use of classifiers is the inability of choosing the appropriate classifier to describe a noun. Whenever students are not sure about which classifier to use, they will use the very common classifier '個' [gɔ:³]. For instance, students may say 一 [yʌt¹] (one) 個 [gɔ:³] (classifier) 車 [tse¹] (car) instead of the correct one 一 [yʌt¹] (one) 部 [bou⁶] (classifier)/ 架 [ga:³] (classifier)/ 輛 [leong⁶] (classifier) 車 [tse¹] (car).

Besides a lack of exposure to the Chinese language, the weaknesses in the use of classifiers by Chinese pupils in Britain may be due to the differences in lexis among the Chinese dialects. It has been mentioned in Chapter 2 that there is a considerable percentage of the Chinese in Britain speaking the Hakka dialect. In the Hakka dialect, people would say 一 [yʌt¹] (one) 隻 [tsak³] (classifier) 人 [yʌn⁴] (person) instead of what Cantonese- or Mandarin-speaking people would say 一 [yʌt¹] (one) 個 [gɔ:³] (classifier) 人 [yʌn⁴]. '隻' [tsɑk³] (classifier) in Cantonese is usually used for describing animals, birds, insects, poultry, etc. It is never used to modify 'people'. If a child speaks Hakka at home but is

TABLE 22 *Wrong words — Strokes confused*

Chinese script with wrong word underlined		Correct character expected	English meaning
1 貴 [*] 用 [youŋ^6]		費 [fai^3]	charges
2 莧 [*] 用 [youŋ^6]		費 [fai^3]	charges
3 賣 [*] 用 [youŋ^6]		費 [fai^3]	charges
4 鼓 [*] 勵 [lai^6]		鼓 [gu:^{2}]	encourage
5 裏 [*] 樂 [lɔk^6]		康 [hɔ:n^1]	healthy and happy
6 稅 [*] 你 [nei^3]		祝 [tsɔk^1]	wish you
7 擧 [goei^2] 辞 [*]		辦 [ba:n^6]	organise
8 兵 [biŋ^1] 球 [kau^4] 兵 [*]		乒 [bʌŋ^1]	table-tennis
9 耐 [*] 心' [sʌm^1]		耐 [nɔi^6]	patient
10 員 [yip^6] 營 [yiŋ^4] 令 [liŋ^6]		夏 [ha:^{6}]	summer camp
11 姊 [*] 甥 [sʌŋ^1]		姨 [yi:^{4}]	nephew
12 成 [*] 績 [tsik^1]		成 [siŋ^4]	results
13 心 [bik^1] 須 [*]		須 [soei^1]	ought to

*Pronunciation is not available as there is no such word in the Chinese script.

taught Cantonese in Chinese school, it is likely that the child can be confused by the two sets of classifiers used in Hakka and Cantonese.

Of the 74 teachers reported by seven Chinese supplementary schools in London, only 6 are Hakka-speaking[3]. It implies that many of the Chinese teachers do not have any knowledge of the Hakka dialect. Since ' 隻 ' [tsak^3] (classifier) is not used in Mandarin either, Chinese teachers will regard the use of ' 隻 ' [tsɔk^3] to describe 'people' as ungrammatical. Hakka-speaking students without being explained the differences between the two Chinese dialects by their teachers may continue to write what they speak at home without realising that the Hakka dialect they write is not considered as grammatical written Chinese which is based on the Mandarin structure.

TABLE 23 *Wrong words — Confusion of homophones*

Chinese script with wrong word underlined		Correct character expected	English meaning
影 [yiŋ²]	現 [yiŋ⁶]	映 [yiŋ²]	to reflect
到 [dou³]	星 [si:⁶]	時 [si:⁴]	by that time
日 [yʌt⁵]	其月 [kei⁴] 時 [si:⁴]	是 [si:⁶]	the date is
是 [si:⁶]	候 [hau⁶]	時 [si:⁴]	the time
有 [yau³] 個 [gɔ:³]	有 月 [lə:n³] [yue⁶]	又 [yau⁶]	two months have
沒 [mu:⁶]	又 [yau⁶]	有 [yau³]	do not have
四 [sai¹]	個 [gɔ:³] 月 [yue⁶]	四 [sei³]	four months
天 [tin¹] 很 [hʌŋ²]	氣冬 [hei³] [doun¹]	凍 [doun³]	The weather is cold
生 [sʌŋ¹]	期 [kei⁴] 日 [yʌt⁶]	星 [siŋ¹]	Sunday
帕 [pa:³]	郎 tsiə³	拍 [pak³]	taking photographs
生 [sʌŋ¹]	年 [niŋ⁴]	新 [sʌŋ¹]	New Year

12	上 [səːn⁶]		你 [tsam¹] 切 [gaː¹]		想 [səːn²]	to wish to join
13	我 [ŋɔ⁵]		渴 [səːn²]		想 [səːn²]	I hope
14	我 [ŋɔː⁵]		帝 [səːn⁴]		想 [səːn²]	I hope
15	尸 [tsi²]		到 [dou³]		知 [tsi¹]道 [dou³]	to know
16	會 [wuei³]		信 [sʌn³]		回 [wuei⁴]	to reply a letter
17	肈 [tsʌŋ²]		快 [fai³]		盡 [tsʌŋ⁶]	as soon as possible
18	直 [tsik⁶]		物 [mʌt⁶]		植 [tsik⁶]	plant
19	好 [gau¹]		錢 [tsin²]		交 [gau¹]	to hand in money
20	遇 [yue⁶]		果 [kwɔ²]		如 [yue⁴]	if
21	兒 [yi:⁴]		個 [gɔ:³]		如果 [yue⁴]果 [kwɔ:²]	if
22	溜 [lau⁴]		冰 [biŋ¹]		溜 [lau⁴]	skating
23	外 [ŋɔi⁶]		生 [sʌŋ¹] 女 [ŋoei²]		甥 [sʌŋ¹]	niece
24	見 [gin³]		個 [gɔ:³] [min⁶]		過 [kwɔ:³]	have met before

Note:
The phonetic symbols for indicating the pronunciation of the Chinese characters are mainly based on those of the International Phonetic Association (IPA). When no equivalents are available in the IPA for some peculiar Cantonese sounds such as [ts] in 參 [tsam¹] (participate), [oeil] in 女 [ŋoei²] (girl) and [ue] in 月 [yue⁵] (moon), reference is made to Bruce's (1986) Cantonese.

TABLE 24 *Lexical differences between Cantonese and MSC*

	Cantonese	MSC	English
1.	成十年	差不多十年	almost ten years
2.	寫信比你	寫信給你	write to you
3.	今日	今天	today

(4) Use of Cantonese expressions in Modern Standard Chinese

Similar to their Hong Kong counterparts, Chinese children in Britain use quite a lot of Cantonese expressions in writing which are not accepted in Modern Standard Chinese which is based on the Mandarin structure. From the sixteen letters written by some primary three students in an examination, 11 Cantonese expressions have been detected. Table 24 shows the lexical differences between Cantonese and Modern Standard Chinese (MSC). The words or expressions underlined indicate the differences between the two language varieties in Chinese.

Although the error analysis is brief, it signifies that Chinese children in Britain have two major problems in learning the Chinese language, namely reading and writing. Since Chinese children in Britain lack the language environment to use the Chinese language, some of the errors they make such as the variations in tones is quite different from their counterparts in Hong Kong. It implies that using the traditional teaching methods in Hong Kong may not help to solve the problems of Chinese children in learning Chinese in Britain. If Chinese language education in Britain aims at improving the Chinese competence of these children, there is a need to have a detailed study of the errors made by Chinese pupils in Britain and develop new methodology in teaching the Chinese language to children of Chinese origin in Britain or in English-speaking societies.

Notes to Appendix 5

1. Source of information: Question 16 in Section 1 of Questionnaire A.
2. Source of information: Question 17 in Section 1 of Questionnaire A.
3. Source of information: Question 28 in Questionnaire B.

Bibliography

ADELMAN, C. *et al.* 1975, Re-thinking Case Study: Notes from the Second Cambridge Conference, 139–150 (publisher and place of publication not known).

Advisory Committee on Chinese Language Instruction in California Public Schools 1962, Chinese language instruction in California public schools. *California Schools* 33, 341–355.

AIJMER, G. 1967, Expansion and extension in Hakka society. *Journal of the Hong Kong Branch of the Royal Asiatic Society* 7, 42–79.

ALATIS, J.E. 1978, *Georgetown University Round Table on Language and Linguistics 1978: International Dimensions of Bilingual Education*. Washington, D.C.: Georgetown University Press.

ALEXANDER, D.J. and NAVA, A. 1976, *A Public Policy Analysis of Bilingual Education in California*. San Francisco, California: R and E Associates, Inc.

——1978, *The How, What, Where, When and Why of Bilingual Education: a Concise and Objective Guide for School District Planning*. San Francisco, California: R and E Research Associates, Inc.

ALITTO, S.B. 1969, The language issue in Communist Chinese education. In C.T. Hu (ed.) *Aspects of Chinese Education*. New York: Teachers College Press.

ALMQUIST, E.M. 1979, *Minorities, Gender and Work*. Lexington, Massachusetts: Lexington Books.

AMBERT, A.N. 1982, The identification of LEP children with special needs. *Bilingual Journal* (Fall) 6(1), 17–22.

AMBERT, A.N. and MELENDEZ, S.E. 1985, *Bilingual Education — A Sourcebook*. New York: Garland Publishing.

ANDERSSON, T. 1972, Bilingual education: the American experience. In Merill SWAIN (ed.) *Bilingual Schooling: Some Experiences in Canada and the United States*. Toronto, Ontario: The Ontario Institute for Studies in Education.

ANDERSSON, T. and BOYER, M. 1976, *Bilingual Schooling in the United States: History, Rationale, Implications and Planning*. Detroit, Michigan: Blaine Ethridge-Books.

ASERAPPA, J.P. 1962, *New Territories Annual Report 1961–62*. Hong Kong: The Government Printer.

——1964, *New Territories Annual Report 1963–64*. Hong Kong: The Government Printer.

ASH, R. 1978, First language teaching in a foreign environment. In *Mother Tongue Teaching and the Asian Community. Occasional Paper 2*. Southhall, Middlesex: SCOPE Communications.

Association of Northern California Chinese Schools (not dated). *Association of Northern California Chinese Schools 1984–1985*. California: Association of Northern California Chinese Schools.

BAISH, B.L. *et al.* 1986, *Working Group on the Collection of Educational Statistics on an Ethnic Basis. Report April 1986*. London: Department of Education and Science.

BAKER, C. 1988, *Key Issues in Bilingualism and Bilingual Education*. Clevedon, England: Multilingual Matters.

BAKER, H. 1964, Clan organization and its role in village affairs: some differences between single-clan and multiple-clan villages. *Aspects of Social Organization in the New Territories*. Royal Asiatic Society Hong Kong Branch, Weekend Symposium, 9th–10th May, 1964.

——1966, The five great clans of the New Territories. *Journal of the Hong Kong Branch of the Royal Asiatic Society* 6, 25–47.

——1968, *A Chinese Lineage Village: Sheung Shui*. London: Frank Cass & Co. Ltd.

——1981, The background to the Chinese in Britain. In *Teaching Chinese Children: a Teacher's Guide*. London: Nuffield Foundation.

BAKER, K.A. and DEKANTER, A.A. 1983, Federal policy and the effectiveness of bilingual education. In Keith A. BAKER and Adriana A. DEKANTER (eds) *Bilingual Education: A Reappraisal of Federal Policy*. Lexington, Massachusetts: Lexington Books.

BARTH, F. 1969, *Ethnic Groups and Boundaries: The Social Organization of Cultural Differences*. Boston: Little, Brown.

BEARDSMORE, H.B. 1986, *Bilingualism: Basic Principles*. Avon, England: Multilingual Matters Ltd.

BELL, S.R. 1986, The 'new' immigration and social education. *Social Education* (March) 50(3), 170–171.

BENEDICT, R. 1935, *Patterns of Culture*. London: Kegan Paul Ltd.

BERRIDGE, V. 1978, East end opium dens and narcotic use in Britain. *The London Journal* (May) 4(1), 3–28.

BEST, J.W. 1977, *Research in Education* (3rd. edition). Englewood Cliffs, New Jersey: Prentice-Hall, Inc.

Bilingual Education Department San Francisco United School District (SFUSD) (n.d.), *Bilingual Education and ESL Programs. Grades K-12*. San Francisco, California: Bilingual Education Department San Francisco Unified School District.

Bilingual Education Office Categorical Support Programs Division 1985, *Legal Requirements for the Implementation of State Bilingual Programs*. Sacramento, California: California State Department of Education.

BIRMAN, B.F. and GINSBURG, A.L. 1983, Introduction: Addressing the needs of language-minority children. In Keith A. BAKER and Adriana A. DEKANTER (eds) *Bilingual Education: A Reappraisal of Federal Policy*. Lexington, Massachusetts: Lexington Books.

BOLTON, E. 1979, Education in a multi-racial group. *Trends in Education* 4, 3–7.

BORG, W. AND GALL, M. 1979, *Educational Research: An Introduction* (3rd. edition). New York: Longman.

BOYD, M. 1971, The Chinese in New York, California, and Hawaii: a study of socioeconomic differences. *Phylon* (Summer), 198–206.

BRAND, D. 1987, The new whiz kids: why Asian Americans are doing so well, and what it costs them. *The Time*, August 31, 1987.

BRIM, J.A. 1970, *Local Systems and Modernizing Change in the New Territories of Hong Kong* (Ph.D. thesis). Michigan: University Microfilms.

BRISK, M. AND WURZEL, J. 1979, An integrated bilingual curriculum model. *NABE (National Association for Bilingual Education) Journal* (Winter) 3(2), 39–51.

BROADY, M. 1952, *The Chinese Family in Liverpool: Some Aspects of Acculturation* (unpublished MA thesis). University of Liverpool.

——1955, The social adjustment of Chinese immigrants in Liverpool. *Social Review* 3, 65–75.

BROOK, M. 1980, The 'mother tongue' issue in Britain: cultural diversity or control? *British Journal of Sociology of Education* 1(3), 237–253.

BRUCE, R. 1986, *Cantonese*. New York: David McKay Company Inc.

Bureau of Bilingual Education New York State Department of Education 1987, *Multilingual Multicultural* (Spring) 9(1).

BURGESS, R.G. 1982, *Field Research: A Sourcebook and Field Manual*. London: George Allen & Unwin.

——1985, *Field Methods in the Study of Education*. London: The Falmer Press.

California State Department of Education 1984, *Bilingual-Crosscultural Teacher-Aides: A Resource Guide*. Sacramento, California: State Department of Education.

CATER, J. 1951, *Annual Departmental Report by the Registrar of Cooperative Societies and Director of Marketing for the Financial Year 1950–51*. Hong Kong: The Government Printer.

Central Statistical Office 1986, *Social Trends 16*. London: Her Majesty's Stationery Office (HMSO).

Centre for Educational Research and Innovation (CERI) 1987, *Immigrants' Children At School*. Paris: Organisation for Economic Co-operation and Development.

Centre for Information on Language Teaching and Research (CILT) 1975, *Less Commonly Taught Languages: Resources and Problems*. London: CILT.

——1976, *Bilingualism and British Education: The Dimensions of Diversity*. London: CILT.

——1986, *Language and Culture Guide 4: Chinese*. London: CILT.

CHAN, E. 1983, *Needs of the Chinese Community in Lothian. A Report by Lothian Community Relations Council*. Lothian: Lothian Community Relations Council.

CHAN, K.S. and TSANG, S.L. 1983, Overview of the educational progress of Chinese Americans. In Don T. NAKANISHI and Marsha HIRANO-NAKANISHI (eds) *The Education of Asian and Pacific Americans: Historical Perspectives and Prescriptions for the Future*. Phoenix: The Oryx Press.

CHANG, F. 1934, An accommodation program for second generation Chinese. *Sociology and Social Research* (July-August), 541–582.

CHANG, P.M. 1983, *Continuity and Change: A Profile of Chinese Americans*. New York: Vantage Press.

CHANG, R. and CHANG, M.S. 1978, *Speaking of Chinese*. New York: W.W. Norton & Company, Inc.

CHANN, V.Y.F. 1976a, *Conference on Chinese in Scotland. May 1976*. London: Hong Kong Government Office (Unpublished paper).

——1976b, *The social and educational background of Hong Kong immigrants in Britain*. Talk at a conference organised by the National Association for multi-racial education in Glasgow in 1976. London: Hong Kong Government Office (Unpublished paper).

——1982, *Chinese Mother Tongue Teaching in the United Kingdom*. London: Hong Kong Government Office (Unpublished paper).

——1984, *Paper to National Conference on Chinese Families in Britain. 'The Silent Minority'*. The Report of the Fourth National Conference on the Chinese Community in Great Britain, November 1982. Huddersfield: National Children's Centre (NCC).

CHAO, Y.R. 1969, *The language problems of Chinese children in America*. New Jersey: Princeton University, N.J. Chinese Linguistic Project (ERIC microfiche: ED 026642).

CHEN, J. 1980, *The Chinese of America*. San Francisco, California: Harper & Row, Publishers.

CHEN, M. 1964, *Intelligence and Bilingualism as Independent Variates in a Study of Junior High School Students of Chinese Descent* (Ed.D dissertation). University of California, Berkeley.

CHEN, P.N. 1970, The Chinese community in Los Angeles. *Social Casework* (December) 51, 591–598.

CHENG, K.M. 1981, *They Like to Stay Apart from Us. A Study into the Chinese Community in the United Kingdom* (B.A. dissertation). (University not known. Available at the Hong Kong Government Office in London.)

CHENG, K.T. 1986, Ten years to grow a tree but a hundred years to educate a person. *Chinese Central High School Special Journal for the 1986 Graduation*. San Francisco, California: Chinese Central High School.

CHEUNG, W.C.H. 1975, *The Chinese Way: A Social Study of the Hong Kong Chinese Community in a Yorkshire City* (M. Phil. thesis). University of York, Department of Social Administration and Social Work.

CHIN, I.S.K. 1972, The Chinese in New York City. *Chinese–Americans: School and Community Problems*. Chicago, Illinois: Integrated Education Associates.

CHIN, L. 1972, Chinese and Public School Teaching. *Chinese–Americans: School and Community Problems*. Chicago, Illinois: Integrated Education Associates.

CHIN, W.T. and SIMSOVA, S. 1982, *Library Needs of Chinese in London*. London: School of Librarianship and Information Studies of the Polytechnic of North London.

The China Journal 1935, Chinese school in London. *The China Journal* 22(1), 46.

Chinatown Planning Council 1985, *A 20th Anniversary Journal of Mainstream Activity*. New York, New York: Chinatown Planning Council.

Chinese Action Group and Quaker Community Relations Committee (CAG & QCRC) 1979, *Chinese in the UK*. Conference (London) December 1978. A Report of the Proceedings of the Conference with Additional Papers on Nationality, Education, Bibliography and Statistics. London: Commission For Racial Equality.

Chinese Bilingual Pilot Program ESEA Title VII San Francisco Unified School District (n.d.). *Bibliography of Project Developed Materials*. San Francisco, California: SFUSD.

Chinese Central High School 1986, *Special Journal for the 1986 Graduation*. San Francisco, California: Chinese Central High School.

Chinese Chamber of Commerce (UK) 1980, *Journal of Chinese Chamber of Commerce (UK) Vol. 1*. London: Chinese Chamber of Commerce (UK).

Chinese Confucius Temple of Los Angeles 1984, *Special Journal in Commemoration of the 32th Anniversary of the Chinese Confucius Temple of Los Angeles and the Birthday of Confucius*. Los Angeles, California: Chinese Confucius Temple of Los Angeles.

Chinese Information and Advice Centre (CIAC) 1984, *Annual Report 83/84*. London: CIAC.

——1985a, *Annual Report 84/85*. London: CIAC.

——1985b, *The Chinese Community in Britain*. A report of the conference held at Conway Hall, London on March 30, 1985. London: CIAC.

CHIU T.N. and So, C.L. 1983, *A Geography of Hong Kong*. Hong Kong: Oxford University of Press.

CHU, T.C. 1987, Planning for a bilingual (Chinese and English) school to educate overseas Chinese children. *The Peimei News* (Chinese newspaper published in New York) May 13, 1987.

CHUN, K.T. 1980, The myth of Asian American success and its educational ramifications. *IRCD Bulletin* 15 (1 & 2), 1–12.

CLOUGH, E. and QUARMBY, J. 1978, *A Public Library Service for Ethnic Minorities in Great Britain*. London: The Library Association.

COLLINS, S. 1957, A Chinese community in Lancashire. In S. COLLINS (ed.) *Coloured Minorities in Britain*. London: Lutterworth.

Commission for Racial Equality (CRE) 1978, *Ethnic Minorities in Britain: Statistical Background*. London: CRE.

——1980, *The EEC's Directive on the Education of Children of Migrant Workers and Its Implications for the Education of Children from Ethnic Minority Groups in the UK*. London: CRE.

——1981, *Mother Tongue Teaching Conference Report 1980*. Sponsored jointly by the Commission for Racial Equality and Bradford College, 9–11 September, 1980. London: CRE.

——1982, *Ethnic Minority Community Languages: A Statement*. London: CRE.

Community Educational Services (n.d.), *The Key is in Action. We Hope You'll Become Involved* . . . (Pamphlet). San Francisco, California: Community Educational Services.

Community Relations Commission (CRC) 1975, *The Chinese Community in the UK*. London: CRC.

——1976, CRC backs EEC on mother tongue. *Education and Community Relations* (March/April) 6(2), 1–2.

COMRIE, B. 1981, *Language Universals and Linguistic Typology*. Oxford: Basil Blackwell.

COOLIDGE, M.R. 1969, *Chinese Immigration*. New York: Arno Press and the New York Times.

COON, C.S. 1954, *The Story of Man*. New York: Alfred A. Knopf, Inc.

CRANE, A. 1975, Practical needs. *Less Commonly Taught Languages: Resources and Problems*. London: CILT.

CREEL, H.G. 1954, *Chinese Thought from Confucius to Mao Tse-tung*. London: Eyre & Spottisorde.

CRISSMAN, L.W. 1967, The segmentary structure of urban overseas Chinese communities. *Man* 2, 185–204.

Cumberland Presbyterian Chinese School (n.d.), *Cumberland Presbyterian Chinese School Summer Classes Enrolment Notice* (Pamphlet). San Francisco, California: Cumberland Presbyterian Chinese School.

CUMMINS, J. 1978, Educational implications of mother tongue maintenance in minority language groups. *Canadian Modern Language Review* 34, 395–416.

——1979/80, The language and culture issue in the education of minority language children. *Interchange* 10, 72–88.

——1980, The entry and exit fallacy in bilingual education. *NABE Journal* 4, 25–60.

——1981, *Bilingualism and Minority-Language Children*. Toronto, Ontario: The Ontario Institute for Studies in Education.

——1981, The role of primary language development in promoting educational success for language minority students. In *Schooling and Language Minority Students: A Theoretical Framework*. Los Angeles, California: Evaluation, Dissemination & Assessment Center, California State University.

——1983, *Heritage language education: a literature review*. Toronto: Ontario Institute for Studies in Education (ERIC microfiche: ED 233588).

CUMMINS, M.H. and SLADE, C. 1979, *Writing the Research Paper: A Guide and Sourcebook*. Boston: Houghton Mifflin.

DAVIS, A. 1978, Language and culture in a multi-cultural society. In Trevor Corner (ed.) *Education in Multicultural Societies*. Thirteenth Annual Conference of the Comparative Education Society in Europe (British Section), Univerisity of Edinburgh, September 1978.

DAVIS, A.M. *et al.* 1982a, Mother tongue: a political issue? In *Issues in Race and Education* 35, 1–2.

——1982b, Mother tongue: education issues. In *Issues in Race and Education* 35, 3–4.

DEFRANCIS, J. 1984, *The Chinese Language: Facts and Fantasy*. Honolulu, Hawaii: University of Hawaii Press.

DEMUTH, C. 1978, *Immigration: A Brief Guide to the Numbers Game*. London: The Runnymede Trust.

DENT, H.C. 1968, *The Education Act 1944 (12th edition)*. London: University of London Press Ltd.

Department of Education and Science (DES) 1966, *The Education of Immigrants (Circular 7/65)*. Circulars and Administrative Memoranda. London: HMSO.

——1967, *Children and Their Primary Schools* (Plowden Report). London: HMSO.

——1971a, *The Education of Immigrants: Education Survey 13*. London: HMSO.

——1971b, *Potential and Progress in a Second Culture*. London: HMSO.

——1972, *The Continuing Needs of Immigrants: Education Survey 14*. London: HMSO.

——1975, *A Language For Life* (Bullock Report). London: HMSO.

——1977, *Education in Schools: A Consultative Document* (Green Paper). London: HMSO.

——1982, *Directive of the Council of the European Community in the Education of the Children of Migrant Workers (Circular 5/81)*. Circulars and Administrative Memoranda. London: HMSO.

——1983, *The Education System of England and Wales*. London: HMSO.

——1984, *Mother Tongue Teaching in School and Community*. London: HMSO.

——1985, *Education For All: The Report of the Committee of Inquiry into the Education of Children from Ethnic Minority Groups* (Swann Report). London: HMSO.

———1987, *The National Curriculum 5–16: A Consultative Document*. London: HMSO.

———1988, *Modern Languages in the School Curriculum: A Statement of Policy*. London: HMSO.

DERRICK, J. 1967, *English for the Children of Immigrants*. London: HMSO.

———1976, Politics of language. In the *Times Educational Supplement*, 13 February, 1976.

———1977, *Language Needs of Minority Group Children*. Slough, Berks: National Foundation for Educational Research in England and Wales.

DICKER, L.M. 1979, *The Chinese in San Francisco: A Pictorial History*. New York: Dover Publications.

DORN, A. and TROYNA, B. 1982, Multiracial education and the politics of decision-making. *Oxford Review of Education* 8(2), 175–185.

DUMMETT, A. 1982, *The National Act — Its Implication for School Students*. ACE Information Sheet. London: Advisory Centre for Education.

Education Department (Hong Kong) 1972, *Annual Summary 1971–1972*. Hong Kong: The Government Printer.

EDWARDS, V. 1984, Language policy in multicultural Britain. In J. EDWARDS (ed.) *Linguistic Minorities, Policies and Pluralism*. London: Academic Press.

———1991, The Welsh speech community. In S. ALLADINA & V. EDWARDS (ed.) *Multilingualism in the British Isles The Older Mother Tongues & Europe*. London: Longman.

ELLIOTT, P. 1981, *Library Needs of Children Attending Self-Help Mother-Tongue Schools in London*. Research Report No.6. London: The Polytechnic of North London School of Librarianship.

ENGLE, P.L. 1975, Language medium in early school years for minority language groups. *Review of Educational Research* (Spring) 45, 284–310.

EPSTEIN, N. 1977, *Language, Ethnicity and the Schools*. Washington, D.C.: The Institute for Educational Leadership.

Equal Opportunities Commission 1977, '*Education in Schools — A Consultative Document*'. *The Response of the EOC*. Manchester: Equal Opportunities Commission.

E.C. (European Commission) Pilot Project 1987, *E.C. Pilot Project: Community Languages in the Secondary Curriculum. Report 1984–1987. The Inclusion of Community Languages in the Normal Curricular Arrangements of Local Education Authority Maintained Schools in England and Wales*. London: Institute of Education University of London.

EEC Sponsored Pilot Project 1979, '*Mother Tongue and Culture*' *in Bedfordshire. First External Evaluation Report, January 1978–September 1978*. [Cambridge]: Cambridge Institute of Education.

———1980, '*Mother Tongue and Culture*' *in Bedfordshire. Second External Evaluation Report, September 1978 – September 1979*. Cambridge: Cambridge Institute of Education.

Evaluation, Dissemination and Assessment Center (EDAC) (n.d.), *Asian and Pacific Island Curricular Materials and Professional Development Materials (Catalog)*. Los Angeles, California: EDAC, School of Education California State University.

EVANS, K.M. 1968, *Planning Small Scale Research*. Windsor: The National Foundation for Educationl Research in England and Wales.

FAN, C.Y. 1981, *The Chinese Language School of San Francisco in Relation to Family Integration and Cultural Identity*. Nankang, Taipei, Republic of China: Institute of American Cultural Academia Sinica.

FESSLER, L.W. 1983, *Chinese in America: Stereotyped Past, Changing Present*. New York: Vantage Press.

FILLMORE, L.W. 1980, Learning a second language: Chinese children in American classroom. In J.E. ALATIS (ed.) *Current Issues in Bilingual Education: the 31st Annual Georgetown University Round Table in Languages and Linguistics*. Washington, D.C.: Georgetown University.

——1982, Language minority students and school participation. What kind of English is needed? *Journal of Education* (Spring) 164(2), 143–156.

FISHMAN, J.A. 1966, *Language Loyalty in the United States*. London: Mouton & Co.

——1970, *Readings in the Sociology of Language*. The Hague: Mouton.

——1980, Bilingualism and biculturalism. *Journal of Multilingual and Multicultural Development* 1(1), 3–14.

FISHMAN, J.A. and LOVAS, J. 1970, Bilingual education in sociolinguistic perspective. *TESOL Quarterly* 4, 3.

FITCHETT, N. 1976, *Chinese Children in Derby*. (Publisher and place of publication not known).

FONG, J. 1971, A letter concerning Chinese school . . . *East/West* July 28, 1971.

——1972, Don't force your kid to go to Chinese school. *East/West* March 29, 1972.

FONG, V. 1976, *Planning for and Development of the Chinese Community in London* (thesis, degree not known). University of California, Department of Architecture.

FOX, L.W. *et al.* 1978a, *Bilingual–Bicultural Program, District 2, 1977–78. Final Report, Title VII*. New York, New York: Community School District 2 (ERIC microfiche: ED 181123).

——1978b, *Final report ESEA Title VII: Program for Achievements in Chinese, English and Spanish (PACES) 1977–78*. (ERIC microfiche: ED 181125).

FREEDMAN, M. 1979, *The Study of Chinese Society: Essays by M. Freedman*. Stanford, California: Stanford University Press.

FU-MO, M.C. 1986, Problems faced by the Chinese schools. *Southern California Council of Chinese Schools 10th Anniversary Special Journal*, 63–64.

FUNG, C.N. 1984, Effects of racism on Chinese kids in school. *Contemporary Issues in Geography and Education* (Spring) 1(2), 41.

FUNG, Y.L. 1947, *The Spirit of Chinese Philosophy*. Kegan Paul, Trench: Truber & Co.

GANS, H.J. 1982, The participant observer as a human being: observations on the personal aspects of fieldwork. In Robert G. BURGESS (ed.) *Field Research: A Sourcebook and Field Manual*. London: George Allen & Unwin.

GARCIA, J.O. and ESPINOSA, R.W. 1976, *Major Student Ethnic Minority Group Concentrations in the California Public Schools*. San Diego, California: School of Education, San Diego University.

GARVEY, A. and JACKSON, B. 1975, *Chinese Children*. Research and action project into the needs of Chinese children. Cambridge: National Educational Research and Development Trust.

GEIGER, T. and GEIGER, F.M. 1975, *The Development Progress of Hong Kong and Singapore*. London: The Macmillan Press Ltd.

General Register Office 1956, *Census 1951: England and Wales General Tables*. London: HMSO.

——1966, *Census 1961: Great Britain Summary Tables*. London: HMSO.

GIBBONS, J. 1982, The issues of the language of instruction in the lower forms of Hong Kong secondary schools. *Journal of Multilingual and Multicultural Development* 3(2), 117–128.

GOLLNICK, D.M. and CHINN, P.C. 1983, *Multicultural Education in a Pluralistic Society*. St. Louis, Missouri: The C.V. Mosby Company.

GORDON, P. and KLUG, F. 1985, *British Immigration Control: A Brief Guide*. London: Runnymede Trust.

Great Britain 1979, *Race Relations Act 1976*. London: HMSO.

Great Britain. Home Office 1974, *Immigration Statistics 1973*. London: HMSO.

——1975, *Immigration Statistics 1974*. London: HMSO.

——1986, *Home Office Circular No. 72/1986: Section 11 of the Local Government Act 1966*. London: HMSO.

Great Britain. Office of Population, Census and Surveys (GB. OPCS) 1974, *Census 1971 Great Britain Country of Birth Tables*. London: HMSO.

——1982, *Labour Force Survey 1981*. London: HMSO.

——1983a, *Census 1981 National Report Great Britain Part II*. London: HMSO.

——1983b, *Census 1981 Country of Birth Great Britain*. London: HMSO.

——1986, *Labour Force Survey 1983 and 1984*. London: HMSO.

——1987, *Labour Force Survey 1985*. London: HMSO.

Great Britain. Parliament. House of Commons. Home Affairs Committee (GB. P. H. of C. HAC) 1985, Second report from the Home Affairs Committee, Session 1984–5. *Chinese Community in Britain* (Vol.1–3). London: HMSO.

Greater London Council Department of Planning and Transportation Intelligence Unit 1974, *1971 Census Data in London's Overseas-Born Population and Their Children*. London: Greater London Council (GLC).

Greater London Council 1983, *1981 Census Data for London: Statistical Series No. 25*. London: GLC.

GRIFFITHS, J. 1982, *Asian Links*. Record of a broadcast series. London: CRE.

GRUBER, K. 1985, *Encyclopedia of Associations*. Detroit, Michigan: Gale Research Company.

GUTHRIE, G.P. 1985, *A School Divided: An Ethnography of Bilingual Education in a Chinese Community*. Hillsdale, New Jersey: Lawrence Erlbaum Associates.

HANS, N. 1949, *Comparative Education*. London: Routledge and Kegan Paul Ltd.

Haringey Chinese Group (HCG) 1985, *Annual Report 1983–85*. London: HCG.

——1986a, *Annual Report 1986*. London: HCG.

——1986b, *A Survey of the Needs of the Chinese living in Haringey* (unpublished report). London: HCG.

HARTFORD, B. *et al.* 1982, *Issues in International Bilingual Education: The Role of the Vernacular*. New York: Plenum Press.

HAYDON, C. 1980, Mother tongue teaching: the outsider. *The Times Educational Supplement* February 22, 1980.

HAYES, J. 1964, A mixed community of Hakka and Cantonese on Lantau island.

Aspects of Social Organization in the New Territories. Royal Asiatic Society Hong Kong Branch, Weekend Symposium 9th–10th May 1964.

HMSO 1965, *Immigrants from the Commonwealth.* London: HMSO.

——1966, *Local Government Act.* London: HMSO.

——1977, *Select Committee on Race Relations and Immigration, Session 1972–3: Education.* London: HMSO.

——1979, *Statutes in Force: Education.* London: HMSO.

HERNANDEZ-CHAVEZ, E. 1978, Language maintenance, bilingual education, and philosophies of bilingualism in the United States. In J.E. ALATIS (ed.) *Georgetown Universtiy Round Table on Language and Linguistics 1978: International Dimensions of Bilingual Education.* Washington, D.C.: Georgetown University Press.

HEYER, V. 1953, *Patterns of Scoial Organization in New York's Chinatown* (Ph.D dissertation). Ann Arbor: University Microfilms.

HICKEY, T. 1991, The Irish speech community. In S. ALLADINA & V. EDWARDS (ed.) *Multilingualism in the British Isles The Older Mother Tongues & Europe.* London: Longman.

HO, K.W. 1977, *Report on Fieldwork Placement with Westminster Community Relations Council from 18th October 1976 to 14th January 1977* (unpublished paper).

HOLMES, B. 1965, *Problems in Education: A Comparative Approach.* London: Routledge & Kegan Paul.

——1979, *International Guide to Education System.* Paris, France: UNESCO (United Nations Educational, Scientific and Cultural Organisation).

——1981, *Comparative Education: Some Considerations of Method.* London: George Allen & Unwin.

——1985, The problem (solving) approach and national character. In K. WATSON and R. WILSON (eds) *Contemporary Issues in Comparative Education.* London: Croom Helm Ltd.

Hong Kong Government 1961, *Hong Kong 1960.* England: HMSO.

——1965, *Hong Kong 1964.* England: HMSO.

——1974, *Secondary Education in Hong Kong over the Next Decade.* Hong Kong: The Government Printer.

——1984, *A Draft Agreement between the Government of the United Kingdom of Great Britain and Northern Ireland and the Government of the People's Republic of China of the Future of Hong Kong.* Hong Kong: The Government Printer.

Hong Kong Government Office (London) 1985, *List of Chinese school/class in the United Kingdom* (pamphlet). London: Hong Kong Government Office.

HOY, W. 1942, *The Chinese Six Companies.* San Francisco, California: California Chinese Historical Society.

Inner London Education Authority (ILEA) 1975, *Some Life Style of Chinese People from Hong Kong and Singapore.* London: ILEA.

——1977, *Multi-Ethnic Education.* Report (6.10.77) by Education Officer. London: ILEA.

——1981, *Language in the Primary School.* London: ILEA Learning Materials Service.

——1982, *Bilingualism in the ILEA — The Educational Implications of the 1981 Language Census* (report). London: ILEA.

——1983a, *The Green Book.* London: ILEA.

——1983b, *Your Guide to the Inner London Education Authority*. London: ILEA.

——1986, *Review of Languages Education*. London: ILEA.

Ilea Research & Statistics 1979, *Report on the 1978 Census of those ILEA Pupils for whom English was not a First Language*. London: ILEA.

——1982, *1981 Language Census*. London: ILEA.

IP, M. 1983, Cooperative roles of the home and school in maintaining ancestral languages and resolving cultural conflicts. In J. CUMMINS (ed.) *Heritage Language Education: Issues and Directions*. Canada: Minister of Supply and Services.

IRIZARRY, R.A. 1980, *Seward Park High School Chinese Bilingual-Bicultural Program. ESEA Title VII. Final Evaluation Report 1979–1980*. Brooklyn, New York: New York Office of Educational Evaluation New York City Board of Education (ERIC Microfiche: ED 202934).

JACKSON, B. and GARVEY, A. 1974, Chinese children in Britain. *New Society* 30(626), 9–12.

JACOB, J.B. 1975, Continuity and Change in the Contemporary Chinese Family. *Asian Survey* 15(10), 882–891.

JEFFERY, G.B. 1949, Problems of independence. *Year Book of Education 1949*. London: Evans Brothers Ltd.

JENNINGS, J. and LOGAN, D.W. 1953, *A Report on the University of Hong Kong*. Hong Kong: Cathay Press.

JONES, D. 1979, The Chinese in Britain: origin and development of a community. *New Community* (Winter) 7(3), 397–402.

——1980, Chinese schools in Britain: a minority's response to its own needs. *Trends in Education* (Spring), 15–18.

JONES, D. 1987, *Hong Kong as a Partner in World Trade*. Hong Kong: The Hong Kong Government Printer.

JONES, I. 1979, Some cultural and linguistic considerations affecting the learning of English by Chinese in Britain. *English Language Teaching Journal* 34(1), 55–61.

JONES, P.E. 1971, *Comparative Education: Purpose and Method*. St. Lucia, Queensland: University of Queensland Press.

JUNG, R.K. 1972, The Chinese language school in the U.S. *School and Society* (Summer), 309–312.

KHAN, V. 1976, Provision by minorities for language maintenance. *Bilingualism and British Education*. London: CILT.

——1977, *Bilingualism and Linguistic Minorities in Britain: Developments, Perspectives*. Briefing paper. London: The Runnymede Trust.

——1978, *Mother-Tongue Teaching and the Asian Community*. Occasional Paper 2. Southhall, Middlesex: SCOPE Communications.

KIANG, W.H. 1948, *The Chinese Student Movement*. Morningside Heights, New York: King's Crown Press.

KLEIMAN, D. 1981, A 'one-room school' teaches a new life. *The New York Times* March 4, 1981.

KLOSS, H. 1971, *Laws and Legal Documents relating to Problems on Bilingual Education in the United States* (ERIC microfiche: ED 044703).

——1977, *The American Bilingual Tradition*. Rowley, Massachusetts: Newbury House Publishers, Inc.

KRAUSZ, E. 1971, *Ethnic Minorities in Britain*. London: MacGibbon & Kee.

KUNG, S.W. 1962, *Chinese in American Life: Some Aspects of their History,*

Status, Problems, and Contributions. Seattle: University of Washington Press.

Kuo, C.L. 1977, *Social and Political Change in New York's Chinatown: The Role of Voluntary Associations.* New York: Praeger Publishers.

Kuo, E. 1972, *Bilingual Socialization of Preschool Chinese Children in the Twin Cities Area* (Ph.D. dissertation). University of Minnesota.

Kuo, E. 1974, The family and bilingual socialization: a sociolinguistic study of a sample of Chinese children in the US. *Journal of Social Psychology* (April) 92(2), 181–191.

Kwok, I. 1980, *The Relationship of Language Orientation and Racial/Ethnic Attitude among Chinese Primary Grade Children.* Outstanding Dissertations in Bilingual Education 1980. Rosslyn, Virginia: National Clearinghouse for Bilingual Education.

Kysel, F. 1983, *1983 Language Census.* London: ILEA.

——1985, *1985 Language Census.* London: ILEA.

——1987, *Ethnic Background and Examination Results 1985 and 1986.* London: ILEA.

Ladlow, D.E. 1980, *Suggestions and Background Information for Teachers of Chinese Children.* Mimeograph.

Lai, H.M. 1971a, The Chinese and public education in San Francisco, Part I. *East/West* August 18, 1971.

——1971b, The Chinese and public education in San Francisco, Part II. *East/West* September 1, 1971.

——1976, Why did the Chinese migrate? Exerpt from 'Blood and sweat in the Golden Mountains.' *East/West* January 1, 1976.

Lai, K.C. 1975, *Problems facing Chinese Immigrants from Liverpool.* Unpublished fieldwork report for the degree of Diploma in Applied Social Studies, University of Hull.

Lai, L. 1975, *Chinese Families in London — A Study into their Social Needs* (unpublished MA thesis). Brunel University.

Lai, S. 1986, My languages. *SiYu* (Chinese community magazine in Manchester) (September) 14, 27–28.

Landes, R. 1965, *Culture in American Education: Anthropological Approaches to Minority and Dominant Groups in Schools.* New York: John Wiley and Sons, Inc.

Lang, O. 1946, *Chinese Family and Society.* New Haven: Yale University Press.

Langton, P. 1979, *Chinese Children in British Schools.* CUES (Centre for Urban Educational Studies) Occasional Paper No. 2. London: ILEA.

Lau, S. 1972, *Elementary Cantonese.* Vol. I. Hong Kong: Hong Kong Government Printer.

Leary, M. 1971, San Francisco's Chinatown. In J.C. Stone and D.P. DeNevi (ed.) *Teaching Multi-cultural Populations.* New York: Van Nostrand Reinhold Company.

Lee, R.H. 1956, The Chinese abroad. *Phylon* (3rd Quarter), 257-270.

——1960, *The Chinese in the United States of America.* Hong Kong: Hong Kong University Press.

Lehmann, W.P. (ed.) 1975, *Language and Linguistics in the People's Republic of China.* Austin & London: University of Texas Press.

Lester, J.D. 1980, *Writing Research Papers: A Complete Guide* (3rd. edition). Glenview, Illinois: Scott, Foresman and Company.

LEUNG, N. 1977, Bilingual education at Seward Park High School. *The China Tribune* (New York local Chinese newspaper) December 2, 1977, 4.

LEVINE, J. 1987, *The Establishment of the Further Professional Option 'Teaching a Community Language' within the University of London Institute of Education PGCE course*. Report of a working party University of London Institute of Education. London: The University of London Institute of Education.

LEWIS, E.G. 1970, Immigrants — their languages and development. *Trends in Education* 19, 25–32.

LEWIS, M.M. 1963, *Language, Thought and Personality in Infancy and Childhood*. London: Harrap.

LI, A.M. 1983, *A Study of the Chinese in London, their Backgrounds, Health Problems and Health Educational Needs* (unpublished diploma project). Polytechnic of the South Bank.

LIELL, P. and SAUNDERS, J.B. 1986, *The Law of Education* (9th edition). London: Butterworths.

Linguistic Minorities Project 1983, *Linguistic Minorities in England. A report by the Linguistic Minorities Project for the Department of Education and Science*. London: University of London Institute of Education.

LITTLE, A. and WILLEY, R. 1981, *Multi-ethnic Education: The Way Forward*. Schools Council Pamphlet 18. London: Schools Council.

LIU, C. 1975, Record-breaking enrollment at New York Chinese School. *East/West* October 1, 1975.

LLANES, J. 1983, Issues and questions in the study of bilingual education in the United States. *Bilingual Education Paper Series* (March) 6(8). Los Angeles, California: EDAC, California State University.

LOMAS, G.B. 1973, *Census 1971 The Coloured Population of Great Britain: Preliminary Report*. London: The Runnymede Trust.

London Kung Ho Association 1985, *London Kung Ho Association Fund-Raising Campaign for the Chinese Education Trust & Purchase of School Property Special Journal*. London: London Kung Ho Association.

LOO, C. 1985, The biliterate ballot controversy: language acquisition and cultural shift among immigrants. *International Migration Review* 19(3), 493–515.

LOUIS, K.K. 1932, Program for second generation Chinese. *Sociology and Social Research* (May–June), 455–462.

LOW, V. 1982, *The Unimpressible Race: A Century of Educational Struggle by the Chinese in San Francisco*. San Francisco, California: East/West Publishing Company, Inc.

LUE, A. 1981, *Community Work among the Chinese in London*. Talk given at the Open Day at the North London Polytechnic on Wednesday, November 4, 1981 to highlight the library needs of the Chinese community.

LUKE, K.K. and RICHARDS, J.C. 1982, English in Hong Kong: functions and status. *English World-Wide: A Journal of Varieties of English* 3(1), 47–64.

LUM, J.B. 1971, *An Effectiveness Study of English as a Second Language (ESL) and Chinese Bilingual Methods* (Ph.D. dissertation). University of California, Berkeley.

LYMAN, S.M. 1974, *Chinese Americans*. New York: Random House.

LYNN, I.L. 1982, *The Chinese Community in Liverpool: Their Unmet Needs with respect to Education, Social Welfare and Housing*. Liverpool: Merseyside Area Profile Group.

MA, M. 1967, *The Riot in Hong Kong*. Hong Kong: Sky Horse Book Co.

MALCOLM, A.H. 1969, Influx of Chinese spurs educators. *The New York Times* November 16, 1969.

MALLINSON, V. 1975, *An Introduction to the Study of Comparative Education* (4th edition). London: Heinemann.

MAY, J.P. 1978, The Chinese in Britain. In C. HOLMES (ed.) *Immigrants and' Minorities in British Society*. London: George Allen & Unwin.

MCCANDLESS, B.R. *et al*. 1956, The relationship of anxiety in children to performance is a complex learning task. *Child Development* 27(3), 333–337.

MCLEAN, M. 1983, Education and cultural diversity in Britain: recent immigrant groups. *Comparative Education* 19(2), 179–192.

MACDONALD, I.V. 1977, *Race Relations: The New Law*. London: Butterworths.

MACKINNON, K. 1991, The Gaelic speech community. In S. ALLADINA & V. EDWARDS (ed.) *Multilingualism in the British Isles the Older Mother Tongues & Europe*. London: Longman.

MACQUOWN, N.A. 1982, *Language, Culture and Education*. Standford, California: Stanford University Press.

MELTZER, M. 1980, *The Chinese Americans*. New York: Thomas Y. Crowell.

MILLER, J. 1983, *Many Voices: Bilingualism, Culture and Education*. London: Routledge & Kegan Paul.

Ministry of Education 1963, *English for Immigrants* (Pamphlet No. 43). London: HMSO.

MITCHELL, R. 1978, *Bilingual Education of Minority Language Groups in the English Speaking World: Some Research Evidence*. Seminar papers No.4. Stirling: University of Stirling, Department of Education.

MOORE, R.L. 1981, *Modern and Westernization in Hong Kong: Patterns of Culture Change in an Urban Setting* (Ph.D. thesis). USA: University Microfilms International.

MORSE, H.B. 1918, *The International Relations of the Chinese Empire*. London: Longman, Green and Co.

MOSER, C.A. and KALTON, G. 1971, *Survey Methods in Social Investigation* (2nd edition). London: Heinemann Educational Books Litmited.

Mother Tongue Project 1984, *Mother Tongue Colloquium. Papers presented to the European Commission, London 26–29 March 1984*. London: Schools Council.

MOULY, G.J. 1970, *The Science of Educational Research*. New York: Van Nostrand Reinhold Company.

MUCKLEY, R.L. 1971, After childhood, then what? An overview of Ethnic Language Retention (ELRET) Programs in the United States (ERIC microfiche: ED 061808).

MYRDAL, G. 1944, *An American Dilemma: The Negro Problem and Modern Democracy*. New York & London: Harper.

NACHMIAS, D. and NACHMIAS, C. 1976, *Research Methods in the Social Sciences*. London: Edward Arnold.

National Association for Multi-Cultural Education (NAME) 1985, *NAME on SWAN*. England: National Antiracist Movement in Education.

National Center for Education Statistics (NCES) 1978, *Geographic Distribution, Nativity, and Age Distribution of Language Minorities in the United States: Spring 1976. National Center for Education Statistics (NCES) Bulletin*

78 B-5. Washington, D.C.: U.S. Department of Health, Education , and Welfare (DHEW).

——1979, *Birthplace and Language Characteristics of Persons of Chinese, Japanese, Korean, Philipino, and Vietnamese Origin in the United States: Spring 1976*. *NCES Bulletin 79B-12*. Washington, D.C.: U.S. DEHW (ERIC microfiche: ED 185810).

National Children's Centre (NCC) 1979, *Report on the Third National Conference on Chinese Children in Britain, April, 1979*. Huddersfield: NCC.

——1984, *'The Silent Minority'. The Report of the Fourth National Conference on the Chinese Community in Great Britain. November, 1982*. Huddersfield: NCC.

National Education Association (NEA) of The United States 1984, *Guide to Curriculum and Cultural Materials For Teaching Asian and Pacific Islander Students*. Washington, D.C.: National Education Association.

National Educational Research and Development Trust (1977) *First National Conference on Chinese Children in Britain*. Huddersfield: NCC.

——1978, *Report of the Second National Conference on Chinese Children in Britain*. Huddersfield: NCC.

National Union of Teachers (NUT) 1977, *Education in Schools: The NUT's Response to the Recommendations in the 1977 Green Paper*. London: NUT.

——1978, *Section 11 — An NUT Report*. London: NUT.

NEE, V.G. and NEE, B. 1973, *Longtime Californ': A Documentary Study of an American Chinatown*. New York: Random House.

New Territories Development Department 1978, *Hong Kong's New Towns, Sha Tin*. Hong Kong: Public Works Department.

New York Best Chinese School 1984, *Introduction to the New York Best Chinese School 1975–1984* (pamphlet). New York: New York Best Chinese School.

New York Bilingual Educators Committee 1987, *The Ninth Annual City-Wide Chinese Parents Conference* (programme). New York: New York Bilingual Educators Committee.

New York Chinese School 1983a, *New York Chinese School Graduates Record 1983*. New York: New York Chinese School.

——1983b, *Supplement on the New York Chinese School* (pamphlet). New York: New York Chinese School.

New York Ming Yuan Chinese School 1987, *Ming Yuan Summer Day Camp 1987* (pamphlet). New York: New York Ming Yuan Chinese School.

The New York Times 1971, Schools for teaching Chinese are on rise here. *The New York Times* May 31, 1971.

NG, A. 1982, *Learning of Chinese by Chinese Immigrant Children* (unpublished B.Phil. dissertation). University of Newcastle-upon-Tyne.

NG, K.C. 1968, *The Chinese in London*. London: Oxford University Press.

NG, R. 1964, Economic life and the family. *Aspects of Social Organization in the New Territories*. Royal Asiatic Society Hong Kong Branch, Weekend Symposium 9th-10th May 1964.

NIXON, J. 1985, *A Teacher's Guide to Multicultural Education*. Oxford: Basil Blackwell.

Nuffield Foundation 1981, *Teaching Chinese Children*. London: The Nuffield Foundation.

Office of Bilingual Bicultural Education 1982, *Basic Principles for the Education of Language Minority Students: An Overview*. Sacramento, California: State Department of Education.

Office of Educational Assessment (OEA) Bilingual Education Unit 1986, *OEA Evaluation Report Project Project CHAMP 1985–1986*. New York: New York Board of Education.

OGBU, J.U. and MATUTE-BIANCHI, M.E. 1986, Understanding sociocultural factors: knowledge, identity and school adjustment. *Beyond Language: Social and Cultural Factors in Schooling Language Minority Students*. Los Angeles, California: EDAC.

OGBURN, W.F. 1964, *On Culture and Social Change*. Chicago: The University of Chicago Press.

——1973, The hypothesis of cultural lag. In A. ETZIONI & E. ETZIONI-HALEVY (eds) *Social Change:Sources, Patterns and Consequences* (2nd. edition). New York: Basic Books, Inc.

O'MALLEY, J. 1982, *Children's English and Services Study: Educational Needs Assessment for Language Minority Children with Limited English Proficiency*. Rosslyn, Virginia: National Clearinghouse For Bilingual Education.

OMOHUNDRO, J.T. and JACOBS, J.B. 1980, *Culture Change and Persistence among the Chinese*. State University of New York, Special Studies Series No. 120. Buffalo, New York: State University of New York.

O'NEIL, J. 1972, *The Role of Family and Community in the Social Adjustment of the Chinese in Liverpool* (MA thesis). Liverpool University.

ORZECHOWSKA, E. 1984, *What it means to be a Bilingual Child in Britain today*. Working paper No.4. London: Centre for Multicultural Education University of London.

OVANDO, C.J. 1983, Bilingual/bicultural education: its legacy and its future. *Phi Delta Kappan* 64(8), 564–568.

OW, Y. *et al.* 1975, *A History of the Sam Yap Benevolent Association in the United States 1850–1974*. San Francisco, California: Sam Yup Benevolent Association.

PARKER, L.L. 1978, Current perspectives. *Bilingual Education: Current Perspectives/Synthesis*. Arlington, Virginia: Center for Applied Linguistics.

PARSONS, T. 1958, Some ingredients of a general theory of formal organisation. In Andrew W. Halpin (ed.) *Administrative Theory in Education*. New York: Macmillan Company.

PAZ, E. 1980, *The Development of Bilingual Education Models*. Bilingual Education Paper Series 3(10).

The Peimei News 1986, Benefits of learning Chinese after school. *The Peimei News* (New York local Chinese newspaper) August 26, 1986.

PERREN, G.E. 1976, *Bilingualism and British Education*. London: CILT.

——1979, *Mother Tongue and Other Languages in Education*. NCLE (National Congress on Languages in Education) Papers and Reports 2. London: CILT.

PETERSON, W. 1978, Chinese and Japanese Americans. In Thomas Sowell (ed.) *Essays and Data on American Ethnic Groups*. Washington, D.C.: Urban Institute.

PHILIPS, M. 1984, Wah Mei School began to provide both remedial and enriched classes. *East/West* November 28, 1984.

POPPER, K.P. 1946, *The Open Society and its Enemy*. London: Routledge.

POTTER, J.M. 1968, *Capitalism and the Chinese Peasant Social and Economic Change in a Hong Kong Village*. Berkeley, California: University of California Press.

Public Law 95–561 1978, *The Bilingual Education Act*. Rosslyn, Virginia: InterAmerica Research Associates, National Clearinghouse for Bilingual Education.

PUREWAL, J.S. and SACHA, G.S. 1976, Mother-tongue — a Sikh view. *Education and Community Relations* (March/April) 6(2), 3.

Quaker Community Relations Committee (QCRC) 1981, *The Chinese in Britain Today*. Weekend Conference on 30 January — 1 February 1981. London: CRE.

RAMIREZ, A.G. 1985, *Bilingualism Through Schooling: Cross Cultural Education for Minority and Majority Students*. Albany, New York: State University of New York Press.

RAND, E. 1981, Bilingual education: contributing to second language programs in the elementary schools. *NCBE Forum*, (November–December) 4(9), 3–6.

REID, E. and MORAWACKA, A. 1984, *The School Language Survey of the Linguistic Minorities Project: The Data in Context. LMP/CLE Working Paper No.7*. London: Institute of Education University of London.

REISNER, E.R. 1983a, The availability of bilingual education teacher. In K.A. Baker and A. DeKanter (eds) *Bilingual Education*. Lexington, Massachusetts: Lexington Books.

——1983b, *Building Capacity and Commitment in Bilingual Education: A Practical Guide for Educators*. Final report as submitted by the Educational Policy Development Center. Jointly published by the Evaluation, Dissemination and Assessment Centers (EDACs) for Bilingual Education: Cambridge, Massachusetts: EDAC, Lesley College; Dallas, Texas: EDAC, Dallas Independent School District; Los Angeles, California: EDAC, California State University.

RIDGE, M. 1981, The new bilingualism: an American dilemma. In Martin RIDGE (ed.) *The New Bilingualism: An American Dilemma*. Los Angeles, California: University of Southern California.

ROHTER, L. 1986, 2 systems of bilingual learning, but which is better? *The New York Times* November 24, 1986.

ROSEN, H. and BURGESS, T. 1980, *Languages and Dialects of London School Children*. London: Ward Lock Educational.

The Runnymede Trust and the Radical Statistics Race Group 1980, *Britain's Black Population*. London: Heinemann Educational.

Runnymede Research Report 1985, *'Education For All': A Summary of the Swann Report on the Education of Ethnic Minorituy Children*. London: The Runnymede Trust.

St. Mary's Chinese Schools 1986, *Special Journal in Commemoration of the 65th School Anniversary*. San Francisco, California: St. Mary's Chinese School.

The San Francisco Chinese Community Citizens' Survey and Fact Finding Committee 1969, *Report of the San Francisco Chinese Community Citizens' Survey and Fact Finding Committee*. San Francisco, California: Office of Mayor.

San Francisco Unified School District (SFUSD) 1967, *Bilingual Education in the San Francisco School District*. San Francisco, California: SFUSD.

———1974, *The Chinese Bilingual Pilot Program, ESEA Title VII, 1974 Program Guide*. San Francisco, California: SFUSD (ERIC microfiche: ED 098282).

———(n.d.) *Bilingual Education Implementation Manual* (Draft). San Francisco, California: SFUSD.

SARASON, S.B. *et al.* 1960, *Anxiety in Elementary School Children*. New York: John Wiley and Sons.

SCHATZMAN, L. and STRAUSS, A.L. 1973, *Field Research: Strategies for a Natural Sociology*. Englewood Cliffs, New Jersey: Prentice-Hall.

Schools Council 1970, *Immigrant Children in Infant Schools*. Schools Council Working Paper 31. London: Evans/Methuen Educational.

———1982, *Education of Children from Ethnic Minority Groups*. Schools Council Pamphlet 19. London: Schools Council.

SEWARD, G.F. 1881, *Chinese Immigration*. New York: Charles Scribner's Sons.

Seward Park High School (n.d.), *Seward Park High School Bilingual-Bicultural Program — Chinese: Description and Evaluation*. (Publisher and place of publication not known. Photocopy available at the New York Public Library Chatham Square Branch).

SHANG, A. 1984, *The Chinese in Britain*. London: Batsford Academic and Educational.

SHARP, D. 1973, *Language in Bilingual Communities*. London: Edward Arnold.

SIMPSON, J.M. 1981, The challenge of minority languages. In E. HAUGEN *et al.* (ed.) *Minority Languages Today*. Edinburgh: Edinburgh University Press.

SIMPSON, R.F. 1966, *Future Development in Education*. Hong Kong: Hong Kong Council for Educational Research Department of Education, University of Hong Kong.

SMOLICZ, J.J. 1981, Culture, ethnicity and education: multiculturalism in a plural society. *World Yearbook of Education 1981 Education of Minorities*. London: Kogan Page Ltd.

SOON, W. 1987, Profile: Chinatown YWCA has popular summer programs — and a waiting list. *East/West News* May 14, 1987.

Southern California Council of Chinese Schools 1986, *Special Journal in Commemoration of the 10th Anniversary*. Southern California: Southern California Council of Chinese Schools.

SPOLSKY, B. 1978, Bilingual education in the United States. In James E. ALATIS (ed.) *Georgetown University Round Table on Language and Linguistics 1978: International Dimensions of Bilingual Education*. Washington, D.C.: Georgetown University Press.

STEWART, P. 1976, *Immigrants*. London: B.T. Batsford.

STONE, J.C. and DeNEVI, D.P. 1971, *Teaching Multi-cultural Populations*. New York: Van Nostrand Reinhold Company.

STRAUSS, A. *et al.* 1969, Field tactics. In George J. McCALL and J. L. SIMMONS (eds) *Issues in Participant Observation: A Text and Reader*. Reading, Massachusetts: Addison-Wesley Publishing Company.

STUBBS, M.W. 1985, *The Other Languages of England Linguistic Minorities Project*. London: Routledge & Kegan Paul.

SUNG, B.L. 1976, *A Survey of Chinese–Americans: Manpower and Employment*. New York: Praeger Publisher.

———1979, *Transplanted Chinese Children*. New York: City University of New York.

SUZUKI, B.H. 1983, The education of Asian and Pacific Americans: an introductory review. In DON T. NAKANISHI and MARSHA HIRANO-NAKANISHI (eds) *The*

Education of Asian and Pacific Americans: Historical Perspectives and Prescriptions for the Future. Phoenix: The Oryx Press.

SWAIN, M. 1972, *Bilingual Schooling: Some Experiences in Canada and the United States.* A report on the Bilingual Education Conference, Toronto, March 11–13, 1971. Toronto, Ontario: The Ontario Institute for Studies in Education.

TAN, S.P. 1982, *Food Ideology and Food Habits of the Chinese Immigrants in London, and the Growth of their Young Children.* Report of a survey 1982. London School of Hygiene and Tropical Medicine Department of Human Nutrition.

TANG, W.T. 1986, Address by Tang at the opening ceremony of the Youth Festival. *Chinese Central High School Special Journal for the 1986 Graduation.* San Francisco, California: Chinese Central High School.

TAYLOR, G. 1976, *The Law of Education* (8th. edition). London: Butterworths.

TAYLOR, M.J. 1987, *Chinese Pupils in Britain.* Windsor, Berkshire: NFER-NELSON Publishing Company Ltd.

TEITELBAUM, H. and HILLER, R. 1977, The legal perspective. *Bilingual Education: Current Perspectives* Vol. 3. Arlington, Virginia: Center for Applied Linguistics.

TOENNIES, F. 1973, From community to society. In E. ETZIONI and E. ETZIONI-HALEVY (ed.) *Social Change: Sources, Patterns and Consequences* (2nd. edition). New York: Basic Books, Inc.

TOM, K.F. 1941, Functions of the Chinese language school. *Sociology and Social Research* (July), 557–561.

TOMLINSON, S. 1983, *Ethnic Minorities in British Schools: A Review of the Literature 1960–1982.* London: Heinemann Educational Books.

TREGAER, T.R. 1955, *Land use in Hong Kong and the New Territories.* Hong Kong: The Government Printer.

TRETHEWAY, A.R. 1976, *Introducing Comparative Education.* Australia: Pergamon Press.

TSAI, S.S. 1983, *China and the Overseas Chinese in the United States 1868–1911.* Fayetteville, Arkansas: University of Arkansas Press.

——1986, *The Chinese Experience in America.* Bloomington and Indianapolis: Indiana University Press.

TSANG, S.L. 1982, *Bilingual Education in a Chinese Community.* Final research report. Oakland, California: ARC Associates (ERIC microfiche: ED 228853)

TSOW, M. 1980, Chinese children and multi-cultural education. *Education Journal* 2(2), 6.

——1981, A tower of babel? Mother tongue? *Mother Tongue Teaching Conference Report 1980.* London: CRE.

——1983, Community education: the unknown perspective . . . Chinese mother tongue classes. *Journal of Community Education* (February) 2(1), 38–44.

——1984, *Mother Tongue Maintenance: A Survey of part-time Chinese Language Classes.* London: CRE.

TSU, J.B. 1977, Chinese bilingual education and Chinese language teaching. *Journal of the Chinese Language Teachers Association* (February) 12(1), 44–54.

——1978, The future of Asian bilingual and bicultural education. *Bilingual Resources* (Fall) 2(1), 8–10.

TUCKER, C.A. 1972, The Chinese immigrant's language handicap.

Chinese–Americans: School and Community Problems. Chicago, Illinois: Integrated Education Associates.

TURABIAN, K.L. 1982, *A Manual for Writers of Research Papers, Theses and Dissertations* (1st. British edition). London: Heinemann.

U.S. Bureau of Census 1970, *Japanese, Chinese and Filipinos in the United States.* Washingtion, D.C.: Government Printing Office.

U.S. Commission on Civil Rights 1978, *Social Indicators of Equality for Minorities and Women.* Washington, D.C.: U.S. Commission on Civil Rights.

U.S. Department of Commerce, Bureau of the Census 1972, *Public Use Samples of Basic Records from the 1970 Census.* Washington, D.C.: U.S. Government Printing Office.

——1983a *1980 Census of Population. Vol. 1 Characteristics of the Population. Chapter C General Social and Economic Characteristics. Part 6 California. Section 1 of 2.* Washington, D.C.: U.S. Government Printing Office.

——1983b *1980 Census of Population. Vol. 1 Characteristics of the Population. Chapter C General Social and Economic Characteristics. Part 34 New York. Section 1 of 2.* Washington, D.C.: U.S. Government Printing Office.

U.S. Department of Health, Education and Welfare, National Center for Education Statistics 1979, Birthplace and language characteristics of persons of Chinese, Japanese, Korean, Filipino, and Vietnamese Origin in the US, Spring 1976. *NCES Bulletin,* 79–144.

U.S. Department of Health, Education and Welfare, Public Health Service 1946–69, *Vital Statistics of the United States.* Washington. D.C.: U.S.. Government Printing Office.

U.S. Department of Justice, Immigration and Naturalization Service 1961–73, *Annual Reports 1961–73.*

VALENTE, W.D. 1980, *Law in the Schools.* Columbus, Ohio: Bell & Howell Company.

VIDICH, A.J. 1969, Participant observation and the collection and interpretation of data. In George J. McCALL and J.L. SIMMONS (eds) *Issues in Participant Observation: A Text and Reader.* Reading, Massachusetts: Addison-Wesley Publishing Company.

VON MALTITZ, F.W. 1975, *Living and Learning in Two Languages: Bilingual-Bicultural Education in the United States.* New York: McGraw-Hill Book Company.

VOS, A.J. and BARNARD, S.S. 1984, *Comparative and International Education for Student Teachers.* Durban, South Africa: Butterworths.

WAGNER, S.T. 1981, The historical background of bilingualism and biculturalism in the United States. In Martin Ridge (ed.) *The New Bilingualism: An American Dilemma.* Los Angeles, California: University of Southern California.

WANG, A.Y. and EARLE, R.A. 1972, Cultural constraints in teaching Chinese students to read English. *Reading Teacher* (April) 25(7), 663–669.

WANG, L.C. 1971, The Chinese community in San Francisco. *Integrated Education: Race and Schools* (March-April) 9(2), 21-28.

WANG, W. 1973, The Chinese language. *Human Communication: Language and its Psychobiological Bases.* Readings from Scientific American. San Francisco, California: W.H. Freeman and Company.

WASSERMEN, P. and KENNINGTON, A.E. 1983, *Ethnic Information Sources of the United States* (2nd. edition). Detroit, Michigan: Gale Research Company.

WATSON, J.L. 1977a, Chinese emigrant ties to the home community. *New Community* (Spring–summer) 5(4), 343–352.

——1977b, The Chinese: Hong Kong villagers in the British catering trade. In James L. WATSON (ed.) *Between Two Cultures*. Oxford: Basil Blackwell.

WHYTE, W.F. 1960, Interviewing in field research. In Richard N. ADAMS and Jack J. PREISS (eds) *Human Organization Research*. Homewood, Illinois: Dorsey Press.

WILLIAMS, B. 1964, Visit to Ho Chung and Sheung Yeung villages in the Sai Kung Area. *Aspects of Social Organization in the New Territories*, Royal Asiatic Society Hong Kong Branch, Weekend Symposium, 9th–10th May 1964, pp. 46–47.

WILLIAMS, R. 1981, *Culture*. London: Fontana Paperbacks.

WISE, J.E. *et al.* 1967, *Methods of Research in Education*. Boston: D.C. Heath and Company.

WISEMAN, J.P. and ARON, M.S. 1970, *Field Projects in Sociology*. Cambridge, Massachusetts: Schenkman Publishing Company, Inc.

WOLFE, T. 1971, The new yellow peril. In JAMES C. STONE and DONALD P. DeNEVI (eds) *Teaching Multi-cultural Populations*. New York: Van Nostrand Reinhold Company.

WONG, B. 1979, *A Chinese American Community: Ethnicity and Survival Strategies*. Singapore: Chopmen Enterprises.

——1982, *Chinatown: Economic Adaptation and Ethnic Identity of the Chinese*. New York: Holt Rinehart and Winston.

WONG, K.Y. and FONG-LEE, M.K. 1980, *Tai Po as a Place of Habitat: A Perception Study*. Occasional Paper No. 11 (November). Hong Kong: The Chinese University of Hong Kong.

WONG, K.T. (n.d.), Problems in learning Chinese overseas. *Chinese News Weekly* 3(6), 8–10.

WONG, L. 1976, From yellow peril to model minority: the Chinese experience. *Civil Rights Digest* (Fall) 9(1), 33–35.

WONG, L.Y.F. 1989, The bilingual/bicultural education of Chinese children in London, New York City and San Francisco. In M. McLEAN (ed.) *Education in Cities: International Perspectives*. Papers presented at the Annual Conference of the British Comparative and International Education Society. London: Department of International and Comparative Education, Institute of Education London University.

——1989a, A comparative study of mother-tongue education for Chinese pupils in Britain and the USA and its implications on language policies in education in Hong Kong. Paper presented at the 6th Annual Conference on Advances and Innovations in Education, organised by the Hong Kong Educational Research Association, November 11–12, 1989 (unpublished paper).

——1989b, Educational problems of Chinese children in British schools. In J. GEACH with J. BROADBENT (ed.) *Coherence in Diversity: Britain's Multilingual Classroom*. London: CILT.

——1989c, Students caught between two languages. In *Hong Kong Standard* (English newspaper of Hong Kong) November 29, 1989.

——1991a, A comparative study of national policies and community initiatives in the maintenance of the Chinese language in London and New York City. In K. JASPAERT and S. KROON (eds) *Ethnic Minority Languages and Education*. Amsterdam: Swets & Zeitlinger B.V.

———1991b, The Hong Kong Chinese speech community. In S. ALLADINA and V. EDWARDS (eds) *Multilingualism in the British Isles, Africa, The Middle East and Asia*. London: Longman.

———1991c, The Vietnamese Chinese speech community. In S. ALLADINA and V. EDWARDS (eds) *Multilingualism in the British Isles, Africa, The Middle East and Asia*. London: Longman.

The World Journal 1985, English tutoring classes for Grades 4–8 new immigrant children. New classes begin on November 5. *The World Journal* November, 1985.

WOO, J. 1985, *The Chinese-speaking Student: A Composite Profile*. New York: New York Bilingual Education Multifunctional Support Center.

WRIGHT, J. 1982, *Bilingualism in Education*. London: Issues In Race & Education.

WRIGHT, J. *et al.* 1978, *A Practical Guide to the Race Relations Act*. London: National Council for Civil Liberties.

WRIGHT, K. 1979, Chinese American history. In George HENDERSON (ed.) *Understanding and Counseling Ethnic Minorities*. Springfield, Illinois: Charles C. Thomas Publisher.

WU, C.T. 1958, *Chinese People and Chinatown in New York City* (Ph.D. thesis). Ann Arbor: University Microfilms.

YAO, E.L. 1979, Min-Ming: a child of a different culture. *Reading Improvement* (Spring) 16(1), 43–49.

———1983, Ethnic awareness of Chinese-American teenagers. *Urban Education* (April) 18(1), 71–81.

YAU, L. 1983, Report on the Chinese Community in Lambeth (unplished). London: Community Relations Council for Lambeth.

YOUNG, J. and DRISCOLL, B.M. 1980, *ESEA Title VII Chinese Bilingual Program. Community School District One. Final Evaluation Report 1979–1980*. New York: Community School District One. (ERIC microfiche: ED 200697).

YWCA 1987, *Chinatown/North Beach YWCA* (pamphlet). San Francisco, California: YWCA.

YU, C.Y. 1976, The 'others': Asian Americans and education. *Civil Rights Digest* (Fall) 9(1), 44–51.

YUAN, D.Y. 1963, Voluntary segregation: a study of New York Chinatown. *Phylon* 24(3), 255–268.

ZO, K.Y. 1978, *Chinese Emigration into the US 1850–1880*. New York: Arno Press.